Robert Shepard
1968

THE GOSPEL
ACCORDING TO
ST. LUKE

A Commentary

THE GOSPEL

according to

ST. LUKE

by

WILFRID J. HARRINGTON, O.P.

NEWMAN PRESS

Westminster, Md.   New York, N.Y.   Glen Rock, N.J.

Amsterdam   Toronto

The Bible text in this publication is from the *Revised Standard Version of the Bible,* copyrighted 1946 and 1952 by the Division of Christian Education, National Council of the Churches of Christ in the U.S.A. and used by permission.

NIHIL OBSTAT:
Rev. Robert E. Hunt, S.T.D.
Censor Librorum

IMPRIMATUR:
✠ Thomas A. Boland, S.T.D.
Archbishop of Newark

July 11, 1967

The Nihil Obstat and Imprimatur are official declarations that a book or pamphlet is free of doctrinal or moral error. No implication is contained therein that those who have granted the Nihil Obstat and Imprimatur agree with the contents, opinions or statements expressed.

Library of Congress
Catalog Card Number: 67-28700

Published by Newman Press
Editorial Office: 304 W. 58th St., N.Y., N.Y. 10019
Business Office: Westminster, Maryland 21157

Printed and bound in the
United States of America

CONTENTS

LIST OF ABBREVIATIONS

Gn	Genesis	Obad	Obadiah
Ex	Exodus	Jon	Jonah
Lv	Leviticus	Mi	Micah
Nm	Numbers	Na	Nahum
Dt	Deuteronomy	Hb	Habakkuk
Jos	Joshua	Zeph	Zephaniah
Jg	Judges	Hag	Haggai
Ru	Ruth	Zech	Zechariah
1,2 Sm	1,2 Samuel	Mal	Malachi
1,2 Kg	1,2 Kings	1,2 Mc	1,2 Maccabees
1,2 Chr	1,2 Chronicles	Mt	Matthew
Ez	Ezra	Mk	Mark
Neh	Nehemiah	Lk	Luke
Tb	Tobit	Jn	John
Jdt	Judith	Ac	Acts
Est	Esther	Rm	Romans
Jb	Job	1,2 Cor	1,2 Corinthians
Ps	Psalms	Gal	Galatians
Prv	Proverbs	Eph	Ephesians
Qoh	Qoheleth	Phil	Philippians
Ct	Canticle of Canticles	Col	Colossians
Wis	Wisdom	1,2 Thes	1,2 Thessalonians
Sir	Sirach	1,2 Tm	1,2 Timothy
Is	Isaiah	Ti	Titus
Jer	Jeremiah	Phm	Philemon
Lam	Lamentations	Heb	Hebrews
Bar	Baruch	Jas	James
Ezek	Ezekiel	1,2 Pt	1,2 Peter
Dn	Daniel	1,2,3 Jn	1,2,3 John
Hos	Hosea	Jude	Jude
Jl	Joel	Ap	Apocalypse
Am	Amos		

PREFACE

Modern study of the gospels has established the significant part played by the apostolic Church and by the evangelists in the presentation of the works and words of the Lord. In the first place, Form-Criticism has made us aware of literary units within the Synoptic gospels and of the frequent loose linking of these units. We no longer seek to trace a strictly logical sequence of thought throughout a gospel or throughout a long passage of it; rather, we recognize that, at times, we have to study a pericope sentence by sentence, for isolated sayings may be joined by a system of catchwords, or may simply have been juxtaposed. We also realize that there was a development of the tradition, a process which has left visible traces in the gospels. It is not only legitimate but illuminating to seek the *Sitz im Leben* of the units of the tradition—the life-situation in which they have arisen. And whereas we are sure that the community did not create the gospel, we do admit that the needs and life of the early Church did influence the selection of the sayings of Jesus and the stories about him.

More recently, *Redaktionsgeschichte* ("redaction-criticism") has drawn our attention to the contribution of the evangelists. They were not entirely free, because they were working with traditional material; but we are aware that they worked with more freedom than we had been wont to believe. Besides, since a gospel is a presentation of the Person and teaching of Jesus, seen and interpreted in the light of the resurrection, it is necessarily theological. And as one who selects, synthesizes and interprets the apostolic tradition, the evangelist, to a greater or lesser degree, is a theologian. In short, the evangelists are authors who wrote with a purpose in view and adapted the material to suit this purpose; we should keep in mind the distinctive scope and viewpoint of each of them.

1

In this Commentary (based on the RSV text, but with an eye to the Greek wherever necessary or helpful) I have endeavored to explain the third gospel as I believe Luke himself meant it to be understood. If I have met with a measure of success, that is thanks to the remarkable contribution of modern New Testament scholarship. My scope is not ambitious. I wish to provide a helpful tool for the serious student of Scripture—seminarians, interested layfolk, pastoral clergy, Sisters engaged in religious education. The work is non-technical and is as self-explanatory as I could make it.

I have thought it well to linger over those parts of the gospel which are proper to Luke—and which, in fact, add up to almost half of the gospel. I have been particularly brief wherever Luke has followed Mark closely, sometimes being content to note Luke's modification of his source. Such passages, I believe, might be more profitably studied at length in a commentary on Mark.

I am very conscious of my debt to a host of New Testament scholars. Because acknowledgment at all points and in every case would soon have become tedious, I have decided to restrict references to occasions of direct quotation. It is hoped that the select bibliography will reasonably, though perhaps not adequately, indicate the extent of my obligation.

I am grateful to Father Thomas C. Donlan, O.P. who has kindly granted me permission to make free use of material taken from *Record of the Fulfillment: The New Testament,* published and copyrighted by The Priory Press, Chicago.

W. J. H.

INTRODUCTION

I. THE AUTHORSHIP OF THE GOSPEL

1. The Testimony of Tradition

The testimony of tradition regarding the authorship of the third gospel is unhesitating: it is the work of St. Luke. The chief witnesses are:

Irenaeus (end of 2nd century):

> Luke, the companion of Paul, wrote the latter's gospel in a book.

Anti-Marcionite Prologue (c. 160-180):

> Luke, a Syrian of Antioch, doctor by profession, was the disciple of the Apostles. At a later date he was the disciple of Paul until the apostle's death. Having served the Lord without fault and never having married, he died, full of the Holy Spirit, at Boeotia, aged 84. As gospels had already been written by Matthew in Judea and by Mark in Italy, Luke, under the impulse of the Holy Spirit, wrote his gospel in the region of Achaia. In the prologue he shows that other gospels had been written before his but that it was necessary to present to the faithful converted from paganism an exact account of the economy of salvation, lest they should be impeded by Jewish fables or caused to stray from the truth by the deceits of heretics.

The Muratorian Canon (end of 2nd century):

> Luke, a doctor and companion of Paul, wrote the third gospel. He himself had not seen the Lord.

3

St. Jerome gives a summary of the traditional data:

> Thirdly, Luke the physician, by nation a Syrian of Antioch, whose praise is in the gospel (cf. 2 Cor 8:18), and who himself was a disciple of the Apostle Paul, wrote in the region of Achaia and Boeotia, seeking material from the ancients, and, as he admits in his preface, writing rather from hearsay than from eyewitnesses.

The main points of the impressive traditional witness come to this: the author of the third gospel is Luke, a companion of St. Paul and a doctor. Present-day scholarship, generally, agrees to accept the tradition. It follows that Luke is also the author of Acts, for Luke and Acts are demonstrably two volumes of the one work.

2. The New Testament Witness

(1) *The Pauline Epistles*

Luke is named three times: Col 4:14; Phm 23f; 2 Tm 4:11.

Col 4:14: "Luke the beloved physician and Demas greet you."
Phm 23f: "Epaphras, my fellow prisoner in Christ Jesus, sends greetings to you, as do Mark, Aristarchus, Demas and Luke, my fellow workers."
2 Tm 4:11: "Luke alone is with me."

Thus, according to Colossians and Philemon Luke was with Paul in Rome during the latter's first captivity (61-63 A.D.), and according to 2 Timothy he was with him during the second Roman captivity (67 A.D.). In Col 4:10-14 the collaborators of Paul are divided into two groups:

(a) Aristarchus, Mark, and Justus, "the only circumcised", i.e. Jews.

(b) Epaphras, Luke, and Demas, who, by implication, are of pagan origin. The designation "beloved physician" (Col 4:14) reveals that Luke belonged to an educated class, and also that his services were appreciated by Paul, especially during the second captivity.

(2) *The Acts of the Apostles*

The "we passages": 16:10-17; 20:5-15; 21:1-18; 27:1-28:16.

In these sections the author of Acts (who, beyond all reasonable doubt, is Luke) writes in the first person—hence the designation "we passages"—obviously as an eyewitness. We gather that Luke met Paul at Troas during the latter's second missionary journey (50-52 A.D.). He went to Macedonia with him, to Philippi, where Paul founded a church (16:10-17). Luke appears to have remained at Philippi because the next "we-passage" occurs in the context of the third missionary journey (53-58 A.D.). Luke joined Paul at Philippi about 57 A.D. (20:5-15) and went with him to Jerusalem. On this occasion Paul was arrested and spent two years as a prisoner at Caesarea, on the Palestinian coast (58-60 A.D.). This afforded Luke ample time to search out sources, oral and written, both for his gospel and for Acts. He accompanied Paul on the journey to Rome 60-61 A.D. (27:1-28:16). There Luke could have met the people mentioned in Col 4:10-14 and Phm 24—especially Mark. Here again the data of the Pauline epistles and of Acts are in perfect accord, and it is clear how a disciple of Paul came to know the Palestinian tradition.

3. Destination and Date

St. Luke dedicated his gospel (and Acts) to a certain Theophilus. The title given to him (*kratiste*—Excellency) indicates a man of high social standing. According to ancient custom the man to whom a book was dedicated was expected to promote its circulation.

Luke certainly wrote for Gentile Christians—this is quite evident from a study of his gospel. Thus he consistently avoids many matters which might appear too specifically Jewish. He omits whole passages: the traditions of the ancients (Mk 7:1-23); the return of Elijah (Mk 9:11-13); the antitheses (Mt 5:21-22,27f, 33-37). Sometimes, instead of suppressing a passage he rearranges it or omits details. For instance, compare Mt 5:38-48 with Lk 6:27-36 and Mt 7:24-27 with Lk 6:47-49. He is also careful to omit or play down anything that might shock his Gentile Christian readers: sayings liable to be misunderstood—"Of that day or hour no one knows . . . nor the Son" (Mk 13:32); the cry

from the Cross: "My God, My God, why hast thou forsaken me?"
(Mk 15:34); sentiments of Jesus like anger, indignation, sorrow
(in this regard compare: "And he looked around at them with
anger, grieved at their hardness of heart" [Mk 3:5] with "And he
looked around on them all" [Lk 6:10]; Lk 19:45f with Mk 11:15-17
and Lk 22:39-46 with Mk 14:32-42); anything which might cast
doubt on the omnipotence of Christ (in this regard compare
"And he could do no mighty work there [in his own country] . . .
and he marvelled because of their unbelief" [Mk 6:5f] with Lk
4:25-30; Lk 4:40 with Mk 1:34 and Lk 5:15f with Mk 1:45).

Luke also omits or changes details that do not redound to the
credit of the Apostles: he has omitted Mk 4:13; 8:22f; 9:10,28f,33f.
Elsewhere he has modified the text of Mark: See Lk 8:24f and
Mk 4:38,40; Lk 18:25f and Mk 10:24-26; Lk 22:31-34 and Mk
14:27-31. This conduct of St. Luke is explained by Father Lagrange: "Luke, because he was addressing Gentiles, especially
Greeks prone to discussions and criticism, did not wish to raise
difficulties for them. . . . He felt that the transition from the Semitic
to the Greek world of ideas would be rendered easier by saying
nothing about matters difficult to understand." [1]

Some scholars date Luke 60-62 A.D. One of their arguments is
that this date is demanded by the date of Acts. Since in the latter
writing (they say) Luke gives no indication of the outcome of
Paul's appeal to Caesar, it follows that Acts must have been written before 63 A.D.—the end of Paul's first captivity. The gospel
is certainly earlier, so it must have been written about 60-62 A.D.

This argument, however, cannot be taken as proving its point.
To do so it would have to show that Luke intended to give the
result of Paul's appeal to Caesar. In fact, the plan of Acts shows
that this lay beyond Luke's purpose, and that the ending of the
book is indeed just as it should be. Luke indicates the plan of
Acts by quoting Christ's own words before his ascension: "You
shall receive power when the Holy Spirit has come upon you; and
shall be my witnesses in Jerusalem and in all Judea and Samaria
and to the ends of the earth" (1:8). Luke followed that plan, and
at the close—having traced the expansion of the Church from
Jerusalem—he has led the great Apostle of the Gentiles to the
capital of the Roman Empire, the center of the world; there, al-

[1] *Évangile selon Saint Luc* (Paris: Gabalda, 1941⁵), p. cxl.

though technically a prisoner, Paul was "preaching the kingdom of God and teaching about the Lord Jesus Christ quite openly and unhindered" (28:31). This is a masterly ending to a book that has shown the triumphal advance of Christianity and is one more proof of the literary artistry of St. Luke. That, then, is obviously the ending that Luke intended. To say that he does not go on to give the outcome of Paul's appeal to Caesar is therefore not a proof that Acts, and consequently Luke, was written before 63 A.D.

The early dating of the gospel is more compellingly excluded by the date of Mark—not earlier than 64 A.D.—and by the fact that Luke has used Mark. Catholic scholars, on the whole, tend to date Luke between 65 A.D. (the probable date of Mark) and 70 A.D. Most Protestant, and not a few Catholic, scholars would put the composition of Luke in the decade 70-80 A.D. Their main reason for doing so is based on the detailed form of the prediction of the destruction of Jerusalem (19:43f; 21:20,24; 23:28-30). Where Mt 24:15 and Mk 13:14 have "abomination of desolation" (cf. Dn 9:27; 11:31; 12:11), Lk 21:20 reads: "When you see Jerusalem surrounded by armies, then know that its desolation has come near." Verse 24 adds that the inhabitants of the city "will fall by the edge of the sword, and be led captive among all nations; and Jerusalem will be trodden down by the Gentiles until the times of the Gentiles are fulfilled". These would seem to be an *ex eventu* clarification of the veiled prophecy of the destruction of Jerusalem in 70 A.D. The argument is not conclusive, however, because the expressions, general in themselves, may well have been suggested by the Old Testament (cf. Dt 28:54; Hos 9:7; Zech 12:3). Luke may have been written shortly before 70 A.D., but in the long run the exact date of the gospel, apart from being uncertain, is hardly a vital question. In the course of the commentary we shall suggest that a date after 70 A.D. is probable.

II. THE LITERARY CONSTRUCTION OF THE GOSPEL

1. The Plan

Luke, like Mark and Matthew, has followed the primitive four-fold gospel plan: *i* Preparation and baptism in Judea, that is, the preaching of John the Baptist and the inauguration of the public ministry of Jesus; *ii* Ministry in Galilee; *iii* Journey from Galilee to Jerusalem; *iv* In Jerusalem: Passion, Death, Resurrection. However, he has made two important changes in this order and so has given to his gospel quite a different bias. By placing at the beginning the long Infancy narrative (chs. 1–2)—which balances the Passion and Resurrection narrative—he has presented the story of Jesus in perfect equilibrium. By his insertion of the long section (9:51–18:14), he has fitted cleverly into the gospel narrative a very important collection of episodes and sayings which are entirely absent from Mark and only partially represented in Matthew. This Lucan section is dominated by the perspective of the Passion, and the journey to Jerusalem is seen as a journey to death (cf. 9:51; 13:22; 17:11). In Luke, then, the story of Jesus falls into three parts:

Prologue (1:1-4)

A. *From the Temple to the Close of the Galilean Ministry* (1:5–9:50)
B. *Journey from Galilee to Jerusalem* (9:51–19:27)
C. *Last Days of the Suffering and Risen Christ in Jerusalem* (19:28–24:53)

Thus, despite the general agreement with Mark and Matthew, the third gospel has a distinctive character. But while the main division is clear, it is not so easy to give a satisfactory arrangement of the details. Our subsequent arrangement of the text respects a complexity that really exists and does not seek to falsify the picture by oversimplification.

2. The Sources

It is universally recognized that Luke has used Mark as a source, indeed that Mark is his chief source, and he has manifestly followed the order of Mark. We may put the relationship between them in schematic form.

	Luke	*Mark*
Prologue	1–2	—
	3:1–6:19 ⟶ 1:1–3:19	
		3:20-35
A. In Galilee 3:1–9:50	*6:20–8:3*	
	8:4–9:50 ⟶ 4:1–6:44 + 8:27–9:40	
		6:45–8:26
B. To Jerusalem 9:5–19:27	*9:51–18:14*	
	18:15–19:27 → 10:13-52	
C. In Jerusalem	19:28–24:53 → 11:1–16:8(20)	

The chief differences that meet the eye (apart from the omission of Mk 6:45–8:26) are the additions made by Luke: 6:20–8:3 and especially 9:51–18:14. It is instructive to see how this last section has, in fact, been inserted into the order of Mark. In Lk 9:18-50 and Mk 8:27–9:40 the sequence of events is: profession of faith by Peter, the Transfiguration, the epileptic, the second prediction of the Passion, who is the greatest, use of the name of Jesus. At this point Luke makes the insertion, comprising some nine chapters, and at the end of it (18:15) he takes up the plan of Mark again, almost where he had left off, so that in Lk 18:15-43 and Mk 10:13-52 the sequence is: Jesus and children, the rich young man, the danger of riches, detachment rewarded, the third prediction of the Passion, the blind man at Jericho.

While it is undoubtedly, and indeed, obviously, true that Luke follows Mark, he does not by any means merely reproduce his source. We may classify the changes he makes under the general headings of *omissions, additions and retouches,* and *transpositions.* Many of these changes are due to the theological plan of Luke.

Omissions. Luke has omitted Markan passages which might not be understood by his readers, such as specifically Jewish matters (Mk 7:1-23; 9:9-13; 10:1-12) or matters which might raise difficulties for them (Mk 3:20f; 7:24-30; 11:12-14,20-25; 6:45-52). Luke avoids Markan passages that occur in another context in his gospel—Mk 1:16-20 (Lk 5:1-11); Mk 3:22-30 (Lk 11:14-23); Mk 4:30-32 (Lk 13:18-21); Mk 6:1-6a (Lk 4:16-30); Mk 8:11-13 (Lk

11:29-32); Mk 9:42-48 (Lk 17:1f); Mk 9:49 (Lk 14:34f); Mk 10: 35-45 (Lk 22:24-27); Mk 12:28-34 (Lk 10:25-28). He also avoids the repetition of closely related narratives and so omits: the parable of the Seed Growing Secretly (Mk 4:26-29), Jesus walking on the waters (6:45-52), the second multiplication of loaves (8:1-10), the anointing at Bethany (14:3-9), the first appearance before the Sanhedrin (14:55-64), the episode of the wine mingled with myrrh (15:23). Further omissions are motivated by reverence towards Jesus: passages in which his human sensibility appears to be too boldly expressed (Mk 1:43; 3:5; 9:36; 10:16,21; 14:33f) or where his knowledge seems to be limited (Mk 13:32; 15:34); and, of course, Mk 3:21. Similarly, the Apostles are spared by leaving aside the following passages: Mk 4:13,38; 5:31; 9:10,28f, 33f; 10:35-45; 14:50. In general, Luke omits the picturesque but unessential details of Mark's narrative. Finally, certain topographical data are omitted in view of the theological plan of the gospel.

Additions and retouches. These are variously motivated by Luke's desire for clarity and by his literary and religious sensibility. So, Lk 4:31; 5:1; 8:24; 19:37; 23:51 (geographical data); 6:15 (explanation of an Aramaic expression); 4:1,40,43; 8:18,30f, 53,55; 9:9; 22:51,69 (varied). Especially notable are 21:20,24. See also 22:45,47f,51. Luke's favorite themes frequently appear: Lk 5:25; 18:43; 19:37; 23:47 (praise); 3:6—cf. Mk 1:3 (universalism); Lk 3:21; 6:12; 9:28; 23:34 (prayer); 5:11,28; 14:26; 18:22,29 (detachment); 4:14; 10:21; 11:13 (the Holy Spirit).

Transpositions. Again the motives are varied. The arrest of the Baptist (3:19f; cf. Mk 1:14; 6:17-20) emphasizes the fact that the Baptist now fades into the background. The expulsion from Nazareth (4:16-30; cf. Mk 6:1-6a), placed by Luke at the beginning of the ministry, symbolizes Israel's rejection of Jesus. The call of the first disciples (5:1-11), placed after the first miracles at Capernaum and not before as in Mk 1:16-20, makes their immediate response more understandable. The introduction of the Sermon (6:17-19) follows after the choice of the Twelve (cf. Mk 3:7-19), so that the discourse itself (6:20-49) can follow immediately and naturally. In the Passion and Resurrection narrative (22:1–24:53) the transpositions seem to assure a more correct literary presentation. The institution of the Eucharist is placed before the

announcement of the betrayal and after the Jewish Passover
(22:14-23) in a logical order (cf. Mk 14:17-25). The announcement of Peter's betrayal is placed at the Supper after another
admonition to the Apostles (22:31-34) and not on the way to
Gethsemane (Mk 14:26-31). For the same reason the question on
precedence (cf. Mk 10:42-44) and the recompense promised to
the Apostles (cf. Mt 19:28) have been added here (Lk 22:24-30).
The narrative of the arrest of Jesus (22:47-53; cf. Mk 14:43-50)
has been rearranged in a better literary style.

Another, and very important, source of Luke comes to light
when we analyze the long section 9:51–18:14 which has been inserted into the plan of Mark. In this part of his gospel Luke has
grouped "under the sign of Jerusalem and the Passion", and in no
strict chronological order, a great bulk of material which did not
come to him via Mark or the Aramaic gospel; whereas—and this
is the significant point—many of these elements are found in
Matthew also. The only reasonable explanation is that, besides
Aramaic Matthew, another common (or partly common) source
was known to Matthew and Luke. An analysis of Lk 9:51–18:14
permits us to distinguish, apart from a large body of material
peculiar to Luke: (a) elements common to Matthew and Luke
and absent from Mark; (b) elements common to Matthew, Mark
and Luke. With regard to (a), there are thirty-three of these elements, simple sayings composed of only a few verses each for the
most part (e.g. Lk 13:24 = Mt 22:1-10; Lk 10:13-15 = Mt 11:21-23).
It is noteworthy that the resemblances between Matthew and
Luke in these passages are relatively more numerous than in passages common to all three synoptists. It is clear that in these cases
Matthew and Luke follow a common source. The material under
(b) is of greater significance, for here we have the question of
doublets. By doublets we mean the passages, generally consisting
of sayings, which are met with more than once in the same gospel
but in a different context. Some of these may be due to repetition
but many of them point to the use of different sources. An examination of these doublets leads to the conclusion that, as a rule,
in the case of each doublet, the first form of the text appears in
parallel passages of the tradition Matthew-Mark-Luke, while the
second form, never found in Mark, frequent in Matthew and
almost always present in Lk 9:51–18:14, points to a tradition

common to Matthew and Luke. Some examples will clarify this statement. The saying "If any man would come after me, let him deny himself and take up his cross and follow me" occurs in Mk 8:34b; Mt 16:24b; Lk 9:23 after the first prediction of the Passion, and in Mt 10:38; Lk 14:27 in another context. The saying "To him who has will more be given . . ." occurs in Mk 4:25; Mt 13:12; Lk 8:18 after the parable of the Measure and in Mt 25:29; Lk 19:26 after the parable of the Talents ("Pounds" in Luke). The conclusion would seem to be inevitable: Mark has no doublet because it follows one source only; the agreement of Matthew and Luke, independently of Mark, postulates another and common source. The passages common to the two evangelists make up, in the main, a collection of sayings and parables; these Matthew has distributed throughout his gospel while Luke has grouped most of them in the long section under review. Luke's three principal sources, then, are: Mark, a Greek translation of Aramaic Matthew and the special source common (more accurately, in part common) to himself and Matthew.

But Luke is not confined to these. We know that he had ample time (the two years 58-60 A.D.) for personal research in Palestine; and not only his own prologue ("having followed all things closely for some time past"), but a study of his gospel as well, affords proof that he did not waste his time. First of all there is the Infancy narrative (1–2), which is proper to Luke and independent of Matthew's first two chapters. The coloring of Lk 1–2 is highly Semitic; it has been suggested that this section is based on a Greek translation of an Aramaic source, while some contend that these chapters were first written in Hebrew. Perhaps the most satisfactory explanation is this: Luke may have had Aramaic sources, but he has written chapters 1–2 of his gospel in a Greek that is modelled on the style of the LXX (the Septuagint, the pre-Christian Greek translation of the Old Testament). These chapters, as they stand, are the work of Luke but, manifestly, he has followed a source of some sort. It is conceivable that our Lady may have been his informant; the two references to her meditation on the things that concerned her Son (2:19,51) would seem to indicate as much.

Not only in the Infancy narrative but throughout his gospel Luke presents to us the fruits of his research. One is quite sur-

prised to discover how much of what we take for granted we owe
to Luke alone. For instance, the lovely parables of the Prodigal
Son, the Good Samaritan, the Pharisee and the Publican, and the
Rich Man and Lazarus are found only in Luke. In the Passion
and Resurrection narrative the third gospel has many additions,
and it may be well to consider some of these in order to appreciate the extent of our debt. In 22:8 it is specified that "John and
Peter" were the disciples sent to prepare for the Last Supper; and
22:15f tells us of our Lord's desire to celebrate that last Pasch
with his disciples. In 22:35-38 he tells them of the hour of the
decisive combat. It is only Luke who informs us of the sweat of
blood at Gethsemane (22:43f) and of Jesus' healing the wound
inflicted by Peter (22:51). He alone tells (23:6-16) that our Lord
appeared before Herod, and of the daughters of Jerusalem who
wept over Christ (23:27-31). Only he speaks of the pardon of the
"good thief" (23: 40-43). While the cry of dereliction on the Cross
is not given in this gospel, we find instead three other sayings of
our Lord: 23:34,43,46. And after the Resurrection it is in Luke
that we read of the delightful episode of the disciples on the way
to Emmaus (24:13-35).

Luke shows certain affinities with John, notably in the Passion
and Resurrection narrative. He cannot have known John and it is
unlikely that John has used Luke; yet the contacts are there,
numerous and varied. It seems that Luke would have known the
Johannine tradition before it had taken final shape in the fourth
gospel. We shall draw attention to these contacts throughout the
Commentary.

Luke shows a curious complexity in his approach to his sources.
He can, and does, follow the order of Mark very closely, while at
the same time he fits it into a new plan. He can depart from that
order when it suits him and make deliberate changes in it. Most
important of all he has had recourse to new sources and, indeed,
the elements proper to Luke make up almost half of the work.
These additions include especially the Infancy narrative and the
special Source section, but they extend, too, to many elements of
the Passion and Resurrection narrative. The Infancy narrative
enables the evangelist to begin the history of Jesus with the annunciation of the birth of the Precursor. The central Source section is the treasury of Luke and there he has grouped the loveliest

parables in the gospels. And in the Passion and Resurrection narrative, as we have seen, the additions of the evangelist are of real importance. We have good reason to be grateful to St. Luke.

3. Language and Style

Luke has the best Greek style among the evangelists and that language is certainly his mother-tongue. St. Jerome testifies: *"Lucas . . . inter omnes evangelistas graeci sermonis eruditissimus fuit."* [2] He often avoids the literary faults he finds in his sources; he chooses more exact Greek words and he usually suppresses foreign words and expressions. It is, however, true that he does not carry out these improvements consistently and, not infrequently, he reproduces his sources just as he finds them. This makes for an unevenness in the style of the gospel that is something of a mystery. The problem which emerges is not so much Luke's paucity of Aramaisms and his frequency of Greek expressions in relation to Mark as the inconstancy of his stylistic changes.

Though Luke has preserved traces of the Aramaic originals of his sources, as a rule he avoids Aramaisms and translates Aramaic words. E.g. instead of "Rabbi" (Mk 9:5; 10:51) he has "Master" (9:33) and "Lord" (18:41); and instead of "Abba" (Mk 14:36) he has "Father" (22:42). On the whole, though Aramaisms are less frequent than in Mark and Matthew, they are nonetheless more in evidence than is commonly suggested, and they bear witness to the Semitic substratum of the gospel.

On the other hand, true Hebraisms are found almost exclusively in Luke. E.g. *egeneto . . . kai* (5:12,17; 8:1; 9:51; etc.), *eleusontai hēmerai* (5:35; 17:22; 21:6; etc.), *kai idou* (2:25; 5:12; 8:41; etc.), *enōpion* (1:15,19,76; 12:6,9; 15:6; etc.), *Hierousalēm* instead of the grecized form *Hierosolyma*. The presence of these Hebraisms is almost certainly due to the influence of the LXX; it seems that Luke has consciously imitated the style of the Greek Bible. This viewpoint is not infrequently contested, however, especially with regard to the Infancy narrative.

An interesting feature of Luke's style is his habit of rounding off one subject before passing on to another; it is a characteristic that might easily lead to misinterpretation. When he says, "Mary remained with her about three months and returned to her home"

[2] St. Jerome, Epist. 19, 4, *Ad Damasum;* PL 22:378.

(1:56), and goes on to tell of the birth of John, he does not mean to imply that Mary had departed before this event—he merely wants to complete the episode of the Visitation before taking up another matter. In chapter 3 he ends his account of the preaching of the Baptist by stating that Herod had John cast into prison (3:19f), and then immediately tells of the baptism of Jesus (3:21f); in other words, he finishes what he has to say about the ministry of John before going on to that of Jesus.

In quite the same way he indicates well in advance matters that will be dealt with later, and so ensures the unity and flow of the narrative. In 1:80 he mentions the sojourn of the Baptist in the desert, and later we learn that it was in the desert that the divine call came to him (3:2). At the close of the temptations the devil departed from Jesus "to return at the appointed time" (4:13), that is to say, the hour of his arrest: "This is your hour and the power of darkness" (22:53; cf. 22:3). In 8:2f we are told of the women who accompanied our Lord on his journeys and these reappear, quite naturally, and with no need of any explanation of their presence, as those who prepare the spices and ointments for the body of Jesus (23:55f). We may also consider 3:20 and 9:9; 5:33 and 11:1; 9:1-6 and 10:1; 9:9 and 28:8; 18:31 and 24:25f; 20:19 and 22:2; 20:25 and 23:2; 21:27 and 22:39.

It is certainly true that the author of the third gospel is the most versatile of the New Testament writers. Left to himself his Greek is excellent, but it is less good when he wishes to be faithful to his sources; and, lastly, he can imitate, perfectly, the style of the LXX. The language and style of the gospel reveal a Christian who is familiar with the Old Testament and an author familiar with the Greek literary style of his time. If the style of the third gospel is complex this is, in great measure, because Luke is undoubtedly a poet. According to a late tradition he was an artist and he is credited with the first painting of our Lady. It is easy to see how the legend could have grown out of the word picture he has drawn of her in his Infancy narrative. And surely it is because of its poetic depth that the same story has inspired, and indeed dominated, Christian art. Speaking still more broadly, we can scarcely realize how different our picture of Christmas would be without these chapters. At the other end of the gospel we find the delightful story of the two disciples and the unknown traveler on the road to Emmaus, while in between there is so much beauty. We should be thankful to St. Luke not only for the treasures he has searched out for us and so carefully preserved, but also for the artistry that went into the setting of these many pearls of great price.

4. The Author

(1) *The Minister of the Word*

(i) *The historian.* Luke's careful wording of his prologue and his dedication of the work to the "excellent Theophilus" introduce a work that does not purport merely to tell us about the Good News; his object is to establish the soundness of the catechetical teaching and, for that reason, his express intention is to weigh his sources. In view of this he shows care in presenting historical data. By the detailed synchronisms prefixed to his narrative of the birth of Jesus (2:1-3) and of the ministry of John (3:1f), he sets these events in the framework of general history. He can, on occasion, correct the chronology of his sources. Thus, while in Mark we are told that the Transfiguration took place six days after Peter's profession of faith at Caesarea Philippi (Mk 9:2), Luke quietly modifies the statement and says: "about eight days after" (9:28); and he regularly qualifies round numbers by adding "about" (1:56; 3:23; etc.). He speaks of Herod as "tetrarch"—his correct title—(9:7) and not, as he was popularly described, as "king" (Mk 6:14). Similarly, he speaks of the "lake of Gennesaret" (5:1) rather than of the "sea of Galilee" (Mk 1:16). He mentions contemporary facts: the massacre of Galileans by Pilate (13:1-3) and the fall of the tower of Siloam (13:4f). It is in the same spirit that he has had recourse to new sources.

We may not, however, judge the work of Luke as we would that of a modern historian; his gospel is not scientific history, nor is it, any more than Matthew and Mark, a biography of Jesus. Even though he has retouched his sources in this respect, he has scarcely anything of the modern passion for precise chronology and detailed topography. He is interested in historical facts but he does not have our regard for "history". If he does promise to write an "orderly account" that order is primarily theological, for his concern is with the things delivered by those who were not merely eyewitnesses of events but "ministers of the word" (1:2).

(ii) *The evangelist.* Luke himself is, first and foremost, a "minister of the word", an evangelist, and his work is, in the strict sense, a "gospel". That is why he has remained faithful to the general plan of Mark, the consecrated plan of the apostolic kerygma. For in the New Testament itself the word "gospel" means the *preaching* of Christ and the evangelist is a *preacher* (Ac 21:8; Eph 4:11; 2 Tm 4:5). When, in the second century, *euaggelion* came to designate the written account of the life and teaching of our Lord, these writings were still regarded as filling a missionary need and served the same purpose as the spoken word: to waken and strengthen faith (cf. Jn 20:31). Similarly, the evangelist, too, is a preacher and behind him stands the whole teaching activity of a living Church; of that Church he is a spokesman. His work is kerygmatic, in the proper sense of that overworked term: to herald Jesus Christ, his works and words. And because this is so an evangelist necessarily has a care for the historical and a certain biographical interest: the good news that he preaches is all concerned with a Person who lived and moved among men and taught them, a man who died at a given time and place, and rose from the dead. The Person of Jesus, seen and interpreted in the light of the Resurrection, is the very center of *Heilsgeschichte* and the presentation of his words and deeds is necessarily theological. While Luke, no doubt because of his Greek background, is somewhat more meticulous than the other synoptists about historical data, his intention remains, fundamentally, kerygmatic and theological.

In short, we might say that Luke was a historian because he was a theologian. His view of the *pragmata*, "the things" (1:1), was colored by his reflections on the relevance of the traditional *logoi*, "teaching" (1:4) for his own time. If this teaching—the sayings of Jesus about the importance of human relationships, about the virtues of patience, perseverance, poverty of spirit, about the necessity of persistence in prayer—did have a far-reaching importance for all time, then it meant that the period after the Resurrection and Ascension had a value peculiar to itself as circumstantially influential for salvation, and not merely as a short interval before the Second Coming. This idea molded Luke's interpretation of the tradition but immediately raised the question of the relationship between Luke's contemporary situation and the life of Christ.

For Luke, salvation had come with Christ; after the Ascension, men would be saved through him and because of what he had accomplished. The events of the life of Christ were decisive for the world, constituting the beginning of the last days. For Luke, too, Christ was the fulfillment of all the promises, in spite of the outward circumstances of his life which blinded the eyes of the Jews to the reality before them. This implied that all that went before Christ was merely preparatory. Yet, preparation, fulfillment in Christ, and eventual universal salvation through him in these last days, though constituting quite distinct epochs, nonetheless, together form one divine plan for the salvation of the world, a plan progressively realized through history.

(2) *The Purpose of Luke*

To appreciate Luke's overall purpose, his second work too must be taken into consideration. Then one can see that his object is to present the definitive phase of God's saving intervention, from the birth of the Baptist to the proclaiming of the gospel in the capital of the Gentile world. His theme is the progress of the Good News from Jerusalem to Rome; it is above all a message of salvation to the Gentiles. Simeon had seen in Christ "a light for revelation to the Gentiles" (2:32) and Paul's last words to the Roman Jews are: "Let it be known to you then that the salvation of God has been sent to the Gentiles: they will listen" (Ac 28:28).

All of this follows, in the plan of God, on Christ's rejection by Israel, for that rejection led to his death and exaltation and to universal salvation (Lk 24:46f). "Thus it is written, that the Christ should suffer and on the third day rise from the dead, and that repentance and forgiveness of sins should be preached in his name to all nations, beginning from Jerusalem" (Lk 24:46f). It is indeed a constant (theological) preoccupation of the evangelist to center his whole gospel around Jerusalem, for Jerusalem is for him the holy city of God and the theater of the great redemptive event, the Passion and triumph of Christ. In Jerusalem the gospel begins (1:5) and in Jerusalem it closes (24:52f). The Infancy narrative has two significant entries into the holy city (2:22-38, 41-50), and it is this same interest that explains why, unlike the natural climax of Matthew (3:2-10), the culminating temptation of our Lord in Luke is at the pinnacle of the Temple (4:9-12). The long central section (9:51–18:14) is presented as a journey to Jerusalem, and to heighten the effect, all other place-names are omitted. The journey outside of Galilee (Mk 6:45–8:26) is not given and Caesarea Philippi is not named as the place of Peter's profession of faith (9:18-22). This concern also explains why Luke has no mention of an apparition of Christ in Galilee. Jesus had come to Jerusalem and there had suffered and died and risen from the dead, and it was from Jerusalem that he was to ascend, finally, into heaven; a departure from the holy city would, in Luke's plan, be an anti-climax. And, consistently, when he came to write his second book he took care to show the Christian message radiating from that same center: "You shall be my witnesses in Jerusalem and in all Judea and Samaria and to the ends of the earth" (Ac 1:8).

Luke, we have seen, is an evangelist rather than an historian; here we may go further and describe him as a theologian of salvation history. For him that *Heilsgeschichte* falls into three periods: i/ the period of Israel; ii/ the period of Christ; iii/ the period of the Church. The Old Testament is the time of preparation for the culminating event of Christ's coming: "The law and the prophets were until John; since then the good news of the kingdom of God is preached" (16:16). Yet, though this is true, the period of Christ is preeminently that of his ministry and the time since the Ascension is that of the Church, looking back to the period of Christ and forward to the Parousia. In this perspective the Ascension, followed by the sending of the Spirit, is more the beginning of Acts than the close of Luke; and Acts itself is more correctly seen as a sequel to the gospel than as a history or the primitive Church. After his account of the infancies of John and of Jesus, Luke turns to the preaching of the kingdom of God in Palestine, first by the Precursor and then by the Messiah; and at the end of his work he has Paul proclaiming the same kingdom at the center of the Roman world. The gospel tells of the mission of Jesus and of the saving event of his death and Resurrection; it ends with his glorification in the Ascension. Jesus had come as the Messiah of his people and had found himself rejected by them. But his mission had not failed: he had brought salvation to a new Israel—repentance and forgiveness of sins must be preached in his name to all nations, beginning from Jerusalem (Lk 24:47).

The outlook of Luke is more striking when we see it in a wider perspective. In the Old Testament view the midpoint of time is marked by the future coming of the Messiah. For Christians this is no longer so: the midpoint of time is now in the past, in the historical life and work of Jesus Christ. There is another difference. For Christians the midpoint of time does not coincide with the Parousia (as it did in the Old Testament perspective); there is a space of time between Christ and the Parousia. These factors account for a certain tension that we find throughout the New Testament writings. There is still an expectation, a looking to the future, as there was in the Old Testament, but that future event (the Parousia) is no longer the center of salvation history; that center is found in an historical event. The New Testament outlook is based on "the thoroughly *positive* conviction that the mighty Christ-event has given a new center to time, and so it roots in the faith that the fulfillment has already taken place, that it is no longer the Parousia but rather the cross and the Resurrection of Christ that constitute the middle point and meaning of all that occurs".[3] Luke, in his gospel, is concerned with that midpoint of salvation history, the Christ-event, which he sees as the climax of the preceding period of Israel. In Acts he deals with the opening moments of the time between the great event and the Parousia, the period of the Church.

III. DOCTRINE

1. Universalism

Luke wrote his gospel for the Gentile Church and so he stressed the universal import of the Good News. This intention is already present in the Infancy narrative, despite its marked Semitic character. It is expressed in the canticle of the angels ("peace among men with whom he is pleased" 2:14), and Simeon saw that the

[3] O. Cullmann, *Christ and Time* (Philadelphia: Westminster Press, 1964), p. 81.

child would be a light to the Gentiles. In his genealogy of Jesus
Luke does not stop at Abraham (as Matthew does) but goes back
to Adam, the father of all men. In his preaching, the Baptist cites
the prophecy of Isaiah: "All flesh shall see the salvation of God"
(Lk 3:6; cf. Is 40:5); Lk 2:30-32 refers to another universalist
text of Second Isaiah (52:10). Jesus' charge to the Twelve, not
to go among the Gentiles or Samaritans (Mt 10:5f), is not recorded by Luke; indeed, Jesus sought hospitality in a Samaritan
village (Lk 9:52). A Samaritan is found among the ten lepers
healed by Jesus—the only one who returns to give thanks (17:11-
19); and, of course, one of the most striking of parables is the
Good Samaritan with its lesson that all barriers fall before the
demands of love (10:30-37). The Jews are warned that they will
be supplanted at the Messianic feast by men from every land.
And the last commission of the Risen Lord is that the gospel
should be preached to all nations (24:47; cf. Mt 28:19f).

Apart from these clear pointers the universalist bearing of the
gospel is also indicated by several deft touches which open up a
wider perspective than the original Palestinian one. The Pharisees tithe not only mint and rue but "every herb" (11:42; cf. Mt
23:23). Not only the fig tree (Mk 13:28) but "all the trees"
(21:29) herald summer. In the parable of the Two Builders
(6:47-48; cf. Mt 7:24-27) Luke has wholly changed the details so
that the story might be readily intelligible to his non-Palestinian
readers. The omissions and explanations we have noted have the
same effect: the gospel for all men is presented in a way that all
men can understand.

2. The Savior

Each of the gospels has its own characteristics, its own peculiar
quality, and these depend, to a large extent, on the manner in
which each evangelist presents the Person of our Lord. For Luke,
Jesus Christ is the Savior of men. He uses the title once only in
his gospel, in the words of the angel to the shepherds: "To you is
born this day a Savior" (2:11). The title is not repeated, it is true,
but it is significant that the evangelist has drawn attention to the
name given to the child at his circumcision—Jesus [= "Yahweh
saves"] (2:21). At any rate the Christ of Luke is throughout, and
before all else, a Savior who is full of compassion and tenderness

and great forgiveness. And the gospel of Luke is a gospel of mercy.

Luke has a gentle soul; it is because of this that he sees so clearly the tenderness of Christ. It is characteristic of him that he has omitted the cursing of the fig tree (Mk 11:12-14; Mt 21:18f) and has given instead the parable of the Barren Fig Tree (13:6-9) —"let it alone this year also". In the same vein of tenderness and mercy he has assembled the three parables of chapter 15: the Lost Sheep, the Lost Coin, the Prodigal Son. Matthew, too, has the first of these but the others are proper to Luke. We are told that God rejoices at the repentance of a sinner (15:7,10); we are shown that love of the divine Father for the prodigal child (15:20). We, too, must have something of the mercy of a forgiving God, and the father's gentle rebuke to the sulking elder son has a message for all of us: "It was fitting to make merry and be glad, for this your brother was dead, and is alive, he was lost and is found" (15:32). The three parables of chapter 15 are addressed to Pharisees and scribes, critical of our Lord's association with sinners (15:2f); a high proportion of Jesus' parables were spoken to the same audience. They witness in a striking way to his solicitude for those blind guides. He sought by every means to open their eyes, for he had come that they too might have life —if they would.

Perhaps nowhere more than in the wonderful passage on the "woman of the city who was a sinner" (7:36-50) do we see Christ as Luke saw him. The Lord does not hesitate between the self-righteous Pharisee and the repentant sinner and his words are clear and to the point: "And so, I tell you, her great love proves that her many sins have been forgiven" (7:47). Luke alone records the words of Jesus to the "good thief" (23:43) and his prayer for his executioners: "Father, forgive them, for they do not know what they do" (23:34). He alone tells of the look that moved Peter so deeply (22:61). Everywhere, at all times, there is forgiveness. It has been well said that the gospel of Luke is the gospel of great pardons.

It is typical of Luke that in his gospel he has paid special attention to women, for in the world of his day the position of women was degraded; and the insistence of the third evangelist is all the more striking when we compare his gospel with Matthew and Mark. Among the women introduced by Luke are: Elizabeth, the mother of the Baptist (1:39-58), Anna, the prophetess (2:36-38), the widow of Nain (7:11-17), the repentant sinner (7:36-50), the women of Galilee who accompanied Jesus on the public ministry, notably Mary Magdalen, Joanna and Susanna (8:2f) who were with him at the end (23:55f), the sisters of Bethany, Martha and Mary (10:38-42). There are, also, the woman who declared the mother of Jesus blessed (11:27f) and the women of Jerusalem who met Christ on his way to Calvary (23:27-31). We find, besides, two parables proper to Luke in which women figure: the Lost Coin (15:8-10) and the Unjust Judge (18:1-8). Finally, it is impossible not to recognize that the person of our Lady is shown in a vivid light in the Infancy narrative. God deigns to inform her of the great thing he is to do in her, and the lingering echo of the angel's "Rejoice! O favored one" is heard already in the *Magnificat.*

The gentle heart of Luke beat for the distressed, the poor, the humble. His sensitive soul perceived the tenderness of Christ. His gospel of mercy and pardon is the gospel of the supreme physician of souls who has told us that "the Son of man came to seek and to save the lost" (19:10). And if the Lord at his birth was hailed as Savior (2:11), it is also true that the last message of Christ to his disciples is a message of repentance and forgiveness: "Thus it is written, that the Christ should suffer and on the third day rise from the dead, and that repentance and forgiveness of sins should be preached in his name to all nations" (24:46f). The message of the third gospel and its purpose have been admirably expressed by Lagrange: "In reading this gospel of mercy and of repentance, of total renunciation motivated by love; in considering these miracles inspired by goodness, this understanding of sin which is not complacency but which brings with it the divine gift of sanctification; in learning to know how a most pure virgin and most tender mother had given birth to the Son of God, and how he had consented to suffer in order to lead men to the Father—in all this the noble Theophilus would perceive the reason for that moral transformation which had taken place before his eyes, and which had doubtless begun in his own heart, and he would judge the reason good and solid: the world had found a Savior."[4]

[4] *Op. cit.,* p. xlvii.

3. The Holy Spirit

Jesus as Messiah is the bearer of the Holy Spirit—this is a truth emphasized by Luke. He means to say that the whole of Jesus' life was supernatural and that he was a prophet in the fullest sense. After the baptism and temptation it is "in the power of the Spirit" that Jesus returned to Galilee and began his Messianic work (4:14), and his very first words were a quotation of Is 61:1f—"The Spirit of the Lord is upon me, because he has appointed me to preach the good news to the poor" (Lk 4:18). The whole public ministry is thus put under the sign of the Spirit and all the works and teachings of Christ must be seen in the light of this introduction.

In the early part of the gospel Luke has named the Holy Spirit very often; in the later chapters such references are rarer, yet there are a number of significant texts. In 10:21 Christ "rejoiced in the Holy Spirit" at the manifestation of his Messiahship to the unworldly. The Holy Spirit is, in the estimation of Jesus, the "good thing", the gift *par excellence* (11:13). Finally, the Risen Christ guaranteed that he would send the "promise of the Father", the "Power from on high", upon his disciples (24:49; Ac 1:8), for the Holy Spirit is the gift of the Risen and Ascended Lord (Jn 7:38f; 14:26). From Pentecost onward the Spirit is the guide and motive power of the Church's mission. The Spirit which moved the Messiah is now poured out by the Risen Lord upon his Church (Ac 1:8; 2:4) and the prophecy of Joel (2:28-32) was fulfilled (Ac 2:17-21); for, indeed, the gift of Pentecost is not for the little circle of disciples only but for all who believe in the name of Christ (cf. 2:38f; 10:44f).

Almost all the persons mentioned in Lk 1–2 are said to be moved by or filled with the Holy Spirit: John the Baptist from his mother's womb (1:15,18), his parents Zechariah (1:67ff) and Elizabeth (1:41ff), as well as Simeon (2:27ff) and Anna (2:36). In all these cases the Holy Spirit is the spirit of prophecy, and throughout Luke the Spirit is presented as a supernatural divine power. Perhaps the clearest text is 1:35 where Mary is told:

> The Holy Spirit will come upon you,
> and the power of the Most High will overshadow you.

The parallelism indicates that here Holy Spirit = Power of the Most High. In other words, Luke shows us the activity of the Spirit rather than the divine Person himself. John, however, tells us that the Holy Spirit is a Paraclete, an Advocate, just like the Son (14:16), and throughout the discourses after the Last Supper it is manifest that the Spirit is a Person, sent by the Father and the Son. But this more developed doctrine of the Trinity is not elaborated in Luke.

4. Prayer

Luke is the gospel of prayer and the supreme example of prayer is given by Jesus Christ himself. This fact is not neglected by Matthew and Mark. According to the three synoptists Christ prayed in Gethsemane; he prayed after the first multiplication of loaves (Mk 6:46; Mt 14:23); he prayed in Capernaum after he had cured many (Mk 1:35). But Luke speaks of the prayer of Christ in eight further circumstances. He prayed at the baptism (3:21), he retired into the desert to pray (5:16), and before choosing his Apostles he spent the whole night in prayer (6:12). He prayed before the confession of Peter (9:18) and later he told Peter that he had prayed specially for him (22:32). He prayed at the Transfiguration, and it was the sight of him in prayer that moved his disciples to ask to be taught how to pray (11:1). He prayed on the Cross for his executioners (23:34). Indeed, we might add that the surrender of his soul to the Father was a prayer (23:46).

Our Lord often recommended prayer to his disciples: persevering prayer like that of the importunate friend (11:5-13) or of the widow before the unjust judge (18:1-8). They must pray to obtain the Holy Spirit (11:13) and, in short, they ought to pray at all times (21:36). Their prayer must be true prayer, like that of the publican (18:13).

Prayer is necessary for all men, for the individual Christian, but it is the special office of the Church to give glory to God. It is, perhaps, not always recognized that the third gospel has furnished the Church with her canticles of praise: the *Benedictus* at Lauds, the *Magnificat* at Vespers, the *Nunc Dimittis* at Compline, and the theme of the *Gloria in Excelsis* in the Mass. But it is not surprising to find these canticles in Luke for the whole of the gospel sheds an atmosphere of joy and peace.

5. Joy and Peace

The coming of the Savior has created an atmosphere of joy and Luke is keenly aware of it. The annunciation of the birth of John includes a promise of joy (1:14), a promise that is fulfilled (1:58), and the yet unborn child leaps for joy in the womb at the presence of the mother of the Messiah (1:41,44). At the greater Annunciation the angel bids Mary rejoice (*Chaire* = "Rejoice!") and her thankful joy finds expression in the *Magnificat* (1:46-55). The birth of Jesus is an event of great joy for the angels who proclaim it and for the people he had come to save (2:10,13f). Later, the crowds rejoiced at the works they had witnessed (3:17). The seventy-two disciples returned, rejoicing, from their mission; Jesus pointed out to them the true motive of joy (10:20) and he himself "rejoiced in the Holy Spirit" (10:21). Zacchaeus received Jesus joyfully (19:6). The disciples rejoiced on the occasion of the entry into Jerusalem (19:37), and after the Ascension they returned to the city with great joy and praised God in the Temple (24:52). The parables of chapter 15 depict the joy of God at the repentance of a sinner.

Peace follows on joy, the peace which Jesus gives (7:50; 8:48), the peace that came into the world at his coming (2:14,29). The canticle of the angels celebrating the birth of the *Rex pacificus* (2:14) is echoed by the disciples when the King of peace enters the holy city in triumph (19:38)—the city that did not receive his message of peace (19:42). It is this same gift of peace that the Risen Christ gave (24:36), the peace which the disciples spread throughout the world (Ac 7:26; 9:31; 15:23). But peace and joy, both, are the fruit of prayer, of close personal union with Jesus Christ the Savior.

6. Rich and Poor

If we were to speak of Luke in modern terms we might describe it as the "social" gospel. The preaching even of the Baptist is given this character, and he points out to the tax collectors and soldiers what their social duty is (3:10-14). But the beatitudes offer the clearest case in point and the differences between Luke and Matthew are instructive. Matthew speaks of the "poor in spirit" (5:3), Luke of the "poor" (6:21). Matthew has "blessed are those who hunger and thirst for righteousness" (5:6) while Luke has "blessed are you that hunger now" (6:21). In both cases Matthew uses the term "poor" and "hungry" metaphorically, but Luke speaks of the really poor and of real hunger.

We must, however, keep the context in view. The poor are not worthy of the kingdom of God by the mere fact of being poor; Luke is careful to indicate that the poor in question are disciples (6:20) and, therefore, they are poor who put their trust in God. The poor who hunger in this life will be satisfied in the next—this is the thought of Ps 107(106):9—"He satisfies him who is thirsty, and the hungry he fills with good things." And the *Magnificat* announces the great social upset that the gospel will bring about: "He has put down the mighty from their thrones, and exalted those of low degree" (1:52).

Luke has many warnings against the danger of riches and he is much more emphatic than the other evangelists on this score: 6:24-26; 12:13-21; 14:33; 16:9,11,19-31; 18:22. It is not the possession of wealth as such that is condemned, rather it is the self-ishness of the rich that it severely censured. The parable of the Rich Fool (12:16-21) gives the moral: "So is he who lays up treasure for himself, and is not rich toward God." A choice must be made, for no man can serve God and mammon (16:13). On the positive side there is the fact that the life of Jesus was lived among the poor. At his birth it was shepherds who came to visit him (2:8), not the Magi of Matthew (Mt 2:1-12). His mother and Joseph gave the offering of the poor (2:24). In short, it is above all in the humble birth of the Son of God and in the penury of his life that poverty is exalted: "Foxes have holes, and the birds of the air have nests; but the Son of man has nowhere to lay his head" (9:58). And this example was efficacious, for Simon and James and John—and so many others—left everything and followed him (5:11).

It is to be expected, then, that Luke insists on renunciation. Confidence is not to be placed in riches (12:13-21) but on God who will provide (12:22-32): "Sell your possessions and give alms" (12:33). The follower of Christ must renounce all: "Whoever of you does not renounce all that he has cannot be my disciple" (14:33), and so the ruler who comes to him is bidden: "Sell all that you have and contribute to the poor . . . and come, follow me" (18:22). In both these texts and in 5:11,28 Luke, unlike the other evangelists, stresses the completeness of the renunciation (cf. Mk 10:21; Mt 19:21). He, too, is the only one of the synoptists who includes the *wife* among the possessions of this world which call for renunciation or detachment on the part of the perfect disciple (14:26; 18:29); here speaks the disciple of St. Paul (1 Cor 7:7,26).

7. The Influence of St. Paul

We are assured that Luke was a disciple of St. Paul and the influence of Paul can indeed be traced in the third gospel. This is not so much a matter of vocabulary—though there are resemblances—or of traditions—though in the account of the institution of the Eucharist (Lk 22:19f; 1 Cor 11:23-25) both follow a similar tradition—as of a common atmosphere of thought and sentiment. Both, for example, insist on the theme of the universality of salvation (Lk 2:30f; 3:23,38; 13:28f; 14:23; 24:46f; Rm 1:16; 1 Tm 2:4; Ti 2:11). This is not to say that the other Synoptics do not make it clear that salvation is offered to all men (and not to the Jews only), but that it is more emphatically the view of Luke as it is of Paul.

The atmosphere of joy that we have noted in Luke is like that of the Pauline epistles. In both we find frequent invitations to serve the Lord in thanksgiving and joy (Lk 5:25f; 10:17; 18:43; 19:37; 24:52f; Phil 4:4; 1 Thes 5:16; Rm 12:12; etc.). In both we find the same pressing exhortation, by word and example, to have recourse to prayer (Lk 3:21; 5:16; 6:12; 9:18,28f; 11:1-13; 18:1-5, 9-14; 22:32; 33:34,46; 1 Thes 5:17; Col 4:2; Eph 6:18; Phil 1:3-6; etc.), and the same manner of indicating the action of the Holy Spirit on the conduct of life (Lk 3:16,22; 4:1,14,18; 10:21; 11:13; 12:10,12; 24:49; Gal 3:2-5,13f; 5:22; 1 Cor 6:11; 12:13; 2 Thes 2:13; Rm 8:2,9; 14:17; etc.).

Luke, alone among the synoptists, gives Christ the title *Kyrios*—7:12,19; 10:1,39,41; 11:39; 12:42; 13:15; 16:8; 17:5f; 18:6; 19:8; 22:61; 24:3,34. In the LXX "Yahweh" was rendered *Kyrios* and the early Christians, from the first, gave this same divine title to

Christ. "Lord", for us, has lost its specific meaning, but the definite signification it had in the primitive Church is brought out by such texts as these: "If you confess with your lips that Jesus is Lord . . . you will be saved" (Rm 10:9), and "every tongue should confess that Jesus Christ is Lord" (Phil 2:11)—in both cases the divinity of Christ is professed. And when Luke uses the title he is writing as a Christian firm in his faith and so applies this Christian title to the Savior—for Jesus was not addressed as "Lord", in this full sense, during his lifetime.

It is not necessarily the influence of Paul only that has moved the evangelist to use the title "Lord" so frequently, for many of the concepts in the epistles go back beyond Paul to the primitive tradition. Such are the divine Sonship of Jesus, the universality of salvation, and the importance of faith as a condition of entry into the kingdom of God. It is precisely these, and similar, ideas that we find in Luke, and not as part of the preaching of the Apostle, but as they figured in his own written sources. Doubtless, in reproducing these concepts, he was influenced by the teaching and expressions of his master. But despite his origin and his education, despite his close contact with Paul, despite the Gentile Christian readers to whom his gospel is addressed, Luke reproduced, substantially, the primitive catechesis, the tradition of the apostolic Church.

IV. THE TEXT

The extant Greek manuscripts of the New Testament offer an enormous mass of material, and to them must be added the ancient versions. The study of the whole represents an immense labor, but scholars have gallantly faced up to the task. As a result, four great categories of texts have been established. This has helped to bring order into the crowded field, though some feel that the approach has been oversimplified and that, in fact, much relevant material (such as scriptural quotations in the early Fathers) has not been taken into account.

The four principal text-forms (with indication of their most notable representatives) are:

(1) The Alexandrian or Neutral Text, represented by the 4th-century Codex Vaticanus and Codex Sinaiticus.

(2) The Western Text, represented by the 5th- or 6th-century Codex Bezae.

(3) The Caesarean Text, represented by the 5th-century Codex Freer and the 7-9th-century Codex Koridethi.

(4) The Byzantine or Koine Text, represented by the great majority of (later) manuscripts. This was the *textus receptus* or "received text" of the Greek Church.

It is universally recognized that whereas the Koine and Western texts show abundant traces of free editorial revision, this is less evident in the Neutral and Caesarean texts, which are the best available for the recovery of the authentic New Testament text. The result of textual criticism, by and large, has been to establish the Alexandrian (Neutral) text as the best text-form.

The King James version of the New Testament (1611) was based upon the *textus receptus*—now acknowledged to be the poorest of the text-forms. In the past century, not only has much new manuscript material come to light, but textual criticism has made remarkable progress; the RSV revisers have made full use of the new scientific knowledge and method. Most influential has been the work of the British scholars B. F. Westcott and F. J. A. Hort, whose *The New Testament in the Original Greek* was published in 1883—a text based mainly on Vaticanus and Sinaiticus. But, in the RSV, other manuscripts have been given due consideration.

The Western text of Acts and, to a lesser extent, Luke, have some striking divergencies, by way of addition and omission, from the other text-forms. Since the normal tendency of Codex Bezae is to embellish and expand, Westcott and Hort regarded as highly significant this manuscript's omission of eight passages of the gospel (Lk 22:19b-20; 24:3,6,12,36,40,51,52). To these passages they gave the name "Western non-interpolations"—meaning that the Western text was the only one which at these points had escaped interpolation. This view is accepted in the RSV which relegates the passages to the margin. However, the present-day tendency is not to judge a variant on the ground of belonging to a particular text-form; each variant must be judged on its own merits. Although, in deference to the RSV text, these "Western non-interpolations" are here placed in brackets, the Commentary will make clear that they are regarded as authentic.

Commentary

PROLOGUE 1:1-4

1 Inasmuch as many have undertaken to compile a narrative of the things which have been accomplished among us, 2 just as they were delivered to us by those who from the beginning were eyewitnesses and ministers of the word, 3 it seemed good to me also, having followed all things closely for some time past, to write an orderly account for you, most excellent Theophilus, 4 that you may know the truth concerning the things of which you have been informed.

In the manner of the Greek writers of his day, Luke dedicates his book to a patron, at the same time setting out the occasion, method, and purpose of the work. He does this in a flawless and elegant Greek which contrasts sharply with the style of the following chapters. It is probable that this prologue was meant to introduce both parts of Luke's work, and the brief reference in Ac 1:1 marks the link between both volumes and suggests the continuity of the whole.

1f. "Many", while not to be taken too literally, must mean more than a few: there had been several narratives of the gospel events, some perhaps of no great extent. Among these documents we must surely number Mark, the Greek version of Aramaic Matthew (a gospel, no longer extant, traditionally attributed to St. Matthew and one of the sources of our canonical gospel of Matthew), and the special source common to Luke and Matthew. The authors of the documents—and Luke is in the same position—had recorded the traditions authoritatively handed on by the "eyewitnesses and ministers of the word"—that is, the Apostles, or, at least, these in the first place. The "word" = the gospel (cf. 8:13,15; Ac 4:4; 6:4; 8:4; 11:19).

3f. Luke has himself decided to write a gospel and so has done thorough preparatory research: he has carefully studied these things "from the beginning" (rather than "for some time past"), which meant going beyond the starting point of the apostolic catechesis, the baptism of Jesus, to the infancy of Jesus and of his

Precursor. His work will be "orderly", with a theological rather than a chronological order. The book is not written for Theophilus but is dedicated to him as its patron. Addressed as "Most Excellent", he is a man of some social standing who will help to circulate the work. He himself can learn from this gospel an appreciation of the solid historical foundation of the teaching he had received: in this very Greek phrase *logoi* stands for "teaching" rather than "things" and *katēchēthēs*, while it can mean "informed", most likely means that Theophilus had been "instructed" as a Christian.

A. From the Temple to the Conclusion of the Galilean Ministry

I. BIRTH AND HIDDEN LIFE OF
JOHN THE BAPTIST AND JESUS 1:5–2:52

Like Matthew, but independently of him, Luke prefaces his gospel with a narrative of the infancy of Jesus; he alone treats of the infancy of the Baptist. This whole section is notably more Semitic than the rest of the gospel and it has been seriously argued that a Semitic (Hebrew or Aramaic) original underlies these chapters. In point of fact there is wide divergence among scholars as to the extent and character of source material and regarding the personal contribution of Luke. It seems that the different viewpoints may be reduced to three—though, admittedly, at the price of oversimplifying the situation.

(1) These chapters are based on a written Hebrew source which, presumably, was known to Luke in Greek translation; thus are explained the many notable Hebraisms throughout the Infancy narrative. In this view the editorial work of the evangelist would be quite restricted.

(2) The whole is a free composition by Luke who deliberately, and successfully, imitated the style of the LXX. Since that version abounds in Hebraisms, their presence in these chapters is to be expected. A strong point of this argument is Luke's undoubted knowledge of the LXX and his penchant for reproducing its flavor.

(3) Luke has drawn on sources—Greek versions of Aramaic traditions. But these have been rewritten by him, and the whole arrangement of the carefully constructed Infancy narrative is his work. In the process, he has not only turned to biblical models but has written "biblical" Greek, and has kept himself deliberately within the framework of the Old Testament.

While it is not possible to make an unqualified choice, the third theory seems more satisfactory than the others. For one thing, it takes seriously Luke's assurance that, in his desire to go behind the traditional opening point of the gospel (the ministry of the Baptist), he sought out existing, trustworthy material (1:1-4). Then, by means of his carefully cultivated Old Testament style, he has reproduced the atmosphere of that moment before the emergence of Christianity. It is a brilliant achievement on the part of one who himself enjoyed the fullness of Christian revelation; but our evangelist is capable of such artistry. As well, there is the helpful consideration of the first twelve chapters of Acts. The Semitic coloring of these chapters is notable and the use of sources (originally Aramaic) is undoubted. Yet it is not possible to identify and delineate the sources; one gets the impression that Luke worked over his material more than once. He was not prepared to transcribe his source (or sources), but rewrote it, and then again modified each episode when he fitted it into his own larger framework. Hence, we cannot put our finger on a basic source or document as such; all now bears the imprint of Luke. It is not unreasonable to assume that his procedure in the Infancy narrative is just the same. In brief, then, the position taken here is that Luke, while leaning on a Greek form of originally Aramaic traditions, has himself written chapters 1–2 of his gospel, and in a style redolent of the Septuagint.

Luke's Infancy narrative is composed in the form of a diptych and has two phases: before the births of John and of Jesus (1:5-38) and the accounts of the birth of both (1:56–2:40). Each of these phases has a complementary episode: the Visitation (1:39-56) in the first case and the Finding (2:41-52) in the other. There are seven episodes in all.

i. Diptych of Annunciations 1:5-56

1. Annunciation of the Birth of John 1:5-25	2. Annunciation of the Birth of Jesus 1:26-38
Introduction of the parents	Introduction of the parents
Apparition of the angel	Entry of the angel
Zechariah troubled	Mary troubled
Fear not . . .	Fear not . . .
Annunciation of the birth	Annunciation of the birth
Q. How shall I know?	Q. How shall this be done?

A. *Reprimand* by the angel	A. *Revelation* by the angel
Constrained silence of Zechariah	Spontaneous reply of Mary
Departure of Zechariah	Departure of the angel
	3. Complementary episode 1:39-56
	Visitation
	Conclusion: Return of Mary

ii. Diptych of Births 1:57–2:52

4. Birth of John 1:57-58	5. Birth of Jesus 2:1-20
Joy at the birth	Joy at the birth
with canticle element	Canticle of angels and shepherds
Circumcision and Manifestation of John 1:59-79	6. Circumcision and Manifestation of Jesus 2:21-35
Manifestation of the "Prophet"	Manifestation of the "Savior"
Canticle: *Benedictus*	Canticle: *Nunc Dimittis*
	Supplementary episode: Anna 36–38
	Conclusion: Refrain of growth 2:40
Conclusion	7. Complementary episode 2:41-52
Refrain of growth 1:80	The Finding in the Temple
	Refrain of growth 2:52

A glance at the plan of the Infancy narrative, as it appears in schematic form, brings home Luke's intention. John the Baptist and Jesus are compared and contrasted, but the greatness of Jesus is emphasized even by the more developed account of his earthly origins. Within the parallel narratives the same point is made. Mary is clearly shown to be far superior to Zechariah and, more explicitly, the Son of Mary is set on a pedestal and towers above the son of Zechariah. The parent cell of these two chapters is the infancy of Jesus and, more precisely, the Annunciation; and it may well be that the infancy of the Baptist is no more than a prelude, composed by Luke in order that the Messiah may be introduced by his Precursor as in the primitive gospel.

These chapters are dominated by the idea of Messianic fulfillment.[5] The different scenes build up to the climax of the entry into the Temple, for Luke saw in that event the formal manifestation of Jesus the Messiah. He has achieved his effect, in large measure, by his use of Dn 9–10 in the annunciations of Zechariah and to Mary and by his use of Mal 3 in the annunciation to Zechariah, the *Benedictus* and the Presentation. Taken together with the pregnant *eplēsthēsan* (1:23,57; 2:6,21f) this use of Messianic texts underlines the arrival of the Messianic age. These chapters are religious history written in the biblical manner. Reflecting on the facts, Luke has rethought them and has recounted them in terms of scriptural precedents—hence a constant echoing of Scripture. This gives rise to what we may term an "allusive theology" that lies beneath the surface throughout.

When the chapters are read on this deeper level it emerges that Luke has wished to present Jesus as a transcendent, divine Messiah. The titles given to him (Great, Holy, King, Light, Glory, Son of God, Savior, Christ the Lord, Lord), when taken together, point in that direction. In short we might say that the assimilation of Jesus to Yahweh is "the final word of the Christology of Lk 1–2".[6] We should note, too, that the transcendent dignity of Jesus sheds a reflected glow on Mary. As mother of the Messiah she is the true daughter of Sion where God has come to dwell among his people—a truth brought out by the use of Zeph 3 and Mi 4–5.

1. ANNUNCIATION OF THE BIRTH OF JOHN 5-25

5 In the days of Herod, king of Judea, there was a priest named Zechariah, of the division of Abijah; and he had a wife of the daughters of Aaron, and her name was Elizabeth. **6** And they were both righteous before God, walking in all the commandments and ordinances of

---

[5] See pp. 282ff.

[6] R. Laurentin, *Structure et Théologie de Luc 1–2* (Paris: Gabalda, 1957), p. 130.

the Lord blameless. 7 But they had no child, because Elizabeth was barren, and both were advanced in years.

8 Now while he was serving as priest before God when his division was on duty, 9 according to the custom of the priesthood, it fell to him by lot to enter the temple of the Lord and burn incense. 10 And the whole multitude of the people were praying outside at the hour of incense. 11 And there appeared to him an angel of the Lord standing on the right side of the altar of incense. 12 And Zechariah was troubled when he saw him, and fear fell upon him. 13 But the angel said to him, "Do not be afraid, Zechariah, for your prayer is heard, and your wife Elizabeth will bear you a son, and you shall call his name John.

14 And you will have joy and gladness,
  And many will rejoice at his birth;
15 for he will be great before the Lord,
  and he shall drink no wine nor strong drink,
  and he will be filled with the Holy Spirit,
  even from his mother's womb.
16 And he will turn many of the sons of Israel to the Lord their God,
17 and he will go before him in the spirit and power of Elijah,
  to turn the hearts of the fathers to the children,
  and the disobedient to the wisdom of the just,
  to make ready for the Lord a people prepared."

18 And Zechariah said to the angel, "How shall I know this? For I am an old man, and my wife is advanced in years." 19 And the angel answered him, "I am Gabriel, who stand in the presence of God; and I was sent to speak to you, and to bring you this good news. 20 And behold, you will be silent and unable to speak until the day that these things come to pass, because you did not believe my words, which will be fulfilled in their time." 21 And the people were waiting for Zechariah, and they wondered at his delay in the temple. 22 And when he came out, he could not speak to them, and they perceived that he had seen a vision in the temple; and he made signs to them and remained dumb. 23 And when his time of service was ended, he went to his home.

24 After these days his wife Elizabeth conceived, and for five months she hid herself, saying, 25 "Thus the Lord has done to me in the days when he looked on me, to take away my reproach among men."

5. Herod the Great reigned from 37 to 4 B.C. "Judea" is to be understood in a broad sense: Herod's territory included Idumaea and Samaria. The division of Abijah is the eighth of the 24 divisions of priests (1 Chr 24:10) who carried out, in turn, the daily service of the temple.

6f. Zechariah and his wife are saintly Israelites who faithfully observed the commandments of God. Elizabeth was barren like Sarah (Gn 16:1ff), Rebekah (25:21), Rachel (30:22), the mother of Samson (Jg 13:2), and Anna the mother of Samuel (1 Sm 1-2), while, like Abraham and Sarah, she and her husband were elderly and, humanly speaking, must remain childless. Hence the child to be born is in a special way the gift of God, a child of grace like Isaac, Samson, and Samuel.

8-10. The gospel begins, as it closes (24:53), in the Temple. Each division of priests served for a week at a time. Because of their number the chief offices were assigned to them by lot. To Zechariah had fallen the highest priestly duty of tending the fire and burning fresh incense on the golden altar which stood before the Holy of Holies. Though there was an offering both morning and evening, the presence of a whole multitude, in the outer courts, suggests the evening offering.

11f. It was an auspicious moment for a divine message, and the messenger of the Lord, Gabriel, suddenly appeared in the place of honor at the right hand of the altar. Zechariah's spontaneous reaction to the heavenly apparition was fear; Luke often refers to similar religious awe: 1:29f, 65; 2:9f; 5:26; 7:16; 8:37; 9:34; Ac 2:43; 5:5,11; 19:17; cf. Dn 10:7.

13f. The angel reassures him (cf. 1:30; 2:10): God has heard his prayer (cf. Dn 10:12). The remainder of the verse makes it clear that the object of the prayer was, indeed, the birth of a son; though, in view of v. 18, this had not been a recent prayer of the old priest. God announces beforehand (cf. 1:31; Gn 17:19; Is 7:14) the significant name of the child: John = "Yahweh is gracious"; and John will indeed herald the age of grace (cf. Jn 1:6). So it is that the natural joy of the father will be transformed into a greater joy, and many others (and not only the neighbors of 1:57f) will rejoice when, in due time, he will stand forth as the greatest of the prophets of Israel (cf. 7:26-28).

15f. John will be great not only by human reckoning but in God's eyes (cf. 7:28); his true greatness is indicated by the role he plays in God's plan. Like the Nazirites (Nm 6:23; Jg 13:4f; 1 Sm 1:11) and the Rechabites (Jer 35), the great ascetics of Israel, John will abstain from strong drink. He will be filled with the Holy Spirit "from his mother's womb"—it is not clear whether

the phrase means "from his birth" or "already in the womb".
Here, as almost everywhere in the Infancy narrative, the "Holy
Spirit" is the spirit of prophecy, and the meaning is that John is
called to be a prophet from (or before) birth, like Jeremiah (Jer
1:5) or the Servant of Yahweh (Is 49:1-5). The verse offers no
support for the common view that John was freed from original
sin in the womb (cf. 7:28). Filled with the prophetical spirit he
will win many Israelites back to their God from the ways of sin
(cf. 3:1-20).

17. It was widely believed (Mal 3:23; Sir 48:10f; Mt 17:10 and
parallels; Jn 1:21) that the Messianic era would be preceded by
the return of Elijah; here it is shown that John is the Elijah who
is to come (cf. Mt 17:12). The verse is a—rather free—citation of
Mal 3:23f: John's preaching of repentance will leave the people
well disposed for the coming of the Lord—*Kyrios* is the Lord of
the Old Testament. Though the evangelist is aware that John is
the forerunner of the *Messiah,* in these chapters he remains faithful to the Old Testament perspective and represents the new
Elijah as the forerunner of Yahweh; such, at least, is the general
view. However, it appears to follow from a closer study of the
narrative as a whole that the "Lord" whose way the Baptist prepares is Jesus himself. The dominant idea of the two chapters is
that of Messianic fulfillment, which is realized at the entry to the
Temple. We may observe the influence of Dn 9–10 and Mal 3 in
the present passage.

18. Abraham (Gn 15:8), Gideon (Jg 6:37), and Hezekiah
(2 Kgs 20:8) requested signs in similar circumstances and were
granted them without reprimand; Zechariah's demand betrays a
certain skepticism which will be punished (v. 20).

19f. Gabriel is named in Dn 8:16; 9:21. Like Raphael (Tb
12:15) he is one of the seven "angels of the Face" of Jewish tradition, who stand in the presence of God. He is sent by God to
bring this "Good News"—*euaggelizesthai* is a favorite word of
Luke (10 times in the gospel and 18 times in Acts). The sign that
Zechariah receives is also a punishment; he will be dumb (and
deaf—v. 62f) until the good tidings are fulfilled.

21f. The ceremony of offering incense was a simple and brief
one and the people who awaited the priestly blessing were
wondering at the delay. When he did come forth the people rec-

ognized in his dumbness the effect of a supernatural vision (Dn 10:7f,15), while he conveyed as much to them by signs.

23-25. Zechariah was not one of the priests who lived in Jerusalem and he left the city when his term of office was over; *eplēthēsan* has certain theological overtones (1:57; 2:6,21f). We are evidently to understand that the child was conceived in the normal way, but it was due to a special intervention of God that it happened despite old age and sterility. Why Elizabeth should have hidden herself during the first five months (cf. v. 26) is not at once clear.

2. ANNUNCIATION OF THE BIRTH OF JESUS 26-38

26 In the sixth month the angel Gabriel was sent from God to a city of Galilee named Nazareth, 27 to a virgin betrothed to a man whose name was Joseph, of the house of David; and the virgin's name was Mary. 28 And he came to her and said, "Hail, O favored one, the Lord is with you!" 29 But she was greatly troubled at the saying, and considered in her mind what sort of greeting this might be. 30 And the angel said to her, "Do not be afraid, Mary, for you have found favor with God. 31 And behold, you will conceive in your womb and bear a son, and you shall call his name Jesus.

32 He will be great, and will be called the Son of the Most High;
   and the Lord God will give to him the throne of his father David,
33 and he will reign over the house of Jacob for ever;
   and of his kingdom there will be no end."
34 And Mary said to the angel, "How can this be, since I have no
   husband?"
35 And the angel said to her,
"The Holy Spirit will come upon you,
and the power of the Most High will overshadow you;
therefore the child to be born will be called holy,
the Son of God.

36 And behold, your kinswoman Elizabeth in her old age has also conceived a son; and this is the sixth month with her who was called barren. 37 For with God nothing will be impossible." 38 And Mary said, "Behold, I am the handmaid of the Lord; let it be to me according to your word." And the angel departed from her.

The close parallel between this and the foregoing passage is obvious from a glance at the plan given above. Both Annunciation narratives, involving an angelic message, are presented in a distinctive literary form. We find Old Testament examples of the form in the messages to Hagar (Gn 16:7-15), to the wife of Manoah (Jg 13:3-20), and to Gideon (6:11-24); this last is particularly instructive as we shall see. In these cases, and wherever the form occurs, we find that always the initiative is God's. Always too, though certain difficulties crop up in the dialogue, the message is taken to be sufficiently clear before the messenger departs.

The best way of showing that Luke has been faithful to the traditional literary form is by setting out a typical text, that of Jg 6:11-21, and by pointing to the more significant parallels:

The angel of the Lord came and sat under the terebinth at Ophrah which belonged to Joash of Abiezer. Gideon, his son, was threshing wheat inside the winepress to keep it hidden from Midian when the angel of the Lord appeared to him and said: "The Lord is with you, Valiant Hero!" Gideon answered him: "Pardon, my lord, if the Lord is with us why then has all this befallen us?" . . . Then the angel of the Lord turned to him and said: "Go in this might of yours and deliver Israel from the hand of Midian; lo, I have sent you." Gideon answered him: "Pray, my lord, how am I to save Israel? My clan is the weakest in Manasseh and I myself am the least in my family." The angel of the Lord answered him: "The Lord will be with you, and you shall smite the Midianites as one man." And Gideon said to him: "If now I have found favor in your sight show me a sign that it is you who speak with me." . . . Then the angel of the Lord reached out the tip of the staff which was in his hand and touched the meat and the unleavened cakes; and fire sprang up from the rock and consumed the meat and the unleavened cakes; and the angel of the Lord vanished (*apēlthen*) from his sight (LXX).

The first striking feature is that the angel does not address Gideon by his proper name; indeed it is obvious that his opening words are anything but a conventional greeting. The angel of the Lord speaks words of hope and promise, and Gideon is designated as the chosen vehicle of that promise; so "Valiant Hero" is a new name which indicates something of the whole purport of the message. And the accompanying phrase, "The Lord is with you", is the guarantee that the promise will be efficacious: the Lord who has chosen Gideon will accomplish his purpose. Gideon does realize that the words concern not only him but also, and more especially, his people. Yet he is perplexed, so he asks a question, and the angel's reply to the question is a more emphatic reiteration of his first words. Gideon next requests a sign and the sign is given him when fire breaks from the rock and consumes the sacrifice he had prepared. Then, straightway (Jg 6:25-27), the "Valiant Hero" set about his task of saving Israel. It is already sufficiently clear that Luke's text is an example of the same literary form, and this alone is enough to justify the use of the one passage to explain the other.

26f. In the sixth month of Elizabeth's pregnancy (1:24,36) Gabriel was again sent by God, with tidings of joy, to a "city" called Nazareth; for the benefit of his Gentile-Christian readers Luke specifies that it is a village of Galilee (cf. Mt 2:23). The angel was sent to a "virgin"—*parthenos* is best taken in the current sense of a young girl of marriageable age; though Luke is aware that Mary is a virgin in the strict sense (v. 35) he is not here insisting on this. She is already betrothed and betrothal was, in Jewish law, a fully valid and binding contract. Yet not until the bridegroom had taken the bride to his home (cf. Mt 1:24)— by custom a year after the espousals—did the couple live as man and wife. In the case of Mary and Joseph this final step was not taken until some time after the birth of John: from Judea Mary returned to *her* home (v. 36). Joseph belonged to the house of David, and so the legal Davidic descent of Jesus is assured. It cannot be shown that Mary was of the family of David, though it is reasonable to think so; she was certainly related to Elizabeth who was of Aaronitic descent (vv. 5,36).

28. The occurrence, in such a Semitically colored narrative, of the Greek greeting formula *chaire* ("Hail") instead of the Semitic "Peace!" is so surprising that one hesitates to accept it at its face value.

On closer inspection we find that Luke has a specific Old Testament passage in mind: Zeph 3:14-17 (cf. Jl 2:21-27; Zech 9:9f)—"Rejoice! Daughter of Zion; sing aloud, Daughter of Jeru-

salem!" The word rendered "Rejoice!"—also occurring in a parallel context of Joel and Zechariah and (apart from Lam 4:21)
nowhere else in the LXX—is *chaire,* the same term used by the
evangelist. Since that Messianic passage of Zephaniah underlies
Lk 1:30f (immediately following), *chaire* in 1:28 must have the
meaning "Rejoice!"—an invitation to rejoice at the advent of
Messianic times (for Gabriel's message does herald the new age).
The RSV rendering of *kecharitōmenē* ("favored one") is preferable to "full of grace" (from the *gratia plena* of the Vulgate).
Here the episode of Gideon is instructive; for in view of the cog-
nate literary form and, indeed, on the basis of the close parallel
between Jg 6:12 and Lk 1:28, we must see that the opening
words of Gabriel cannot be just a conventional greeting. Nor can
kecharitōmenē be, primarily, a reference to the personal holiness
of Mary, a compliment. We may reflect that Gideon was given a
new name, "Valiant Hero", a name that was already a pledge of
victory for his people. It is a name which contained the substance
of the angel's message and which pointed to the work that Gideon
was to accomplish. In Mary's case, the context of the angel's
message is Messianic and she is present in her Messianic role.
What Gabriel announces is that she has been chosen to play an
essential part in God's plan. Thus, much better than "full of
grace" is the portentous name "Favored One". This title not only
preserves all that "full of grace" might imply of personal sanctity
(Mary is endowed with grace in a permanent fashion), but points
to the source of that fulness; for the favor that will make of Mary
the Favored One *par excellence* is the Messianic motherhood, the
divine maternity. And now, too, the statement "the Lord is with
you" falls into place. Coming after "full of grace"—as this is commonly understood—it is unnecessary, even banal. But once it is
recognized that the new name designates a function allotted by
God, then the assurance that the Lord will be with the chosen
one is a guarantee of the effective accomplishment of the divine
purpose. Gideon, we may recall, received just such an assurance.
So Gabriel's opening words, as Luke had understood them, are
best rendered: "Rejoice, O Highly Favored One, the Lord is with
you."

29. Mary was "greatly troubled", not like Zechariah (v. 12) by
the appearance of the angel, but at his words. We can surely

leave aside an interpretation going back to St. Ambrose to the effect that the modesty of the young virgin was troubled; Audet rightly characterizes this opinion as "not being very complimentary either to Mary or to her visitor".[7] The common view, that Mary's humility was disturbed, is not satisfactory—her humility is seen in her unhesitating *Fiat* and in her *Magnificat:* serene and direct, quite forgetful of self. The best explanation is the obvious one: Mary is "troubled", perplexed, because she does not yet understand for what purpose and to what extent she has been favored by God.

30f. The angel proceeds to enlighten her. His opening words are a close parallel of his initial salutation: "Fear not" corresponds to "Rejoice", "Mary" replaces "Favored One", and "you have found favor with God" echoes "the Lord is with you". Next follows the message: the Favored One is to conceive and bear a son and she will give to this son the name of Jesus (cf. Gn 16:11; Is 7:14). The text of Zephaniah is again enlightening: "The King of Israel, the Lord, is in your midst (literally, in your womb). . . . Fear not, Zion . . . the Lord your God is in your midst (literally, in your womb)" (3:15-17). We notice the same reassuring "fear not", and the parallel also explains the tautology of Luke: "You will conceive *in your womb*" (cf. 1:13)—an echo of a phrase (*beqirbeh*) which occurs twice in the passage of Zephaniah. Admittedly, we have to turn to the Hebrew text rather than to the LXX; a more literal version of the passage may have been known to Luke. Like Hagar (Gn 16:11) and the mother of Immanuel (Is 7:14), Mary will impose the name on the child: Jesus means "Yahweh saves".

32f. The angel describes her son and his destiny in terms borrowed from the Old Testament, especially from the oracle of Nathan (2 Sm 7:12-16), the first in a chain of prophecies in which the Messiah appears as a son of David. In view of the background, the title "Son of the Most High" and the reference to an everlasting kingdom do not look beyond the horizon of Jewish Messianic expectation (cf. Is 9:6; Dn 7:14). It is clear that the son of Mary will be the Messiah but it does not follow that he will be divine. At this stage everything is still within the limits of the Old Law, but Luke will go on to explain that the intervention

[7] J.-P. Audet, "L'Annonce à Marie" in *Revue Biblique* 63 (1956), p. 361.

of the Holy Spirit will mean that Jesus must be named "Son of God" in an altogether new sense.[8]

34. Like Zechariah (v. 18) Mary asks a question—and her words have embarrassed countless commentators.

A common (Roman Catholic) view is that Mary had made a vow of virginity and had entered into a compact with Joseph to that effect. This interpretation, which cannot be traced back beyond Ambrose (4th century), seems unsatisfactory on several grounds. Admittedly, the question is unexpected, but the problem it has created is due in large measure to the fact that our understanding of it has been clouded by the intrusion of later ideas. To state that Mary had made a vow of virginity surely betrays a later (Christian) mentality, and the anachronism is not very effectively redeemed by the substitution of "intention" or the like. This approach to the text is ultimately due to a preoccupation that is apologetical rather than exegetical, a concern to uphold the doctrine of the virgin birth. But this is not Luke's preoccupation. The very next verse shows that he takes the virginal conception for granted, but his interest does not bear on it directly. We have to look at things from his point of view and keep the Old Testament background in mind. We should consider that Mary was a young Jewish girl with her people's high regard for marriage. Moreover, she was already betrothed and so was about to enter the married state; but she was not yet living with Joseph. Now here precisely is the point of Mary's question. She had understood that the conception of which the angel spoke was to take place without delay, and not only the parallel with Gideon but the context itself indicates that she had understood correctly. As one betrothed she naturally felt that it would come to pass in the normal way; her perplexity is due to the fact that she is not yet married. And that is just what her question implies: "How can this be since I am not in the married state?" The very last objection that should be raised against this interpretation is that it does less than justice to our Lady. Its strength is that it makes no unwarranted assumption and is not colored by apologetical preoccupations—these are the weakness of other explanations. And whatever one may wish to believe, it is not easy to reconcile an intention to remain a virgin with the fact that Mary was betrothed; to suppose that

[8] See pp. 284f.

Joseph also was of the same mind is gratuitous and leaves us with two problems instead of one.

Another suggestion, that of a special revelation, is no more than a theological *deus ex machina*—which, moreover, makes the question utterly pointless. But, on the other hand, to believe that Mary, *after* she had understood from the angel how the wonderful child was to be conceived, resolved to remain a virgin, is a different matter altogether. And in these changed circumstances her resolve was one that a man like Joseph would appreciate and respect (cf. Mt 1:18-25). Another solution is to regard the question as a literary technique of Luke: it marks the change from the Old Testament level of vv. 32f and opens the way for the explanation (v. 35) that what is about to happen is something entirely new. In this view the verse tells us nothing about Mary's understanding of the mystery. Since we take the position that the Infancy narrative, as it stands, is the work of Luke, we have no difficulty in accepting v. 34 as an editorial link-verse. But the evangelist has put the question in the mouth of Mary and it should be interpreted as a question of hers. It does indeed serve as a transition to the further elucidation of the angel but that is not its only role; it still needs to be explained, and we have ventured an explanation.

35. Again the angel speaks, this time in answer to Mary's question. "Holy Spirit" and "Power of the Most High" stand in parallelism; the Spirit is the divine power or energy. In Is 11:2 we read that the Spirit of Yahweh will rest on the Messianic prince; here the Spirit will come upon her who is the mother of the Messiah. Already in Gn 1:2 the Spirit of God hovered over the waters about to perform the great work of creation; here that divine power overshadows Mary, about to perform a new and wondrous creation, a conception wrought by the direct action of God (cf. Jn 1:14). It is possible that there is an allusion to Ex 40:35—the overshadowing Spirit and the presence of the child in the womb of Mary recall the cloud that abode upon the tent of meeting and the glory of Yahweh that filled the tabernacle. But is this to read too much into *episkiazein* ("overshadow"), the one word common to both texts? In v. 35b the word *hagion*, "holy", causes some difficulty. The verse might be rendered: "That is why the child to be born will be holy; he will be called Son of

God." The presence of "holy", which occurs, also unexpectedly, in 2:23, is due to the influence of Dn 9 in the one case and of Mal 3 in the other. In Dn 9:24 the Messianic times will be marked, among other ways, by the consecration of a Holy One. (While it is not clear whether Daniel refers to the consecration of a holy place or of a holy person, Luke was entitled to select the second sense which, moreover, seems to have been a current Jewish interpretation.) With this "Holy One" in mind in v. 35, he thus insinuates that the angel's message was the signal for the inauguration of the Messianic age. In v. 32 we have noted that "Son of the Most High" is a title within the Jewish Messianic perspective and does not necessarily imply divinity. Here the situation is quite other; *dio kai,* "that is why", points back to the action of God: the Holy One will be Son of God in a quite new sense, because he will be conceived by the power of God alone. Though it is evident that this fact implies a virginal conception, it is not less obvious that the virginal conception as such is secondary in the context.

36f. In accordance with the literary form of angelic message, Mary, like Gideon and like Zechariah, is given a sign, a guarantee of the authenticity of the message—though, in her case, the sign is unsolicited. V. 37 is an almost verbatim quotation of God's words to Abraham in relation to the promised birth of Isaac (Gn 18:14).

38. In Mary's consent we may see the true pattern of her humility. If she had been troubled and if she had asked a question it is because she had been perplexed. Now that she knows the divine purpose she accepts that purpose unhesitatingly and with perfect simplicity. If heroics would be out of place at such a moment so, no less certainly, would a protestation, even a suggestion of unworthiness. Mary was too completely God's to think of herself at all. Mary was now aware of the divine purpose—but did she *understand* it? Above all, did she realize that the child to be born of her would be divine? The answer is not obvious. We know that the disciples had not grasped this truth during the lifetime of their Master; it needed the Resurrection to open their eyes. We have good reason, then, to ask if Mary was aware, from the beginning, of the divinity of her Son. If, yet again, we look to the essentials of Luke's narrative, we find that his attention first bears on the child whose birth he announces, then on the motherhood of Mary, and lastly on the manner of her maternity. In other words, the central fact, and the source of the others, is the Incarnation; and this, by definition, means that God became Man. It forms the kernel of the angel's message, and if Mary had not grasped this she had not really understood the message. But, according to the principles of the literary form in question, she ought to have understood the question before the departure of the angel, and Luke's treatment of the matter implied that she had. Here not only the Gideon text, but the calling of Moses (Ex 3:10-12), Isaiah (Is 6:1-13), and Jeremiah (Jer 1:4-10), is relevant. We may maintain, therefore, not gratuitously but by sound exegetical method, that at the moment of the Incarnation, Mary believed that the child then and there conceived within her was divine. This, however, is not to claim that she was fully enlightened (cf. 2:19,50,51); and we are told that her *Fiat* was essentially an act of *faith* (1:45)—which included, in its object, the divinity of Christ, but glimpsed in the darkness that is a necessary feature of faith. Little by little she came to realize that God's thoughts and ways are not those of men for she, too, can have understood only in a human way. And all the while, a strange paradox: the most obvious fact about her Son, the Son of God, was that he was utterly human.

"Today, God has become a human embryo; tomorrow he will leave behind the frugal comfort of Nazareth and be born in a stable; he will flee from his enemies. In the home of his parents, simple peasants, God will live the humble life of a little child; he will grow into adolescence just like others, and he will become a tradesman whom nothing, absolutely nothing, marks off as different from any other. He is so much one of them that when he takes it into his head to play the rabbi his cousins believe him to be out of his mind (Mk 3:21) and his neighbors, the people of Nazareth, refuse to take him seriously (6:1-16). He is a God who allows himself to be arrested, who does not refute the false charges made against him, and who is nailed to a cross between two criminals. And there, in the midst of general disillusionment, Mary will renew her act of faith: despite appearances, this crucified one, her Son, this man about to draw his dying breath, is God. For so it was that once before, then as now standing all alone in a world unaware of the most solemn event in its history, she had made her first act of faith.[9]

But, on Easter morning, she saw, in a blaze of light, all that had been shrouded in darkness and she tasted to the full the Messianic joy already promised in Gabriel's "Rejoice".

3. COMPLEMENTARY EPISODE 39-56

39-44. The Visitation

39 In those days Mary arose and went with haste into the hill country, to a city of Judah, 40 and she entered the house of Zechariah and greeted Elizabeth. 41 And when Elizabeth heard the greeting of Mary, the babe leaped in her womb; and Elizabeth was filled with the Holy Spirit 42 and she exclaimed with a loud cry, "Blessed are you among women, and blessed is the fruit of your womb! 43 And why is this granted me, that the mother of my Lord should come to me? 44 For behold, when the voice of your greeting came to my ears, the babe in my womb leaped for joy."

39. The "city of Judah", in view of the determination "hill country", must be in the neighborhood of Jerusalem; a tradition, going back to the sixth century, points to the delightfully situated village of Ain Karim, five miles west of the city. The "haste" of Mary was inspired by friendship and charity; the journey would have taken some four days.

40f. At Mary's greeting Elizabeth felt the infant move in her womb (cf. Gn 25:22); as an inspired prophetess ("filled with the Holy Spirit"), she understood that he had leaped for joy at the presence of the mother of the Messiah (v. 44). It nowise follows that the unborn babe enjoyed the use of reason or (as has been claimed) that he was then and there cleansed of original sin (cf. v. 15). What did happen is that the Baptist's mother was able to perceive a special significance in an occurrence that she would otherwise have regarded as fortuitous.

[9] S. Lyonnet, "Le récit de l'Annonciation et la Maternité Divine de la Sainte Vierge" in *L'Ami du Clergé* 66 (1956), p. 39.

42-45. Enlightened by the prophetic spirit, Elizabeth is aware of Mary's secret: she is the mother of her "Lord", that is, of the Messiah. That is why she is "blessed among women", a Hebraism (cf. Jdt 13:18) meaning the most blessed of all women. She went on to praise Mary's unhesitating acquiescence in God's plan for her—her great faith. Elizabeth's expression of unworthiness at the signal honor of this visit echoes that of David in the presence of the ark of Yahweh (2 Sm 6:9); but the influence of the passage (2 Sm 6:2-11) on the Visitation narrative, and Luke's consequent presentation of Mary as the true ark of the covenant, must remain doubtful.

45-56. The Magnificat

45 "And blessed is she who believed that there would be fulfillment of what was spoken to her from the Lord."

46 And Mary said,
"My soul magnifies the Lord,
47 and my spirit rejoices in God my Savior,
48 for he has regarded the low estate of his handmaiden.
For behold, henceforth all generations will call me blessed;
49 for he who is mighty has done great things for me,
and holy is his name.
50 And his mercy is on those who fear him
from generation to generation.
51 He has shown strength with his arm,
he has scattered the proud in the imagination of their hearts,
52 he has put down the mighty from their thrones,
and exalted those of low degree;
53 he has filled the hungry with good things,
and the rich he has sent empty away.
54 He has helped his servant Israel,
in remembrance of his mercy,
55 as he spoke to our fathers,
to Abraham and to his posterity for ever."

56 And Mary remained with her about three months, and returned to her home.

Three Old Latin manuscripts, and some texts of Irenaeus, Origen, and Nicetas attribute the *Magnificat* to Elizabeth; all other witnesses attribute it to Mary. In form a thanksgiving psalm, it is a catena of Old Testament reminiscences and leans especially on the canticle of Hannah (1 Sm 2:1-10); hence (like

the *Benedictus*) it is even more Semitic in tone than the rest of
these two chapters. Lagrange warns that the literary quality of
the *Magnificat* has too often been exaggerated. It is unlikely that
the hymn represents the *ipsissima verba* of Mary and it may well
be Luke's composition. Since there is no clear reference to the
Messianic birth—and this is surprising in view of the angel's message and the words of Elizabeth—it is more likely that it represents his adaptation of a psalm from the circle of the "poor of
Yahweh", the saints of Judaism. The *anawim*, or "poor", assumed
a large place in the religious life of Israel after the Exile. The
term expresses an attitude of mind: a willing openness to God,
humility before God (cf. Zeph 2:3; 3:11f; Lk 6:20); the poor man
(*anaw*) is regarded as Yahweh's client, one who abandons himself entirely to God and puts his trust in him. It is easy to understand that a psalm from such a milieu would already marvelously
conform to the outlook of this "handmaid of the Lord" (Lk 1:38).
But, whatever its origin, the attribution of the *Magnificat* to Mary
by an inspired writer gives us an assurance that it truly represents
her sentiments.

46-48. Elizabeth had blessed Mary as mother of the Messiah;
Mary gives the glory, in joyful thanksgiving, to the God who had
blessed her and, through her, Israel: "My soul magnifies the
Lord." The rest of the opening cry of joy (v. 47) echoes the
words of Habakkuk: "I will rejoice in the Lord, I will joy in the
God of my salvation" (Hb 3:18; cf. 1 Sm 2:1; Ps 35[34]:9). God
has looked with favor upon his handmaid, she who is the most
perfect of the "poor of Yahweh". Her entire submission to God's
will (cf. 1 Sm 1:11) has won for her, the Favored One, everlasting glory.

49f. Immediately, she turns her attention to the Almighty, the
holy and merciful God (cf. Dt 10:21; Ps 111[110]:9) who has
done great things for her. In truth, "the steadfast love of the Lord
is from everlasting to everlasting upon those who fear him" (Ps
103[102]:17).

51-53. The interest now switches to Israel and to the manifestation of God's power, holiness, and goodness in favor of his
people (cf. Pss 118[117]:15; 89[88]:10; 103[102]:17; 1 Sm 2:7f;
Sir 10:14; Jb 12:19; Ezek 21:26; Ps 107[106]:9). These verses are

not concerned with the past, or not with the past only, but represent God's action at all times: what he has done to Mary and what he, through her as mother of the Messiah, has done for Israel, shows forth his manner of acting. He does mighty deeds with his arm, the symbol of his strength, when he reverses human situations—the proud, the mighty and the rich he has humbled, destroyed and left empty, while he has raised up and blessed with good things the poor of this world (the *anawim*). None of this, to be sure, is brought about by a social revolution which sets one in the place of the other; the change follows on God's attitude toward those who ask humbly and toward those who believe that they have the right to demand. The great reversal is finally effected in the perfect stage of the kingdom, the life to come.

54f. These closing verses, in the mouth of Mary, point to the final intervention of God. His sending of the Messiah is the crowning act of his gracious treatment of Israel, that people which, through his covenant with Abraham (Gn 17:7), had become his "Servant" (Is 41:8f; cf. Ps 98[97]:3; Mi 7:20). Mindful of his great mercy, he has fulfilled the promise made to the patriarch: a promise made to one man is accomplished in a woman, the Daughter of Zion. Yet it is surprising, especially with the words of Elizabeth in mind, that the saving act of God is not presented in more explicit terms. We have suggested that this is so because Luke has worked-over an older psalm. At any rate, the *Magnificat* stands between the Old Testament and the New and, like the rest of Luke's Infancy narrative, captures the atmosphere of that unique moment.

56. The concluding verse has often been misunderstood. Though Luke immediately begins to describe the birth of John (v. 57), it does not follow, as it seems it must, that Mary had departed before the child was born. Typically (cf. 1:64-67; 3:19f; 8:37f), the evangelist is rounding off one theme before passing to another. The Visitation episode did close with the departure of Mary, so he mentions it at the end; the birth of John is a distinct episode. We may surely take for granted that our Lady remained as long as Elizabeth had need of her: she, *the* handmaid of the Lord, was happy to serve others. Mary returned "to *her* home", that is to say, she had not yet begun to live with Joseph.

4. THE BIRTH AND MANIFESTATION OF JOHN 57-80

57f. The Birth of John

57 Now the time came for Elizabeth to be delivered, and she gave birth to a son. **58** And her neighbors and kinsfolk heard that the Lord had shown great mercy to her, and they rejoiced with her.

57f. The birth of John marks the fulfillment of the angel's message to Zechariah. The completion (*eplēsthē*) of Elizabeth's term of pregnancy (cf. Gn 25:24) suggests, too, the fulfillment of Messianic times (cf. Lk 2:6,21f.). The rejoicing of the neighbors and kinsfolk is already an accomplishment of the promise of v. 14.

59-66. The Circumcision of John

59 And on the eighth day they came to circumcise the child; and they would have named him Zechariah after his father, **60** but his mother said, "Not so; he shall be called John." **61** And they said to her, "None of your kindred is called by this name." **62** And they made signs to his father, inquiring what he would have him called. **63** And he asked for a writing tablet, and wrote, "His name is John." And they all marvelled. **64** And immediately his mouth was opened and his tongue loosed, and he spoke blessing God. **65** And fear came on all their neighbors. And all these things were talked about through all the hill country of Judea; **66** and all who heard them laid them up in their hearts, saying, "What then will this child be?" For the hand of the Lord was with him.

59-62. Circumcision was prescribed for the eighth day after birth (Gn 17:12; Lv 12:3). It had become customary to name the child on that day and to celebrate the occasion by a party to which relatives and neighbors were invited. There is no need to suppose that Elizabeth had learned the child's name by revelation, for Zechariah, though deaf as well as dumb (v. 62), could still have managed to inform her (cf. v. 63).

63f. Zechariah confirmed his wife's declaration. Thereupon he found himself able to speak again and his first words were a hymn of praise, that is, the *Benedictus*.

65f. Before giving the text of the canticle, Luke, in his usual style, rounds off the episode. The closing remark of v. 66 is a biblical expression (cf. Jer 26:24; Ac 11:21).

67-79. The Benedictus

67 And his father Zechariah was filled with the Holy Spirit, and prophesied, saying,

68 "Blessed be the Lord God of Israel,
    for he has visited and redeemed his people,
69 and has raised up a horn of salvation for us
    in the house of his servant David,
70 as he spoke by the mouth of his holy prophets from of old,
71 that we should be saved from our enemies,
    and from the hand of all who hate us;
72 to perform the mercy promised to our fathers,
    and to remember his holy covenant,
73 the oath which he swore to our father Abraham, **74** to grant us
    that we, being delivered from the hand of our enemies,
    might serve him without fear,
75 in holiness and righteousness before him all the days of our life.
76 And you, child, will be called the prophet of the Most High;
    for you will go before the Lord to prepare his ways,
77 to give knowledge of salvation to his people
    in the forgiveness of their sins,
78 through the tender mercy of our God,
    when the day shall dawn upon us from on high
79 to give light to those who sit in darkness and in the shadow of death,
    to guide our feet into the way of peace."

67. Zechariah, as so many others in this narrative, is inspired by the Spirit of prophecy. His canticle, like the *Magnificat,* is a chain of Old Testament quotations and reminiscences and gives an even stronger impression of being a pre-existing psalm put, by Luke (though with some adaptations), in the mouth of Zechariah. This is true especially of the first part (vv. 67-75) which is markedly Jewish in tone; the remainder may be a composition of Luke's. Yet, vv. 78f might be considered the natural conclusion of the original psalm, in which case vv. 76f form an insertion of the evangelist. The *Benedictus* is loosely appended to the narrative; it is significant that if the canticle were removed v. 80 would fit smoothly after v. 66. But the inspired writer has judged that this canticle reflects the mind of the old priest at that moment. As it stands, the first part of it (vv. 68-75) praises God's great actions in the history of his people; the second part (vv. 76-79) turns to the son of Zechariah and foreshadows his office and his preaching.

68f. The hymn opens, like Jewish prayers, with the praise of God (cf. Pss 41[40]:14; 72[71]:18; 106[105]:48). "Visit" is a biblical term which indicates a divine intervention that may be inauspicious or, more generally, favorable (Ex 4:31; Ru 1:6; Pss 65[64]:10; 80[79]:15; 106[105]:4). In the present context the visitation and deliverance refer to the sending of the Messiah, the "horn of salvation"—horn is the symbol of strength (cf. 1 Sm 2:1,10; Pss 18[17]:3; 75[74]:5)—of the house of David. In the New Testament David is called "servant (of God)" only in v. 69 and Ac 4:25.

70f. Sent in accordance with the prophecies (cf. 2 Sm 7), the Messiah will be God's means of saving his people from their enemies (cf. Pss 18[17]:18; 106[105]:10; 2 Sm 22:18). In Ac 3:21 Luke gives an almost exact equivalent of v. 70.

72-75. Then will be the overflowing of God's great mercy (Mi 7:20) when, in remembrance of his covenant (Ex 2:24; Pss 105[104]:8f; 106[105]:45) and of his oath to Abraham (Jer 11:5), his people can serve him, unmolested and without fear, all their days.

76f. These verses, addressed to the infant Baptist, point to his vocation of prophet and Precursor. Where Jesus is the "Son of the Most High" (v. 32), John is the "prophet of the Most High". Moreover, the "Lord" whom John "goes before" is, in the context of these chapters and given the influence of Mal 3 here and at vv. 16f, the Messiah assimilated to Yahweh. John will declare to this Lord's people that true salvation consists in the forgiveness of sins (cf. Lk 3:3; Ac 10:37; 19:4); salvation in terms of remission of sins is a favorite theme of Luke (cf. Lk 3:8; 5:32; 13:3; Ac 3:19,26; 5:31; 10:43; 13:38) and its occurrence here strongly supports the view that these verses were inserted by him. Even more compelling, in this respect, is the fact that the mission of the Apostles is presented in identical language; for they, like the Baptist, will make known to the people that salvation, through remission of sins, is to be found in Jesus (cf. Ac 2:36; 4:10,12; 5:31f; 10:42; 13:23f,26,38).

78f. This passage could well be the conclusion of vv. 68-75. But in its present context, v. 78 indicates that the true salvation is the fruit of the loving mercy of God and will be brought from on high by the "rising Sun"—*anatolē* (Mal 3:20; cf. Is 60:1), that

is, the Messiah or Messianic age. *Episkepsetai,* "will visit", is a
better attested reading than *epeskepsato,* "has visited". More satisfactory than the RSV is the *Jerusalem Bible* rendering of v. 78b:
"who from on high will bring the rising Sun to visit us". The
"shadow of death" is thick darkness (Is 9:1; 42:7), the darkness
of sin which will be dissipated by the Messianic light (cf. Jn 1:5).
That same Sun will guide men along the right way of true peace,
the faithful service of God (vv. 74f).

80. The infancy story of the Baptist closes with a "refrain of
growth" (cf. 2:40,52) indicating his physical and spiritual development (cf. Jg 13:24f; 1 Sm 2:26). In typical Lucan style, reference to John's sojourn in the desert prepares the way for his next
appearance (Lk 3:2). The "wilderness" is that of Judah, in the
neighborhood of the Dead Sea. Though it has been argued that
the verse suggests a link between the Baptist and the Essene
establishment of Qumran (situated in that area), the only necessary conclusion from Luke's statement is that John must have
known the Qumran settlement.

5. THE BIRTH OF JESUS 2:1-20

2:1-7. The Birth

1 In those days a decree went out from Caesar Augustus that all
the world should be enrolled. 2 This was the first enrollment, when
Quirinius was governor of Syria. 3 And all went to be enrolled, each
to his own city. 4 And Joseph also went up from Galilee, from the city
of Nazareth, to Judea, to the city of David, which is called Bethlehem,
because he was of the house and lineage of David, 5 to be enrolled
with Mary, his betrothed, who was with child. 6 And while they were
there, the time came for her to be delivered. 7 And she gave birth to
her first-born son and wrapped him in swaddling cloths, and laid him
in a manger, because there was no place for them in the inn.

Throughout the first chapter of his gospel, while dealing with
the annunciations of the births of John and of Jesus, and with the
birth of the Baptist, Luke's narrative has remained within the
Jewish world. Now, at the beginning of the second chapter, when
he comes to the birth of him who is "a light for revelation to the
Gentiles" (2:32), his perspective opens, if only for a moment, onto
the Gentile world. His eyes have glanced from the Jerusalem of

the beginning of his gospel to the Rome of the last chapter of
Acts. The birth of the Savior of all men is fixed—though perhaps
too vaguely for our taste—on the calendar of world history.

1. Augustus was Emperor from 30 B.C. to 14 A.D. The general
census of the Roman Empire ("all the world" = the *orbis Ro-
manus*) was a means of tax assessment; Luke sees it as the provi-
dential means of assuring that Jesus would be born in Bethlehem.
There is evidence for a census in Gaul in 12 B.C. and there was
provision for the taking of a census in Egypt every fourteen years;
the series seems to have begun between 10 and 9 B.C. According
to Tacitus (*Annal.* 1, 11) a *Breviarium Imperii* in Augustus' own
hand found at his death gave not only the number of regular and
auxiliary troops and the strength of the navy, but provided sta-
tistics on the provisions of dependent kingdoms, on direct and
indirect taxation, and on recurrent expenditure; this information
must have resulted from a general census which, of course, need
not have been carried out simultaneously in all parts of the Empire. The possibility of a Roman census in the domain of Herod
the Great has been questioned. But Augustus knew that Herod,
a puppet king, must bow to his wishes and, besides, there was a
distinct coolness in their relations following Herod's unauthorized
campaign against the Nabataeans, 9-8 B.C. In view of the evidence it is reasonable to suppose that Luke is standing on sound
historical ground when he refers to the edict of Augustus.

2. The celebrated chronological difficulties raised in this verse
are still unsolved. It is widely accepted, on the sole authority of
Josephus (*Ant* XVII, 13, 5; XVIII 1, 1; *Bj* VII, 8, 1), that a census
was held in 6-7 A.D. when Publius Sulpicius Quirinius was legate
of Syria, and that it was resisted by the Zealots under Judas the
Galilean (*Ant* XVII, 10, 5; cf. Ac 5:37). If this dating is accepted
we must look for an earlier census carried out by Quirinius. On
the evidence of inscriptions from Venice, Tivoli and Antioch of
Pisidia, it has been argued that he was legate of Syria between
4 and 1 B.C., and also that he had a special commission to carry
out a census in Palestine from 10 to 8 B.C. Tertullian (*Adv.
Marcionem* 4, 19) attributes the nativity census to Sentius Sa-
turninus, legate of Syria from 8 to 6 B.C.; he could well have
completed a census begun by Quirinius. The truth of the matter
is that the available evidence is an inadequate basis for any firm

conclusion; but, by the same token, it is too scanty to convict Luke of historical inaccuracy—a charge that has often been levelled at him.

3. Though their own method of census-taking did not demand the journey to a man's place of origin, the Romans tended to respect local custom. Egyptian papyri tell of a Roman census carried out in an analogous fashion in that country and specify that married women, too, had to present themselves for enrollment (cf. v. 5). Palestinian custom must have been similar.

4f. Joseph, of the house of David, went from his home in Nazareth to the birthplace of his ancestor (1 Sm 16:1). Although Joseph had taken Mary to his home (cf. Mt 1:24), and she was therefore his wife in the full legal sense, Luke, by referring to her as "betrothed" delicately hints that Joseph was not the father of Jesus. The readings "wife" of some versions and "betrothed wife" of many manuscripts and of the Vulgate—which are presumably meant to account for Mary and Joseph traveling together—show that the evangelist's refinement was not always appreciated.

6f. No indication is given of the time spent in Bethlehem, nor does the text necessarily mean that Joseph had taken his wife on the long journey just when she was about to give birth to her child. The term "firstborn son" has in mind (or echoes) the law prescribing the consecration of the firstborn male to God (Ex 13:12; 34:19; cf. Lk 2:23); an only son is "firstborn" in this technical sense. For Lk 2:4-7, cf. Mi 5:1f. Most likely because of an exceptional influx of travelers due to the census, the *khan*—a hostelry in which men and beasts settled themselves as best they could—was full. Since we are told that the newborn baby was laid in a manger, we learn that Joseph and Mary, perhaps in search of privacy more than anything else, found shelter in a stable of some sort. A tradition going back to the second-century Justin Martyr (*Dial.* 78) specifies a cave. These circumstances emphasize the lowliness and poverty that surrounded the birth of Jesus: nothing here suggests the power and glory of his divinity. The observation that Mary, by herself, wrapped the infant in swaddling cloths is to be understood in the same sense, though this last detail may also be Luke's way of suggesting that the manner of birth was miraculous. At the same time, his delicate touch is far removed from the heavy-handed treatment of the apocryphal gospels, whose authors lose no opportunity of empha-sizing the virginity of Mary and the miracle of the birth. Through-out the Infancy narrative it is evident that Luke is convinced of the perpetual virginity of Mary, but nowhere does this fact obtrude itself.

8-20. Annunciation to the Shepherds

8 And in that region there were shepherds out in the field, keeping watch over their flock by night. 9 And an angel of the Lord appeared to them, and the glory of the Lord shone around them, and they were filled with fear. 10 And the angel said to them, "Be not afraid; for behold, I bring you good news of a great joy which will come to all the people; 11 for to you is born this day in the city of David a Savior, who is Christ the Lord. 12 And this will be a sign for you: you will find a babe wrapped in swaddling cloths and lying in a manger." 13 And suddenly there was with the angel a multitude of the heavenly host praising God and saying,

14 "Glory to God in the highest,
and on earth peace among men with whom he is pleased!"

15 When the angels went away from them into heaven, the shep-herds said to one another, "Let us go over to Bethlehem and see this thing that has happened, which the Lord has made known to us." 16 And they went with haste, and found Mary and Joseph, and the babe lying in a manger. 17 And when they saw it they made known the saying which had been told them concerning this child; 18 and all who heard it wondered at what the shepherds told them. 19 But Mary kept all these things, pondering them in her heart. 20 And the shepherds returned, glorifying and praising God for all they had heard and seen, as it had been told them.

In Lk 7:22 we learn that one of the signs given to the Baptist whereby he might know that Jesus was indeed the Messiah was that "the poor have good news preached to them". So it was that the first announcement of Jesus' birth was made to simple shepherds: these, the poor and humble, despised by the orthodox as non-observers of the Law, are granted and accept the revela-tion which the leaders of Israel will reject.

8. Bethlehem lies at the edge of the desert of Judah and the shepherds in question, living in the open, were nomads—like the bedouins of today who frequent the same desert region.

9. An angel suddenly appeared to a group of them as they guarded their flocks by night, and they found themselves sur-

rounded by a brilliant light; the "glory of the Lord", an expression frequent in the Old Testament (cf. Ex 13:21; 16:10), accompanies a heavenly manifestation. "Fear", religious awe, was the natural reaction (cf. Lk 1:12,29; Mk 16:5).

10-12. But, just like Zechariah and Mary, the shepherds too were reassured. The angel's message is an announcement of good news (*euaggelizomai* is a favorite word of Luke) and joy to all the people of Israel; for, despite the initial setting of the birth of Jesus in the framework of world history (2:1), the universalist note is not again struck in this episode (as it will be in v. 32) and the horizon closes on the limits of the Jewish world. "This day"—the long awaited day of Israel's salvation—has dawned; a newborn child is the Savior (*soter* is used of Jesus only here in the Synoptics; but cf. Ac 5:31; 13:23) who has brought salvation. This Savior is "Christ the Lord"—the title *Christos Kyrios* occurs once only in the LXX (Lam 4:20) and nowhere else in the New Testament: he is the Messiah endowed with lordship and dominion (cf. Is 9:5). However, it would seem that Luke, in the context of the angelic message and the presence of divine glory, intends something more; and the figure of Augustus (2:1) has relevance here too. "Lord", in the LXX a divine title rendering the name "Yahweh" of the Hebrew text, was, together with the title "Savior", claimed by the emperors (and other kings) and was granted to the gods. In the teeth of such arrogant usurpation, the evangelist asserts that this helpless infant is not only Messiah but Savior and Lord as well, thus quietly claiming, for all who would discern, that he is divine. Like Zechariah (1:18,20) and Mary (1:36) the shepherds were given a sign: "Let them go and see for themselves that they are not the victims of illusion; they shall find a child in a manger, not left naked and abandoned as they might expect to find a child who had been put in such an odd cradle, but properly clothed in swaddling bands." [10]

13f. Just as unexpectedly as the first angel had appeared, he was now joined by a great host of the army of heaven, chanting a song of praise. The short canticle is closely related to the acclamation of the crowd at Christ's triumphal entry into Jerusalem (19:38). It differs from the latter in not being addressed to the

---

[10] M.-J. Lagrange, *The Gospel of Jesus Christ* (London: Burns & Oates, 1938), p. 38.

Messiah but to God who had sent him. It would seem that "Glory to God" expresses not so much a wish ("let God be glorified") as a statement, a recognition of the significance of the hour, an acknowledgment of the saving act of God. Though *eudokia*, "favor", "good pleasure", is widely attested, the weight of manuscript evidence upholds the genitive *eudokias*. The current translation "peace to men of goodwill" (based on the Vulgate), referring to human goodness, fails to convey the true meaning; the renderings "with whom he is pleased" and "who enjoy his favor", pointing exclusively to the divine benevolence, suit the term and the context. We may observe, too, a close parallel between both members of the couplet: Glory—peace; the highest— earth; God—men. The sense is that, through the birth of the Messiah, God is glorified in heaven (that is, his power and mercy are manifest) and, on earth, the men whom he loves receive the divine blessing of peace, the peace which the Savior has brought.

15f. Marvelling at their strange experience, stirred to excited anticipation by the angel's words, the shepherds, with the song of the heavenly choir still ringing in their ears, set out in haste for Bethlehem. There they discovered that the facts (*hrēma*, literally, "word" in the Hebraic sense of "thing", "event"; cf. 1:37,65) were just as the angel had described.

17f. Naturally, they spoke freely of what they had seen, and of the things that had been told them, but we do not learn whether the wonder of the hearers led to an acceptance of the angel's words.

19. But one, at least, forgot none of these happenings: Mary kept in her heart the events and words (*hrēmata*) and pondered over them (cf. 2:51; Gn 37:11; Dn 7:28). Luke is, perhaps, reminding us that she is the ultimate source of his Infancy narrative; but, also, his words imply that her understanding of these events was not at once complete but could develop.

20. In his customary way, he winds up the episode by indicating the return of the shepherds to their flocks, and their joyful thanksgiving is a favorite theme of his.

6. CIRCUMCISION AND MANIFESTATION OF JESUS
21-40

21. The Circumcision

21 And at the end of eight days, when he was circumcised, he was called Jesus, the name given by the angel before he was conceived in the womb.

This is parallel to 1:59-63, the circumcision of John, and here, too, the emphasis is on the bestowal of the name. Born under the Law (Gal 4:4), Jesus submitted to the observances of the Law (cf. Gn 17:12; Lv 12:3). Do we tend to lose sight of the full implication of the Incarnation? The fact that he submitted to the ceremony of circumcision and, in general, to all the legal observances, harmonizes perfectly with his role of Messiah as it had been decreed by his Father. Since he had come not to conquer the enemies of Israel by great power and prodigies but to redeem sinners by his death, he must, until that death, conform to the practices of pious Israelites. He is, indeed, the model of *anawim,* the pious souls of Israel, he who is, in perfect measure, "gentle and humble in heart" (*anaw*)—Mt 11:29. The splendor of the angelic manifestation at his birth was not reflected in his Person: he is the infant, lying helpless in a manger, a babe who must be circumcised on the eighth day. It was the father's right to name his child (cf. Lk 1:62) and in this case, too, the heavenly Father had bestowed the name, indicated beforehand by the angel (1:31). The name of Jesus ("Yahweh saves") was not unknown; it had been borne by Joshua (it is the same) and by Jesus ben Sirach, author of *Ecclesiasticus.* But here is something new, a name that suits perfectly the character of that Savior announced to the shepherds, he who is Christ the Lord.

22-28. Jesus Is Presented in the Temple

22 And when the time came for their purification according to the law of Moses, they brought him up to Jerusalem to present him to the Lord **23** (as it is written in the law of the Lord, "Every male that opens the womb shall be called holy to the Lord") **24** and to offer a sacrifice according to what is said in the law of the Lord, "a pair of turtledoves, or two young pigeons." **25** Now there was a man in Jerusalem, whose name was Simeon, and this man was righteous and devout, looking for the consolation of Israel, and the Holy Spirit was upon him. **26** And it had been revealed to him by the Holy Spirit that he should not see death before he had seen the Lord's Christ. **27** And inspired by the Spirit he came into the temple; and when the parents brought in the child Jesus, to do for him according to the custom of the law, **28** he took him up in his arms and blessed God and said,

In vv. 22-24 Luke has combined two requirements of the Law: the purification ceremony after childbirth, and the consecration of the firstborn to the Lord. Thus, somewhat loosely, he can speak of "their" purification—that is, of Mary and Jesus. It is convenient to consider the ceremonies separately for they are, in fact, distinct.

22a, 24. According to Lv 12:2-4, a mother was purified forty days after the birth of a son; she was required to make an offering of a lamb for a burnt offering and of a young pigeon or a turtledove for a sin offering. A poor woman could substitute another pigeon for the lamb (Lv 12:6-8); Mary's was the offering of the poor. The "purification" regarded strictly ritual uncleanness (contact with a corpse, for example, meant ritual uncleanness for a priest) and did not, of course, imply a moral fault in childbirth. Mary, like her Son, fulfilled the observances of the Law, even to the making of a sin offering.

22b-23. If Luke has mentioned the purification of Mary it is only because it happened to be associated with the presentation of Jesus in the Temple. The firstborn son (he "that opens the womb") belonged to the Lord (Ex 13:2,12) but was redeemed, bought back, by the payment of two Temple shekels (Nm 18:15f) —about two dollars in modern money. It is nowhere laid down that the child should be taken to the Temple and presented there, yet the fact that Jesus was so presented is obviously of great importance for Luke, who appears to have in mind the dedication of Samuel (1 Sm 1:11,22-28). We should recall that *eplēsthēsan*, "accomplished" (v. 22; cf. 1:23,57; 2:6,21), has more than the banal significance of the completion of a specified period and, in the context of the Infancy narrative, suggests the end of the time of waiting and the arrival of the Messianic age. In v. 23 *hagion*, "holy", is unexpected. The verse is a rather free citation of Ex 13:2,12 but the word "holy", which does not occur in the Exodus text, has come from Luke, who has inserted it also in 1:33b. Its presence in the latter case is due to the influence of Dn 9:24—the consecration of a "Holy One" which will mark the inauguration of the Messianic age—while its occurrence in our verse establishes a contact between Dn 9 and another Messianic text, Mal 3, for this last stands behind his description of the Presentation. Since in 1:16f and in the *Benedictus* he presents the Baptist as the messenger, the Elijah, who will prepare the way of Yahweh (Mal 3:1,23), it must follow that the "Holy One" who is presented in the Temple is none other than the Lord: "Behold, I send my messenger to prepare the way before me, and the Lord whom you seek will suddenly come to his Temple" (Mal 3:1): Lagrange comments: "Their arrival in the Temple courts, though attended with so little ceremony, was nevertheless an event of sublime importance, for then was fulfilled the promise of Malachi which foretold how the Lord would enter his Temple for the first time. It was fitting, therefore, that he should be greeted by one of the representatives of the prophets." [11]

25-28. This role was filled by Simeon, a pious Israelite who awaited, with faith and patience, the fulfillment of the hope of Israel, its "consolation" (cf. Is 40:1; 49:13; 51:12; 61:2). He, too, like so many others in these chapters, had received the Spirit of prophecy. The same Holy Spirit had assured him that he would not die until he had seen the Messiah (the anointed one of the Lord; cf 4:18). Now the Spirit moved him to visit the Temple and revealed to him that the infant who was at this moment being presented there was indeed the longed-for Messiah. Full of joy and thanksgiving, he took the child into his arms, and then intoned his thanksgiving hymn.

29-32. The Nunc Dimittis

29 "Lord, now lettest thou thy servant depart in peace,
    according to thy word;
30 for mine eyes have seen thy salvation
31 which thou hast prepared in the presence of all peoples,
32 a light for revelation to the Gentiles,
    and for glory to thy people Israel."

The *Nunc Dimittis* is the third canticle given to us by Luke alone and, like the others, it is used daily in the liturgy. In v. 29

[11] *Ibid.*, p. 39.

despota is best rendered "Master". Simeon realizes that, in view of the fulfillment of the promise made to him (v. 26), death must be near; he can die in peace, like Abraham (Gn 15:15), but more privileged than Abraham. His cup of joy has been filled to over-flowing because he has gazed upon the "salvation of God" (cf. 3:6; Is 40:5), the Messiah whom God had sent to save his people. And not his own people only: salvation is destined for the Gen-tiles too (cf. Is 52:10; 2:1-4; 42:6; 49:6). This Messianic salvation is not only a beacon which shines before the nations, it is a brightness which dissipates the darkness and enlightens them. But since salvation comes from Israel (cf. Jn 4:22), and was made manifest through the chosen people, it redounds to the glory of Israel. In this passage, for the first time in the Infancy narrative, we look explicitly (cf. 2:1) beyond Jewish limits to a universalist horizon—salvation for all men; but still the perspec-tive is that of the Old Testament, the vision of Second Isaiah.

33-35. The Prophecy of Simeon

33 And his father and his mother marvelled at what was said about him; 34 and Simeon blessed them and said to Mary his mother,
    "Behold, this child is set for the fall and rising of many in Israel,
    and for a sign that is spoken against
35 (and a sword will pierce through your own soul also),
    that thoughts out of many hearts may be revealed."

33. The previous prophetic words of Simeon were a manifesta-tion of divine power and, as such, met with astonishment, the customary reaction throughout Luke and Acts (Lk 1:62; 2:18,33; 4:22; 8:25; 9:43; 24:12,41; Ac 2:7; 3:12; 4:13; 7:31). Here (cf. Lk 2:27,41,43,48) Luke names Joseph as the father of Jesus; in view of 1:26-38 he can manifestly mean no more than legal paternity.

34f. Simeon speaks again and his gaze, after that fleeting sweep (vv. 31f), has come back to rest on Israel. He blessed Mary and Joseph—the privilege of age—and spoke again prophetically, ad-dressing his words to her whose mother's heart would feel most keenly the fate of her Son (v. 35a). Though the infant has come as the Savior of his people (v. 11), he will be rejected by many of them (cf. Jn 1:11), for he will stand as a sign of contradic-tion, a stone that can be a stumbling block (Is 8:14f) or corner-stone (Is 28:16; Ps 118[117]:22f) according as men turn their backs on him or accept him (cf. Lk 20:17f; Ac 4:11; Rm 9:33; 1 Pt 2:6-8). In his presence there can be no neutrality, for he is the light that men cannot ignore (cf. Jn 9:39; 12:44-50), the light that reveals their inmost thoughts and forces them to take part for him or against him. V. 35a appears to be a parenthesis which associates Mary with the sad and painful aspect of the career of the Messiah, a veiled presage of the great sorrow which was to be hers in full measure when she stood at the foot of the Cross (Jn 19:25-27). But it may be that Mary is here portrayed as the Daughter of Zion, and the words of v. 35a are to be explained as a reminiscence of Ezek 14:17 which describes the sword of God passing through the land as an avenging force. In Luke's mind, the sword which will divide Israel, consuming the wicked and leaving Mary and the faithful remnant unharmed, is the revealing word (cf. Heb 3:12f) brought by Jesus.

36-38. Anna the Prophetess

36 And there was a prophetess, Anna, the daughter of Phanuel, of the tribe of Asher; she was of great age, having lived with her husband seven years from her virginity, 37 and as a widow till she was eighty-four. She did not depart from the temple, worshipping with fasting and prayer night and day. 38 And coming up at that very hour she gave thanks to God, and spoke of him to all who were looking for the redemption of Jerusalem.

After a prophet a prophetess—the delicate hand of Luke—and, once again (implicitly this time), the Spirit of prophecy. Anna, now eighty-four, having lost her husband seven years after an early marriage, had preferred to remain a widow—a choice that was highly regarded in Israel (cf. Jdt 8:4-8; 16:22f). She practically lived in the Temple, so uninterrupted were her prayers; a typical saint of Judaism, one of the *anawim*, the "poor of Yahweh", she is also an example to Christian widows (cf. 1 Tm 5:5,9). Her prophetic instinct enabled her to recognize the infant Messiah and, gratefully, she spoke of him to those who, like Simeon and herself, looked for the true salvation of Jerusalem (Is 52:9), that is, of Israel.

39f. Return to Nazareth

39 And when they had performed everything according to the law

of the Lord, they returned into Galilee, to their own city, Nazareth.
40 And the child grew and became strong, filled with wisdom; and
the favor of God was upon him.

The return to Nazareth serves to round off Luke's narrative.
As at the close of the Baptist's Infancy narrative (1:80), so here
(v. 40) we find a "refrain of growth". The growth and development was not only physical but intellectual as well: though "filled
with wisdom", Jesus grew in wisdom daily (cf. 2:52); his wisdom
is exemplified in the next scene.

7. COMPLEMENTARY EPISODE 41-52

This last episode forms an epilogue to the Infancy narrative
proper. It is the only glimpse we are permitted into the hidden
life and has for Luke a significance beyond that of showing the
increasing wisdom of Jesus (v. 40).

41-50. Jesus in the Temple

41 Now his parents went to Jerusalem every year at the feast of the
Passover. **42** And when he was twelve years old, they went up according to custom; **43** and when the feast was ended, as they were returning, the boy Jesus stayed behind in Jerusalem. His parents did not
know it, **44** but supposing him to be in the company they went a
day's journey, and they sought him among their kinsfolk and acquaintances; **45** and when they did not find him, they returned to Jerusalem,
seeking him. **46** After three days they found him in the temple, sitting
among the teachers, listening to them and asking them questions;
47 and all who heard him were amazed at his understanding and his
answers. **48** And when they saw him they were astonished; and his
mother said to him, "Son, why have you treated us so? Behold, your
father and I have been looking for you anxiously." **49** And he said to
them, "How is it that you sought me? Did you not know that I must
be in my Father's house?" **50** And they did not understand the saying
which he spoke to them.

The incident of the boy Jesus lost and found in the Temple
had, in the primitive catechesis, taken on the form of a Pronouncement Story, finding its climax in the pronouncement of
Jesus (v. 49).

41f. The Law obliged all men who had reached the age of

puberty to go to the Temple three times yearly—for the feasts of Passover, Pentecost and Tabernacles (Ex 23:14-17; 34:23f; Dt 16:16f). Women and children were not bound by this law (but women did freely acompany their husbands) and the law itself was not literally observed by those at some distance from Jerusalem: an annual journey to one feast sufficed in practice. Rabbinical ruling was that a boy was not bound to make the pilgrimage before the completion of his thirteenth year, but it was customary for the parents to take him with them at an earlier age. The text does not necessarily imply that this was the first visit of Jesus to the Temple (apart from 2:22).

43-45. It was not obligatory to remain for the whole term of the feast (here the seven days of unleavened bread), but most pilgrims did remain until the end. As a Jewish boy of twelve, Jesus was well able to look after himself and his parents would naturally have taken for granted that he was with one of the scattered groups of the returning Nazareth caravan. Usually, the pilgrims set out late in the day and the first stage would have been a short one of, perhaps, some three hours—the "day's journey" (v. 44) need not be taken too literally. When it had become clear to Joseph and Mary that the boy was not with the caravan they returned to Jerusalem, searching for him.

46f. At last they found him, "after three days", that is, on the third day (cf. Mk 8:31), sitting among the doctors of the Law. It was customary for the rabbis to teach in the surroundings of the Temple: the pupils sat on the ground "at the feet" of their teacher, as Paul had sat before Gamaliel (Ac 22:3). But here we are presented rather with a discussion among a group of rabbis, one which naturally attracted some attention. The intelligent questions of Jesus won him a hearing and these "teachers of Israel" (Jn 3:10) were soon lost in wonderment at the unusual wisdom of this twelve-year-old boy. "We can imagine their grave faces lighting up with a smile when he asked a question that embarrassed the wisest of them or when he answered intelligently; they loved to discover among the young the promise of future teachers of Israel." [12]

48. The relief of the parents was intense: *exeplagēsan*, "they

[12] M.-J. Lagrange, *Évangile Saint Luc* (Paris: Gabalda, 1941⁵), p. 96.

were overcome", and Mary's reproach was the spontaneous expression of the pain she had suffered.

49. Jesus' reply, the first and only words of his recorded in these chapters, might be paraphrased: "Where would you expect a child to be but in his father's house?" The phrase, *en tois tou patros mou* (literally "in the things of my Father") could mean "about my Father's affairs", but here the far more satisfactory rendering is "in my Father's house"; the French *chez mon Père* admirably expresses the Greek phrase. The significance of the reply is that Jesus declares that God is *his* Father (in contrast to his legal father, v. 48); at twelve years of age he is conscious of his divine Sonship. It follows that the claims of this Father must override all other demands; so his mission will break the natural ties of family (cf. Mk 3:31-35). Furthermore, the episode may be regarded as a prolongation of the Presentation: the child who had been presented is now, as Son of God, at home in the Temple. The close of the Infancy narrative anticipates the close of the gospel: Jesus, now in the house of his Father (v. 49), will, by his glorification—his Passion, death, Resurrection and Ascension (chs. 23-24), return to his Father. His last words are, in fact, an echo of his first words: "Father, into thy hands I commit my spirit" (23:46)—he will abide with his Father forever (cf. 9:51).

50. The full implication of his words was not immediately apparent and unfolded itself gradually. This statement, while manifestly pointing to a limitation in Mary's understanding of her Son, does not conflict with her belief in his divine Sonship; the enigmatic saying, which sums up his mission and the manner of his return to his Father, could be understood only with time.

51f. The Hidden Life

51 And he went down with them and came to Nazareth, and was obedient to them; and his mother kept all these things in her heart.
52 And Jesus increased in wisdom and in stature, and in favor with God and man.

51. But the hour for the breaking of family ties was not yet; until the beginning of his public ministry Jesus was to remain quietly in Nazareth, humbly obedient to his earthly parents. Joseph is never again mentioned and, apparently, had died before

Jesus set out on his mission. Mary's pondering on these *hrēmata,* events and words (v. 19), surely brought a growth in her understanding of the mystery of her Son. If we must insist on the full humanity of Christ—including human limitations—we should certainly not attempt to make Mary less human, especially in the face of the plain statements of Scripture.

52. The "refrain of growth", an echo of v. 40, underlines the complementary nature of the Finding in the Temple (cf. Jn 20:31; 21:25); the verse is practically a quotation of 1 Sm 2:26. Luke has very clearly marked the physical development of Jesus: *to brephos,* "the baby" (2:16), *to paidion,* "the child" (v. 40), *Iesous ho pais,* "the boy Jesus" (v. 43), "Jesus" (v. 52). Here (cf. v. 40) we learn that his human mind, too, developed. The reality of the Incarnation, the authentic humanity of Jesus, demanded such development and set limits to his human knowledge; again Scripture is formal (cf. Heb 2:17; 4:15; 5:7; Mk 13:32). And God looked with complacency on his Incarnate Son, who also attracted the favor of men (cf. Prov 3:4). Thus the Infancy narrative, which has subtly intimated the divine nature of the Messiah, closes with an emphatic assertion of the reality of Christ's humanity.

THE LITERARY FORM OF LK 1–2

Though an integral part of the gospel, the first two chapters of Luke, in content and in style, stand out from the rest of it. We have subscribed to the view that these chapters are the work of Luke who has adapted and rewritten earlier, traditional material. This is not the only view of the matter, as we have seen, but whatever theory of literary construction one adopts, the question of literary form remains and must be faced. It has become fashionable to describe Luke's Infancy narrative as *midrash.*[13] The use of the term does at least recognize the influence of Old Testament texts on the form of the Infancy gospel and acknowledges the presence of a distinctive method, but the designation, applied to Lk 1–2, or to any part of it, is unfortunate. These chapters are not *midrash* and it is not helpful to characterize them as such.

[13] See p. 294.

The fundamental principle of *midrash* is the actualization of a biblical text. If this were to be verified in Lk 1–2 we should have to say that these chapters—or certain episodes—have grown out of specific biblical texts. In fact, what we have found is that the author, starting with episodes in the infancy of John and of Jesus, has described them in terms of Old Testament analogies and in Old Testament language. Where *midrashic* development flows from the biblical text, Luke has used biblical language to illustrate, and interpret, the events with which he deals. The procedure is very different in each case. And even if, as is probable, the Baptist Infancy story in Luke's own free composition, he modeled it on his narrative of Jesus—this is not *midrash*.

But how might we describe the literary form of Lk 1–2? It seems that the verdict of a recent scholar, at the close of a long study of *midrash,* is very sound. "Perhaps the best classification of our material is simply *Infancy narrative,* for these chapters seem to have been written in the tradition of infancy stories, biblical and extra-biblical, sharing with them many of their motifs." [14]

Throughout his Infancy narrative, even more than in the rest of his gospel, Luke is concerned, not with the facts only, but, in a special way, with the meaning of the facts. In the Introduction we have noted his theological preoccupations and will have cause to draw attention to them throughout the commentary. But what are we to say on such matters as the nature of the apparitions to Zechariah and to Mary? Did Gabriel really appear in both cases? Perhaps—but it is more likely that Luke (as, no doubt, his sources had done), has presented genuine spiritual experiences in a traditional and consecrated style. What we do learn is that Zechariah received intimation of the birth of a remarkable son. And we do accept that Mary was called by God—and knew herself to be called—to play an essential role in God's plan of salvation, to be the mother of his Messiah. This is the essential factor; the manner in which God's will was made known is secondary. *A fortiori,* the angelic announcement to the shepherds is to be understood in the same manner as the other two annunciations; and the canticle of the angels, like the other canticles of the narrative, is meant to bring out the spiritual significance of the episode.

[14] A. G. Wright, "The Literary Genre 'Midrash'" in *Catholic Biblical Quarterly* 28 (1966), p. 456.

It was Luke's express intention to compile a narrative of "the things which have been accomplished among us" (1:1); he assures us that he is dealing with facts. We should take him at his word, while keeping in mind that his concern is the significance of the facts. It was his intention to write history but we must not forget that, in the Infancy narrative above all, he is writing history in the biblical manner. And to the Hebrews, history was the mighty acts of God, the God who is Lord of history. Faith was the background of history, and events were the inbreaking of spiritual purpose and power upon the day-to-day affairs of men. Caird has seen that this is the atmosphere of Luke's Infancy narrative:

"This method of writing history does not allow any easy answer to the modern historian's question: What actually happened? Luke certainly believed that he was dealing with real events, and it would be hypercriticism to doubt that behind these two chapters there is a substratum of the same sort of historical fact as we find described in a more down-to-earth manner in the remainder of the gospel. Equally clearly Luke does not content himself with that which the television camera and microphone could have recorded. He would not have been a better historian had he done so. All history is an attempt to find pattern and meaning in a section of human experience, and every historian worthy of the name raises questions about man's ultimate destiny and the meaning of all history to which, as an historian, he can provide no answers. The answers belong to the realm of theology; and into this realm of metahistory Luke and the other evangelists are concerned to lead us. Whether we like it or not, we must be content to live with a measure of uncertainty as to where fact ends and interpretation begins. Of one thing, however, we may be sure—Luke was no simpleton. We do him a grave injustice if we suppose that, when he wrote in an elevated and imaginative style, he was naive enough to take his own poetry with pedantic literalness!" [15]

[15] G. B. Caird, *The Gospel of St. Luke* (Harmondsworth, Middlesex: Penguin Books, 1963), pp. 47f.

II. PREPARATION OF THE MINISTRY OF JESUS 3:1—4:13

The prologue has introduced the Messiah and his herald and has indicated a first manifestation of both; now the time has come for a public manifestation, a proclamation that the age of fulfillment has begun. So John steps forward to prepare the way, to open the hearts of men. He is the link between the Old Covenant and the New; he himself belongs to the former (7:28; 16:16). He speaks his lines before the curtain and when it is raised the stage is held by one mightier than he.

3:1-20. Preaching and Witness of John the Baptist
(Mk 1:1-8; Mt 3:1-12)

1 In the fifteenth year of the reign of Tiberius Caesar, Pontius Pilate being governor of Judea, and Herod being tetrarch of Galilee, and his brother Philip tetrarch of the region of Ituraea and Trachonitis, and Lysanias tetrarch of Abilene, 2 in the high-priesthood of Annas and Caiaphas, the word of God came to John the son of Zechariah in the wilderness; 3 and he went into all the region about the Jordan, preaching a baptism of repentance for the forgiveness of sins. 4 As it is written in the book of the words of Isaiah the prophet,

"The voice of one crying in the wilderness:
Prepare the way of the Lord,
make his paths straight.
5 Every valley shall be filled,
and every mountain and hill shall be brought low,
and the crooked shall be made straight,
and the rough ways shall be made smooth;
6 and all flesh shall see the salvation of God."

7 He said therefore to the multitudes that came out to be baptized by him, "You brood of vipers! Who warned you to flee from the wrath to come? 8 Bear fruits that befit repentance, and do not begin to say to yourselves, 'We have Abraham as our father'; for I tell you, God is able from these stones to raise up children to Abraham. 9 Even now

76

the axe is laid to the root of the tree; every tree therefore that does not bear good fruit is cut down and thrown into the fire."

10 And the multitudes asked him, "What then shall we do?" 11 And he answered them, "He who has two coats, let him share with him who has none; and he who has food, let him do likewise." 12 Tax collectors also came to be baptized, and said to him, "Teacher, what shall we do?" 13 And he said to them, "Collect no more than is appointed you." 14 Soldiers also asked him, "And we, what shall we do?" And he said to them, "Rob no one by violence or by false accusation, and be content with your wages."

15 As the people were in expectation, and all men questioned in their hearts concerning John, whether perhaps he were the Christ, 16 John answered them all, "I baptize you with water; but he who is mightier than I is coming, the thong of whose sandals I am not worthy to untie; he will baptize you with the Holy Spirit and with fire. 17 His winnowing fork is in his hand, to clear his threshing floor, and to gather the wheat into his granary, but the chaff he will burn with unquenchable fire."

18 So, with many other exhortations, he preached good news to the people. 19 But Herod the tetrarch, who had been reproved by him for Herodias, his brother's wife, and for all the evil things that Herod had done, 20 added this to them all, that he shut up John in prison.

1f. Luke is at great pains to date exactly the ministry of the Baptist; his real purpose is thereby to date the beginning of our Lord's ministry. His elaborate synchronization serves to set the gospel event in the framework of world history (cf. 1:5), and describes the political situation in Palestine. The reign of Tiberius began on 19 Aug 14 A.D.; the 15th year would be—in the Roman system—19 Aug 28–18 Aug 29. It is more likely that Luke follows the Syrian calendar with its year beginning on Oct 1. In this case the short period 19 Aug–30 Sept would be reckoned as the first year of Tiberius and the 15th year of his reign would be 1 Oct 27–30 Sept 28. Thus it seems that we can put the preaching of the Baptist, and the beginning of the ministry of Jesus, in the years 27-28 A.D. Pontius Pilate was procurator 26-36; his territory included not only Judea but also Idumea and Samaria. Herod Antipas, son of Herod the Great and Malthake, was tetrarch of Galilee (and Peraea) 4 B.C.–39 A.D. Philip, son of Herod the Great and Cleopatra (not the famous Egyptian queen) was tetrarch of Ituraea, Trachonitis, Auaranitis, Batanaea and Gaulinitis (territories NE of the sea of Galilee) from 4 B.C. to 34 A.D. Lysanias (not of Herod's family) was tetrarch of Abilene (NW of Damascus) until c. 37 A.D.; two inscriptions have shown that Luke had not erred in respect of Lysanias. Caiaphas was high priest from 18 to 36; he was son-in-law of Annas who had been high priest from 6 to 15. The latter's influence was very great (five of his sons and his son-in-law had been high priests) and that is why Luke can associate him with Caiaphas and speak of "the high priesthood of Annas and Caiaphas" (cf. Jn 18:13-24; Ac 4:6). In the manner of the Old Testament prophets, John (who had already been marked as a prophet, 1:15) is now solemnly called to his mission (cf. Jer 1:1,5,11; Hos 1:1; Jl 1:1). For the "wilderness" cf. 1:80.

3-6. "All the region about the Jordan" and the "wilderness" (v. 2) most likely refer to the same area north of the Dead Sea, in the neighborhood of Jericho. John is presented as an itinerant preacher whose message was repentance with a view to forgiveness of sins, an anticipation of the Christian message (24:47). "John's baptism was a prophetic sign denoting the preparation for a coming divine judgment of a penitent and faithful people of God."[16] Luke, unlike Mark and Matthew, continues the quotation of Isaiah on to v. 5 (Is 40:3-5) and so introduces a universalist note ("all flesh"); cf. 2:30-32.

7-9. Luke makes no reference to the asceticism of John and does not mention the concourse of people flocking to him for baptism (cf. Mk 1:6f; Mt 3:4-6). Though the audience is different (Luke has "the multitudes" in place of "the Pharisees and Sadducees" of Matthew), vv. 7-9 agree almost verbatim with Matthew 3:7-10. The term "brood of vipers" would more aptly describe the Pharisees and Sadducees (Mt 3:7; cf. 12:34; 23:33) than the crowd. Those who came for baptism were worldly-wise (Mt 10:16), seeking to escape the wrath, the ultimate judgment of God. An external rite will not save them; there must be a change of heart, a manifest change, whose fruit will prove its genuineness. Nor will the fact that they are children of Abraham avail them (cf. Jn 8:39); God is under no compulsion to save them and can, out of the very stones of the desert, raise up a new Israel (the Aramaic original doubtless had a play on *abnayya*, "stones" and *benayya* "sons"). As it is, the ax of Messianic judg-

---

[16] G. W. H. Lampe, "Luke" in *Peake's Commentary on the Bible* (London: Nelson, 1962²), 721c.

ment already threatens the fruitless trees, but there is yet time for repentance (cf. Lk 13:6-9). But if there is no change of heart the trees will be cut down and cast into the fire: those who fail to grasp this opportunity cannot expect to escape punishment.

10-14. This is a passage peculiar to Luke which explains the character of the repentance required as a preparation for the kingdom: it is a thoroughgoing conversion finding expression in the observance of the commandments and in works of charity. This teaching reflects the exhortations of the Old Testament prophets, while v. 11 suggests the sharing of property in the primitive Jerusalem Church (Ac 2:44f). The recommendation to tax collectors and soldiers (most likely troops of Herod Antipas in whose territory John was preaching) is more specific in view of the special temptation of their way of life.

15. This verse is peculiar to Luke. The common opinion that John was the Messiah, a view explicitly rejected by the Baptist, is also reflected in the fourth gospel (cf. Jn 1:19f; 3:27); both John and Luke emphasize the subordinate role of the Baptist.

16f. Almost textually the same as Matthew 3:11f, but in Luke the preceding verse has turned the statement into a disclaimer of Messianic dignity. John declares himself unworthy to be a slave of the coming Messiah; and the water baptism of John is only a preparation for the Messiah's baptism with its bestowal of the Holy Spirit (cf. Ac 1:5; 11:16). Spirit and fire stand in apposition ("the fire of the Spirit") and refer to the outpouring of the Holy Spirit of Ac 2:3.

17. This verse shows the Messiah in his role as judge: he will separate grain—the new Israel which he will gather to himself (cf. Ap 14:14-16)—from chaff. According to the primitive method, still in practice among Palestinian Arabs, the threshed grain is tossed into the air so that the wind blows aside the chaff. The fire (not that of v. 16) is the final wrath of God (Is 66:24).

18-20. Following a summary account of John's preaching—he "evangelized" the people—comes a typically Lucan conclusion: before turning to Jesus he closes the ministry of John. He thereby suggests that the last spokesman of the Old Testament had finished when the preaching of Jesus began (cf. Mk 6:17-29; Mt 14:3-12). The tetrarch who had the Baptist imprisoned is Herod Antipas (cf. 3:1) who had married Herodias, divorced wife of his brother Herod Philip. With the departure of John from the scene, the period of Israel is ended; now begins the period of Christ.

21f. The Baptism of Jesus
(Mk 1:9-11; Mt 3:13-17; Jn 1:29-34)

21 Now when all the people were baptized, and when Jesus also had been baptized and was praying, the heaven was opened, **22** and the Holy Spirit descended upon him in bodily form, as a dove, and a voice came from heaven, "Thou art my beloved Son; with thee I am well pleased."

Each of the evangelists has insisted on an aspect of this event. For Mark it is first and foremost the beginning of the public ministry of the Savior; the Spirit of God descends on Christ as he had come upon the Judges of Israel to give them the strength to acomplish their mission (cf. Jg 3:10; 6:34; 11:29; 14:19). For Matthew, preoccupied with the relationship between the Old Law, and the New Law which fulfills the former, it is the meeting of prophet and Messiah. For Luke, who closely follows Mark, it is a scene of prayer and a meeting of God with humanity. John stresses the illumination of the Baptist, who recognizes in the one whom he baptizes the Son of God who will "baptize with the Holy Spirit".

21. In Luke's passage Jesus is baptized as one of the people, so, perhaps, identifying himself with the people of Israel. John is not named and Jesus holds the stage. He prays as he does at all the decisive turning-points in Luke's gospel.

22. This verse adds that the Holy Spirit descended "in bodily form"—Luke underlines the reality of the theophany. In place of the reading (given above) which combines the beginning of Ps 2:7 (the Messianic king) with an echo of Is 42:1 (the suffering Servant), some witnesses give the whole of Ps 2:7: "Thou art my Son, today I have begotten thee" (Codex Bezae, Old Latin, Justin, Origen); the accepted reading is better attested.

23-38. The Genealogy
(Mt 1:1-17)

23 Jesus, when he began his ministry, was about thirty years of age, being the son (as was supposed) of Joseph, the son of Heli **24** the son of Matthat, the son of Levi, the son of Melchi, the son of Jannai, the son of Joseph, 25 the son of Mattathias, the son of Amos, the son of Nahum, the son of Esli, the son of Naggai, 26 the son of Maath, the son of Mattathias, the son of Semein, the son of Josech, the son of Joda, 27 the son of Joanan, the son of Rhesa, the son of Zerubbabel, the son of Shealtiel, the son of Neri, 28 the son of Melchi, the son of Addi, the son of Cosam, the son of Elmadam, the son of Er, 29 the son of Joshua, the son of Eliezer, the son of Jorim, the son of Matthat, the son of Levi, 30 the son of Simeon, the son of Judah, the son of Joseph, the son of Jonam, the son of Eliakim, 31 the son of Melea, the son of Menna, the son of Mattatha, the son of Nathan, the son of David, 32 the son of Jesse, the son of Obed, the son of Boaz, the son of Sala, the son of Nahshon, 33 the son of Amminadab, the son of Admin, the son of Arni, the son of Hezron, the son of Perez, the son of Judah, 34 the son of Jacob, the son of Isaac, the son of Abraham, the son of Terah, the son of Nahor, 35 the son of Serug, the son of Reu, the son of Peleg, the son of Eber, the son of Shelah, 36 the son of Cainan, the son of Arphaxad, the son of Shem, the son of Noah, the son of Lamech, 37 the son of Methuselah, the son of Enoch, the son of Jared, the son of Mahalaleel, the son of Cainan, 38 the son of Enos, the son of Seth, the son of Adam, the son of God.

In juxtaposition to his relation of Sonship to God, Luke now presents Christ's human ancestry. Since he is taken to be, and is legally, the son of Joseph, his ancestry is traced through Joseph. This intention is unmistakably expressed in v. 23; and those who, disturbed by the dissimilarities with Matthew's genealogy (1:1-17), have sought to show that Luke traced the descent of Jesus through Mary have had to do violence to this text. Luke, having declared that Joseph was only the reputed father of Jesus, proceeds to trace the descent of Joseph; Matthew does the same, though each gives a different name for the father of Joseph. No reasonable understanding of the genealogies is possible without taking into consideration two facts: first, that ancient Semitic ideas of kinship differed greatly from our own; secondly, that both Matthew and Luke are concerned to show that Jesus was a son of David in the eyes of the Jewish Law. But, according to Jewish ideas, there was no objection to the inclusion of adoptive or legal parents in a genealogical tree. This meant that ancestry could be traced along different lines and Matthew and Luke, working independently, have in fact done just that. While Matthew does not go beyond Abraham, Luke, with his universalist view, goes back to Adam: Jesus is Savior not only of the chosen people but of all mankind. Luke has 76 names (against Matthew's 42). Those from Jesse to Adam he could have worked out from the Septuagint; but for the first part of the list, which traces the Davidic ancestry of Jesus through David's son Nathan (2 Sm 5:14; 1 Chr 3:5; 14:4; Zech 12), he must have had a special source. In his genealogy "Jesus appears not only as the heir of David but as the one towards whom all history converges. All men can call themselves his brethren, with better right than the Israelites, since the relationship goes back to the point where all men came from God".[17]

4:1-13. Temptation in the Wilderness
(Mt 4:1-11; Mk 1:12f)

1 And Jesus, full of the Holy Spirit, returned from the Jordan, and was led by the Spirit 2 for forty days in the wilderness, tempted by the devil. And he ate nothing in those days; and when they were ended, he was hungry. 3 The devil said to him, "If you are the Son of God, command this stone to become bread." 4 And Jesus answered him, "It is written, 'Man shall not live by bread alone.'" 5 And the devil took him up, and showed him all the kingdoms of the world in a moment of time, 6 and said to him, "To you I will give all this authority and their glory; for it has been delivered to me, and I give it to whom I will. 7 If you, then, will worship me, it shall all be yours." 8 And Jesus answered him, "It is writen,

'You shall worship the Lord your God,
and him only shall you serve.'"

9 And he took him to Jerusalem, and set him on the pinnacle of the temple, and said to him, "If you are the Son of God, throw yourself down from here; 10 for it is written,

'He will give his angels charge of you, to guard you,'

11 and

'On their hands they will bear you up,
lest you strike your foot against a stone.'"

12 And Jesus answered him, "It is said, 'You shall not tempt the Lord your God.'" 13 And when the devil had ended every temptation, he departed from him until an opportune time.

1f. Luke agrees with Matthew in giving a description of the temptations of Christ, but with Mark (unlike Matthew) he de-

[17] M.-J. Lagrange, *op. cit.*, p. 126.

clares that Jesus was tempted throughout the whole of the 40 days, the three temptations given here being the climax of the trial. The period of 40 days recalls the fasts of Moses (Ex 34:28) and Elijah (1 Kg 19:8) and perhaps also Israel's 40 years of desert wandering. The Holy Spirit had descended on Jesus at the moment of his baptism (Lk 3:22), and it is "full of the Holy Spirit" and led by the Spirit that he goes into the wilderness. It is not implied that he received the fullness of the Spirit only at the baptism—the Spirit descended on him, not in him (3:22), and he was "holy" from the moment of his conception: Jesus is, in fact, the bearer of the Holy Spirit. Luke shares the Johannine view that Jesus was the bearer of the Spirit in a unique sense and that he bestowed this Spirit only after his "glorification" (Jn 7:39)— hence the emphasis on the action of the Spirit throughout Acts. In vv. 3-12 Luke is very close to Matthew except that he inverts the order of the last two temptations. Matthew's order is more logical, and it can scarcely be doubted that Luke has deliberately changed the order so that the series may end at Jerusalem; this is in keeping with his special theological interest in the holy city.

3f. "Son of God" is an echo of the heavenly voice of 3:22—the devil is aware that Jesus is the Messiah (but not that he is divine). He seeks to get Jesus to use his miraculous powers in his own interest, to show himself disobedient to the will of God. Jesus replies by quoting Dt 8:3. That saying, in its Deuteronomical context, urges the Israelites to abandon themselves to the providence of God who can sustain them, if necessary, with manna in place of bread. Jesus declares his confidence in his Father and his detachment from anything but that Father's will.

5-8. In v. 5, in contrast to Matthew, the mountain is not mentioned—though it is suggested in the expression *anagagōn* ("leading up")—perhaps because, in Luke, "the mountain" is more stylized than in the other gospels and seems to have a fixed meaning: "It is the place of prayer, the scene of secret revelation, of communication with the unseen world. No temptations can take place on it nor any public preaching." [17a] The addition proper to Luke, "for it has been delivered to me, and I give it to

[17a] H. Conzelmann, *The Theology of St. Luke* (New York: Harper & Row, 1960), p. 29.

whom I will" (v. 6b), echoes the opinion of the fourth gospel on the dominion of Satan, the "prince of this world" (Jn 12:31; 14:30; 16:11; 1 Jn 3:8) and the view of Apocalypse that he gives this dominion to whom he wills (Ap 13:2-4). Jesus can receive this authority if he acknowledges himself the vassal of Satan. But if this authority has been delivered to Satan (as he admits), he is not from the beginning the "prince" of this world; dominion over the world is ultimately reserved for the Messiah (Ps 2:6,8). The question is, from whom will the Messiah receive his dominion: here and now from Satan, or from God, but only after suffering and death? Will Jesus be a Messiah according to the worldly expectation of the Jews, or as a Suffering Servant? Again quoting a phrase of Deuteronomy (Dt 6:13), Jesus makes his unequivocal choice. And in the context it is seen that what is at stake is not only the obedience of the Messiah but his obedience unto death.

9-12. The pinnacle of the Temple is probably the southeast corner of the enclosure wall, about 300 feet above the Kidron valley. In the first temptation Jesus was asked to relieve his own hunger by working a miracle; now he is asked to put himself in a danger that will call forth God's intervention on his behalf. Adroitly, the tempter quotes Ps 91(90):11f—if the just man (of the psalm) displays such confidence in God, how much greater should be the trust of his Messiah. Nothing in the context suggests that this was meant to be a display of power manifest to the people. What the devil seeks is that confidence should be turned into presumption. Jesus' reply (Dt 6:16) implies that he refuses to abuse the divine power in order to escape death; he implicitly accepts God's purpose that the Messiah must suffer and die in order to enter into his glory (Lk 24:26).

13. ". . . had ended every temptation"—the temptation is ended decisively and the devil departs. Henceforth there will be no temptation in the life of Jesus—until the moment indicated by the "opportune time", the moment of his Passion (22:3,53; cf. Jn 13:2,27; 14:30). "A period free from Satan is now beginning, an epoch of a special kind in the center of the whole course of redemptive history. What is now beginning, therefore, is not the last times, but the interval between the period of the Law, or of Israel, and the period of the Spirit, or of the Church." [18]

An important factor, in any interpretation of the Temptation

[18] H. Conzelmann, *op. cit.*, p. 28.

narrative, is its place between the Messianic inauguration of Jesus at his baptism and the opening of his public ministry. In this context the temptation is seen as the attempt of Satan to cause Jesus to disobey the will of God at the very moment when he is about to begin his Messianic work. The kernel of the narrative doubtless goes back to Jesus himself, but the narrative, as we read it in our gospels, is a composition of the primitive Church. It may be that the triple scene of Matthew and Luke has been constructed on the analogy of the temptation of the people of Israel in the desert—the citations from Deuteronomy are significant. While Israel, in the desert, had "tempted" Yahweh and so had shown itself disobedient, Christ has remained faithful. It is thus that he represents the true Israel. "The episode describes the kind of Messiah Jesus was, and by implication what kind of society the Church, the New Israel is: it lives by the word of God, it does not challenge God's promises, and it adores and serves God alone and not the world. Jesus rejects in anticipation the temptations to which his Church will be submitted." [19]

The temptation story assures us that Jesus was tempted by Satan and that the temptations bore on his Messianic role. The evangelists have presented the temptation in a highly dramatic form, but it should not be doubted that the action of the drama took place entirely within the mind of Jesus. A detail like the "very high mountain" (Mt 4:8) from which the tempter could show Jesus, "in a moment of time" (Lk 4:5), all the kingdoms of the world and their splendor definitely gives the impression that Satan had conjured up before Jesus an image of earthly glory. Jesus was tempted where he was, in the desert (it is clearer in Mt 4:1,11 than in Luke's narrative that Jesus was to be found, at the close of the temptation, just where he had been at the beginning), and the devil did not appear in visible, bodily form. We must not confuse literary dress with theological implication; and what the text does bring out is the object of Satan's attack: his attempt to undermine the Messiah's full acceptance of the will of God. But while the temptation is not to be understood as an external event in which Satan took bodily shape and in which Jesus moved from place to place, it remains true that the temptations were real (cf. Heb 4:15), that they came from without, penetrating the imagination of Jesus without troubling his soul.

[19] J. L. McKenzie, *Dictionary of the Bible* (Milwaukee: Bruce, 1965), p. 879.

III. THE GALILEAN MINISTRY 4:14–9:50
(Mk 1:14–9:41)

In this section of his gospel Luke follows Mark closely, apart from the omission of Mark 6:45–8:26 and the addition of Luke 6:20–8:3.

14f. The Beginning of the Galilean Ministry
(Mk 1:14f; Mt 4:12-17)

14 And Jesus returned in the power of the Spirit into Galilee, and a report concerning him went out through all the surrounding country. 15 And he taught in their synagogues, being glorified by all.

These verses are a heading for what follows; they provide a survey of the whole of the first period of the ministry of Jesus. The "power of the Spirit" has reference to the miracles that Jesus will work (cf. 4:36; 5:17; 6:19; 8:46). Jesus' preaching in the synagogues sets the pattern for the constant practice of Paul (cf. Ac 13:5,14,44; 14:1; etc.).

16-30. Jesus in Nazareth
(Mk 6:1-6a; Mt 13:53-58)

16 And he came to Nazareth, where he had been brought up; and he went to the synagogue, as his custom was, on the sabbath day. And he stood up to read; 17 and there was given to him the book of the prophet Isaiah. He opened the book and found the place where it was written,

18 "The Spirit of the Lord is upon me,
because he has anointed me to preach good news to the poor.
He has sent me to proclaim release to the captives
and recovering of sight to the blind,
to set at liberty those who are oppressed,
19 to proclaim the acceptable year of the Lord."

20 And he closed the book, and gave it back to the attendant, and

86

sat down; and the eyes of all in the synagogue were fixed on him. 21 And he began to say to them, "Today this scripture has been fulfilled in your hearing." 22 And all spoke well of him, and wondered at the gracious words which proceeded out of his mouth; and they said, "Is not this Joseph's son?" 23 And he said to them, "Doubtless you will quote to me this proverb, 'Physician, heal yourself; what we have heard you did at Capernaum, do here also in your own country.'" 24 And he said, "Truly, I say to you, no prophet is acceptable in his own country. 25 But in truth, I tell you, there were many widows in Israel in the days of Elijah, when the heaven was shut up three years and six months, when there came a great famine over all the land; 26 and Elijah was sent to none of them but only to Zarephath, in the land of Sidon, to a woman who was a widow. 27 And there were many lepers in Israel in the time of the prophet Elisha; and none of them was cleansed, but only Naaman the Syrian." 28 When they heard this, all in the synagogue were filled with wrath. 29 And they rose up and put him out of the city, and led him to the brow of the hill on which their city was built, that they might throw him down headlong. 30 But passing through the midst of them he went away.

At this point Mark (1:16-20) gives the call of the first disciples; Luke instead deals with the preaching of Jesus in his own village (cf. Mk 6:1-6a) and his rejection. His intention is to trace symbolically the course of Christ's mission; he preaches the good news and his own people refuse to accept him. The inaugural scene has been composed by Luke from different sources which relate to three different visits of Jesus to his own people. Firstly (4:16-22) a visit in which he was well received; then the same episode as Mark 6:1-6a and Matthew 13:53-58; and finally, in vv. 25-30, a reference to the close of the Galilean ministry. The whole passage, with its hint of acceptance by the Gentiles, is a synopsis of the gospel and Acts sketching the pattern of the fate of Jesus and of his gospel.

16f. "Where he had been brought up" looks back to 2:29,51 and forward to v. 24. As a faithful Israelite he had regularly attended divine service in the synagogue each sabbath. The service consisted of prayers, and readings (with commentary) from the Law and the prophets. The readers were well-instructed members of the community or visitors known to be versed in Scripture. Jesus was handed the scroll of Isaiah and quickly found the passage he had in mind: 61:1f.

18f. Luke cites (freely) from the LXX; Jesus would have read the Hebrew text and then given an Aramaic version since Hebrew was no longer understood by the people. It is not clear where the first sentence ends, but it seems best to put a full stop after *echrisen me* ("he anointed me") as in the LXX: "The Spirit of the Lord is upon me because he has anointed me. He has sent me to preach good news to the poor . . ." At the beginning of his mission Jesus is consecrated by an anointing, not with oil like the kings and priests of the Old Testament, but with the Holy Spirit (cf. Ac 10:38). "To set at liberty those who are oppressed" is added from Is 58:6. The text of Isaiah effectively sketches the work of Jesus, the works of the Messiah (cf. 7:22). The "year" is the jubilee year *par excellence* (cf. Lv 24:10-13), the Messianic era, the age of salvation.

20-22. When he had read the passage of Isaiah, Jesus sat down to comment on it; Luke has skillfully suggested the expectant atmosphere. Jesus tells his audience that the prophetic words have been fulfilled as they listened to them: he himself is the Spirit-anointed proclaimer of the Lord's year of grace. Their reaction is wonder and puzzlement: they think well of this Jesus whom they knew, they are lost in admiration at his gracious words—but can he, humble son of the humble Joseph, really apply to himself the words of Isaiah and put himself forward as such an extraordinary personage?

23f. Most probably this reply of Jesus answers an objection raised by the people of Nazareth on a later visit—hence the reference to miracles at Capernaum which does not, obviously, fit in the context of an inaugural appearance. In its present situation, v. 23 refers to a demand that Jesus should back his claim by miracles and v. 24 explains why he cannot do this: he shares the fate of every prophet—rejection by his own people. Besides, he consistently refused to support his Messianic claims by signs (cf. the temptation): he demanded faith.

25-27. The passage, vv. 25-30, with its description of a violent reaction of the people, really belongs to the close of the Galilean ministry. Not accepted by his own people, Jesus, like his great prophetic predecessors, will turn to the Gentiles who, by implication, will receive him.

28-30. The people rise in fury when they understand him to mean that the benefits they have rejected will be offered to the Gentiles (cf. Ac 13:46,50). The fate of Jesus at the hands of his own people is foreshadowed, but his hour is not yet come (cf. 9:51; Jn 7:30,45; 8:59). In v. 29 the phrase "the brow of the hill on which their city was built" raises a question: there is apparently no topographical feature which corresponds to this description. But perhaps the difficulty is due to a misconception—the implication that a high precipice is meant. In fact, recent explorations have disclosed a rock formation, hidden by later occupation, which could fit the passage of Luke. The casting down would doubtless have been a prelude to death by stoning (cf. Ac 7:28).

31-44. Ministry at Capernaum
(Mk 1:21-39; cf. Mt 4:23-25; 7:28f; 8:14-17)

31 And he went down to Capernaum, a city of Galilee. And he was teaching them on the sabbath; **32** and they were astonished at his teaching, for his word was with authority. **33** And in the synagogue there was a man who had the spirit of an unclean demon; and he cried out with a loud voice, **34** "Ah! What have you to do with us, Jesus of Nazareth? Have you come to destroy us? I know who you are, the Holy One of God." **35** But Jesus rebuked him, saying, "Be silent, and come out of him!" And when the demon had thrown him down in the midst, he came out of him, having done him no harm. **36** And they were all amazed and said to one another, "What is this word? For with authority and power he commands the unclean spirits, and they come out." **37** And reports of him went into every place in the surrounding region.

38 And he arose and left the synagogue, and entered Simon's house. Now Simon's mother-in-law was ill with a high fever, and they besought him for her. **39** And he stood over her and rebuked the fever, and it left her; and immediately she rose and served them.

40 Now when the sun was setting, all those who had any that were sick with various diseases brought them to him; and he laid his hands on every one of them and healed them. **41** And demons also came out of many, crying, "You are the Son of God!" But he rebuked them, and would not allow them to speak, because they knew that he was the Christ.

42 And when it was day he departed and went into a lonely place. And the people sought him and came to him, and would have kept him from leaving them; **43** but he said to them, "I must preach the good news of the kingdom of God to the other cities also; for I was sent for this purpose." **44** And he was preaching in the synagogue of Judea."

31f. At v. 31 Luke takes up the thread of Mark's narrative. Jesus "went down" from Nazareth to the low-lying Capernaum and taught in the synagogue. Though Luke describes the people's reaction to the authoritative teaching of Jesus, he does not, for his Gentile readers, draw a comparison with the teaching of the scribes.

33. "The spirit of an unclean demon"—a spirit who was an unclean demon.

34. "What have you to do with us?" is a Hebraism (cf. Jg 11:12; 2 Sm 16:10; 19:22; Lk 4:34; Jn 2:4) meaning: "Why do you meddle with us?" The demon feels that Jesus will destroy his dominion over men. By calling Jesus the "Holy One of God", the demon (like Satan in 4:3) recognizes his Messiahship. The silence imposed by Jesus falls into the pattern of the "Messianic secret" so manifest in Mark.[20]

35. Luke softens the description of Mark by his assurance that the departing demon did not harm the man.

36f. The astonishment of the viewers is due to the ease with which Jesus had cast out the evil spirit: his authority is manifest. His victory over Satan at the temptation now finds more concrete form in his manifest power over these satanic spirits (cf. Lk 11:20).

38f. Since Luke gives the call of the first disciples after the Capernaum episode, and not before it as Mark does, he here omits the names Andrew, James and John (cf. Mk 1:29); for that matter, Simon is introduced abruptly. "They besought him for her" replaces Mark's "they told him of her": Jesus does not need to be informed (cf. 9:47). He drives out a bodily fever as easily as he had expelled a demon.

40f. At sunset, when the sabbath had ended, the sick were brought to him; reference to imposition of hands is proper to Luke. At v. 41 (cf. v. 35) we have evidence of the "Messianic secret"; "Son of God" is evidently equivalent to Messiah ("Christ") (cf. Mk 3:11).

42-44. Luke cannot mention "Simon and those who were with him" (cf. Mk 1:36) since he has not yet given the call of the disciples, so he speaks of "people" who sought Jesus and wanted to keep him with them. Curiously, contrary to his general tendency, Luke omits the Markan detail that Jesus prayed in the "lonely place". Here he is preoccupied with making it clear that

[20] See pp. 286ff.

the preaching of Jesus cannot be confined to one place. Luke further specifies that this is the "good news of the kingdom of God" (cf. Mk 1:38). He also clarifies the ambiguous phrase of Mark: "That is why I came out"—(from the Father? from Capernaum?)—by the emphatic "I was sent for this purpose". In v. 44 the variant reading "Galilee" is doubtless a correction, and the weight of manuscript evidence is in favor of "Judea"—used in a wide sense, meaning the whole of Israel (cf. 7:17; Ac 10:37; 28:21).

5:1-11. The Call of the First Disciples
(Mk 1:16-20; Mt 4:18-22)

1 While the people pressed upon him to hear the word of God, he was standing by the lake at Gennesaret. 2 And he saw two boats by the lake; but the fishermen had gone out of them and were washing their nets. 3 Getting into one of the boats, which was Simon's, he asked him to put out a little from the land. And he sat down and taught the people from the boat. 4 And when he had ceased speaking, he said to Simon, "Put out into the deep and let down your nets for a catch." 5 And Simon answered, "Master, we toiled all night and took nothing! But at your word I will let down the nets." 6 And when they had done this, they enclosed a great shoal of fish; and as their nets were breaking, 7 they beckoned to their partners in the other boat to come and help them. And they came and filled both the boats, so that they began to sink. 8 But when Simon Peter saw it, he fell down at Jesus' knees, saying, "Depart from me, for I am a sinful man, O Lord." 9 For he was astonished, and all that were with him, at the catch of fish which they had taken; 10 and so also were James and John, sons of Zebedee, who were partners with Simon. And Jesus said to Simon, "Do not be afraid; henceforth you will be catching men." 11 And when they had brought their boats to land, they left everything and followed him.

Luke has left until now the call of the first four disciples, which Mark has at the very beginning of the ministry (Mk 1:16-20); their immediate response, prepared by the rumor of his ministry (Lk 4:14,44), is psychologically more understandable. The passage is composite and we may distinguish three elements: (a) a detailed setting of a discourse of Jesus (vv. 1-3) parallel to Mk 4:1f; (b) a miraculous catch of fish (vv. 4-10a); (c) the call of Simon (vv. 10b-11), related to Mark 1:17,20.

1-3. "Lake of Gennesaret" is Luke's more precise designation of the popularly named "sea of Galilee" (cf. Mk 1:16; 7:31). Throughout Luke the "lake" is more a theological than a geographical factor: it is the place of manifestations which demonstrate the power of Jesus (cf. 8:22-25).

4f. Simon's words underline the miraculous nature of the subsequent catch: since the night, the proper time for fishing, has yielded nothing, this daytime attempt is, humanly speaking, doomed to failure.

6f. The "partners" are named in v. 10.

8f. "Simon Peter", here only in Luke, is found in the epilogue of the fourth gospel (cf. Jn 21:2,3,7,11). Peter, profoundly moved by the miracle, sank on his knees and spontaneously declared his unworthiness in face of this supernatural intervention; he addresses Jesus as "Lord" instead of "Master" (v. 5). It does not follow that he, at this stage, recognized Jesus as Messiah: he acknowledged his miraculous power. The reaction of Peter, who had already witnessed the miraculous healing of his mother-in-law (4:38f), has seemed strange to some who have not recognized, or do not admit, that the present scene is not in its proper chronological setting.

10f. James and John are overcome by the same religious awe and Jesus speaks the reassuring words: "Do not be afraid" (cf. 1:13,30; 2:10). The symbolism of the miraculous catch is now made clear: henceforth Peter will be a fisher of men; already he stands forth as the leader. The implied call is, however, not addressed to him alone; the others too follow Jesus (v. 11). Luke specifies that they left "all" (cf. 5:28; 11:41; etc.).

12-16. The Healing of a Leper
(Mk 1:40-45; Mt 8:1-4)

12 While he was in one of the cities there came a man full of leprosy; and when he saw Jesus, he fell on his face and besought him, "Lord, if you will, you can make me clean." **13** And he stretched out his hand, and touched him, saying, "I will; be clean." And immediately the leprosy left him. **14** And he charged him to tell no one; but "go and show yourself to the priest, and make an offering for your cleansing, as Moses commanded, for a proof to the people." **15** But so much the more the report went abroad concerning him; and great multitudes gathered to hear and to be healed of their infirmities. **16** But he withdrew to the wilderness and prayed.

Here Luke takes up again the thread of Mark which he had dropped in order to insert 5:1-11. He omits the very human sentiments of Jesus (Mk 1:41,43) and carefully avoids stating that Jesus could no longer openly enter a town (Mk 1:45).

12. Leprosy is a term which in the Bible covers a variety of skin diseases (Lv 13); one classified as a leper was an outcast (Lv 13:45f). According to the Mosaic Law (Lv 14:2-32), only a priest could officially declare a former leper clean; the cure was not regarded as complete until it had been duly acknowledged as such. "He charged him to tell no one"—the Messianic secret again. Luke adds, characteristically, that Jesus withdrew to pray (v. 16).

5:17–6:11. CONFLICT WITH THE SCRIBES AND PHARISEES [21]

Luke, following the exact order of the text of Mk 2:1–3:6, and departing little from its words, gives a series of five disputes between Jesus and his adversaries: on forgiveness of sins (5:17-26); on eating with publicans and sinners (vv. 27-32); on fasting (vv. 33-38); concerning the plucking of ears of grain on the sabbath (6:1-5); concerning healing on the sabbath (vv. 6-11). These are arranged in progressive order. At the cure of the paralytic, the opposition was latent; the scribes and Pharisees "question in their hearts" (5:22). During the meal in the house of Levi they addressed the disciples, though they were really attacking Jesus (v. 30). With regard to fasting, they questioned Jesus about an omission of his disciples (v. 33), but in the case of the ears of grain on the sabbath the charge is a direct violation of the Law (6:2). In the last episode the adversaries spy on Jesus (v. 7) and then meet together to plot his destruction (v. 11).

17-26. On Forgiveness of Sins
(Mk 2:1-12; Mt 9:1-8)

17 On one of those days, as he was teaching, there were Pharisees and teachers of the law sitting by, who had come from every village of Galilee and Judea and from Jerusalem; and the power of the Lord

[21] See pp. 288ff.

was with him to heal. 18 And behold, men were bringing on a bed a man who was paralyzed, and they sought to bring him in and lay him before Jesus; 19 but finding no way to bring him in, because of the crowd, they went up on the roof and let him down with his bed through the tiles into the midst before Jesus. 20 And when he saw their faith he said, "Man, your sins are forgiven you." 21 And the scribes and the Pharisees began to question, saying, "Who is this that speaks blasphemies? Who can forgive sins but God only?" 22 When Jesus perceived their questionings, he answered them, "Why do you question in your hearts? 23 Which is easier to say, 'Your sins are forgiven you,' or to say, 'Rise and walk'? 24 But that you may know that the Son of man has authority on earth to forgive sins"—he said to the man who was paralyzed—"I say to you, rise, take up your bed and go home." 25 And immediately he rose before them, and took up that on which he lay, and went home, glorifying God. 26 And amazement seized them all, and they glorified God and were filled with awe, saying, "We have seen strange things today."

Throughout, Luke has omitted the vivid details of Mark.

17f. More logically, he mentions the presence of Pharisees and teachers of the law at the beginning, and not later as in Mark 2:6. Luke uses the terms *nomodidaskalos*, "teacher of the Law" (cf. Ac 5:34), and *nomikos*, "lawyer" (Lk 7:30; 10:25; 11:45f,52f; 14:3), but also the more usual *grammateus*, "scribe" (5:21,30; 6:7; etc.). The presence of Pharisees and scribes from Judea and Jerusalem seems surprising. However, the climax of the conflicts (6:11) points to a time very much later than the earlier stages of the Galilean ministry; for Mark 2:1–3:6 (Luke's source) is a pre-existing literary unit which illustrates the growth of opposition to Jesus. The reading *auton*, "him" ("the power of the Lord was with him") is unquestionably original and the variant *autous*, "them" ("the power of the Lord was present to heal them") is a scribal correction, perhaps because *kyrios*, "Lord", was taken to refer to Christ. The sense is that the power of God enabled Jesus to work miracles.

19. Luke substitutes a tiled roof (more intelligible to his Gentile readers) for the earthern roof of a Palestinian house (Mk 2:4).

20. Jesus acknowledges the faith of the men, that is, their trust and confidence in his power. His declaration of the forgiveness of the paralytic's sins must be understood against the background

of the contemporary belief in a link between disease and sin (cf. Jn 5:14; 9:2).

21. The forgiveness of sins was regarded as God's prerogative (cf. Ex 34:6f; Is 43:25f; 44:22), not granted even to the Messiah.

22-25. The healing of the sick man proves that Jesus is not a blasphemer as his accusers had alleged, for God would not grant the power of healing to a blasphemer; therefore, also his claim to forgive sins is true. Here for the first time (as in Mark) Jesus calls himself "Son of man"; he claims that he has brought down on earth the very source of pardon which hitherto had existed only in heaven.

25f. Luke alone mentions the glorifying of God by the healed man and the fear (religious awe in the presence of the supernatural) of the bystanders.

27-32. Call of Levi; Eating with Sinners
(Mk 2:13-17; Mt 9:9-13)

27 After this he went out, and saw a tax collector, named Levi, sitting at the tax office; and he said to him, "Follow me." **28** And he left everything, and rose and followed him.

29 And Levi made him a great feast in his house; and there was a large company of tax collectors and others sitting at table with them. **30** And the Pharisees and their scribes murmured against his disciples, saying, "Why do you eat and drink with tax collectors and sinners?" **31** And Jesus answered them, "Those who are well have no need of a physician, but those who are sick; **32** I have not come to call the righteous, but sinners to repentance."

In the parallel passage of the first gospel this man is named "Matthew" (Mt 9:9). Typically, Levi is said to have left "everything" (cf. Mk 2:15).

29f. Luke delicately speaks of "tax collectors and others" (cf. Mk 2:15); it is the Pharisees and scribes who describe these others as "sinners". The disciples, and not Jesus himself as in Mark 2:16, are blamed.

31f. Luke adds that sinners are called "to repentance" (cf. Mk 2:17): the following of Jesus demands a sincere conversion.

33-39. On Fasting
(Mk 2:18-22; Mt 9:14-17)

33 And they said to him, "The disciples of John fast often and offer prayers, and so do the disciples of the Pharisees, but yours eat and drink." 34 And Jesus said to them, "Can you make wedding guests fast while the bridegroom is with them? 35 The days will come, when the bridegroom is taken away from them, and then they will fast in those days." 36 He told them a parable also: "No one tears a piece from a new garment and puts it upon an old garment; if he does, he will tear the new, and the piece from the new will not match the old. 37 And no one puts new wine into old wineskins; if he does, the new wine will burst the skins and it will be spilled, and the skins will be destroyed. 38 But new wine must be put into fresh wineskins. 39 And no one after drinking old wine desires new; for he says, 'The old is good.'"

33. With his "they said to him" (that is, the scribes and Pharisees), Luke links this incident more closely to the preceding one (cf. "the people" of Mark 2:18); he also adds that the disciples of John "offer prayers". Though the only fast enjoined by the Law was for the Day of Expiation (Lv 16:30), the Pharisees fasted on Mondays and Thursdays (cf. Lk 18:12).

34. In Palestine wedding celebrations usually lasted a week; during that time obligations like fasting ceased for all members of the wedding party. Likewise the disciples of Jesus rejoice while their Master is with them.

35. It would seem that the early Church understood the image of v. 24 as an allegory—Jesus is the bridegroom—and, in the light of the Passion, added v. 35. A time for fasting, that is, for sorrow, will come when the bridegroom is "taken away", that is, will have gone to his death.

36. This manner of introducing a parable is peculiar to Luke (cf. 13:6; 14:7; 18:1; 20:9). He has quite changed the parable: Mark (2:21) says that the patching of an old garment with a piece of unshrunken cloth will only make the tear worse; in Luke the piece is torn from a new garment, so that it is the new that suffers. He thus assimilates the first parable to the second.

37f. In the parable of the New Wine Luke follows Mark closely: the new is destroyed by contact with the old. The parables illustrate a contrast between the old spirit and the new: there can be no question of taking something from the gospel and adding it to

Judaism (the one would suffer without profit to the other); nor can the gospel be contained within the framework of Judaism; there must be new wineskins for the new wine. The disciples of Jesus, going their own way (v. 33), have the good sense not to ruin a new garment for the sake of an old one, nor to put new wine into old skins.

39. Peculiar to Luke; it is best considered as an independent logion added here by means of the catchword (*oinos*) *neos,* "new (wine)" (vv. 37f). While its original sense is not obvious, Luke would appear to understand it as reinforcing the message of the parables, the incompatibility between old and new, and as a defense of the independent conduct of the disciples.

6:1-5. The Plucking of Ears of Grain on the Sabbath
(Mk 2:23-28; Mt 12:1-8)

1 On a sabbath, while he was going through the grainfields, his disciples plucked and ate some ears of grain, rubbing them in their hands. 2 But some of the Pharisees said, "Why are you doing what is not lawful to do on the sabbath?" 3 And Jesus answered, "Have you not read what David did when he was hungry, he and those who were with him: 4 how he entered the house of God, and took and ate the bread of the Presence, which it is not lawful for any but the priests to eat, and also gave it to those with him?" 5 And he said to them, "The Son of man is lord of the sabbath."

1f. Many manuscripts read "On the second first sabbath" (on the second sabbath after the first)—to be regarded as a secondary reading. Rubbing ears of grain in the hand was, in rabbinical casuistry, interpreted as reaping and so an infringement of the sabbath rest (cf. Ex 34:21).

3f. Jesus refers to David's action (1 Sm 21:1-6): he and his men, fleeing from Saul's anger, ate the "bread of the Presence" (the twelve loaves, renewed each sabbath, placed in the Holy Place of the sanctuary and eaten by the priests only [Lv 24:5-9]); this scriptural precedent indicates that positive law must yield to genuine human need. Luke omits the inexact detail "when Abiathar was high priest" (Mk 2:26; cf. 1 Sm 21:1-6; 2 Sm 8:17); he also omits Mark 2:27.

5. The Son of man, who can forgive sin (Lk 5:24), also claims the right to dispense his disciples from the divine law of sabbath observance; in practice, this amounts to a declaration that he is introducing a new order in which the sabbath observance will no longer have place. Codex Bezae transfers v. 5 after v. 10 and in its place makes the interesting insertion: "On the same day, seeing one working on the sabbath, he said to him: 'Man, if indeed you know what to do, blessed are you; but if you know not, you are accursed and a transgressor of the Law.'" Some have judged this to be an authentic saying of Jesus, but he could scarcely have spoken in these terms to a Jew who would have regarded the Law as the ultimate norm. The saying shows the influence of Pauline doctrine (cf. Rm 14:12,23).

6-11. Healing on the Sabbath
(Mk 3:1-6; Mt 12:9-14)

6 On another sabbath, when he entered the synagogue and taught, a man was there whose right hand was withered. **7** And the scribes and the Pharisees watched him, to see whether he would heal on the sabbath, so that they might find an accusation against him. **8** But he knew their thoughts, and he said to the man who had the withered hand, "Come and stand here." And he rose and stood there. **9** And Jesus said to them, "I ask you, is it lawful on the sabbath to do good or to do harm, to save life or to destroy it?" **10** And he looked around on them all, and said to him, "Stretch out your hand." And he did so, and his hand was restored. **11** But they were filled with fury and discussed with one another what they might do to Jesus.

6. At once Luke intimates that this incident has also to do with the sabbath observance; he adds that Jesus taught in the synagogue and, strangely, he adds the typically Markan detail that the man's *right* hand was withered (cf. Mk 3:1).

8. Again Luke goes beyond Mark (3:3) in stating that Jesus knew their thoughts.

10. On the other hand he plays down the reactions of Christ (anger and grief)—Mark 3:5.

11. Mark 3:6 certainly refers to the close of the ministry (the whole conflict passage is a literary unit reproduced as such by Mark); Luke softens this impression by suggesting less specific action against Jesus. He does not mention the Herodians (Mk 3:6); but in 13:31, at a much later stage, he refers to Herod's plan to kill Jesus.

6:12-49. THE PREACHING OF JESUS

12-16. Choice of the Twelve
(Mk 3:13-19; Mt 10:1-4)

12 In these days he went out into the hills to pray; and all night he continued in prayer to God. **13** And when it was day, he called his disciples, and chose from them twelve, whom he named apostles; **14** Simon, whom he named Peter, and Andrew his brother, and James and John, and Philip, and Bartholomew, **15** and Matthew, and Thomas, and James the son of Alphaeus, and Simon who was called the Zealot, **16** and Judas the son of James, and Judas Iscariot, who became a traitor.

Luke has switched about two Markan passages (Mk 3:7-12 and 3:13-19) so that the choice of the Twelve, followed by a concourse of the people, sets the scene for the inaugural discourse (6:20-49). "The idea of choosing the Twelve could not have been suggested to Jesus by the presence of the crowd; it had quite another bearing. The matter was so grave that it had to be preceded by a long prayer. And since Jesus must afterward, in Luke, address to his disciples and to the crowd a discourse on the new spirit, especially the spirit of charity, it was necessary that the crowd should be present to hear it. Jesus with God, with the Twelve, with the crowd whom he heals and teaches, that is the order which Luke judged most appropriate." [22]

12. He emphasizes the importance of the choice of the Twelve by the night-long prayer of Jesus (cf. 9:28f; 11:1; 22:41); throughout Luke, "the mountain" is a place of prayer or revelation.

13. Instead of Mark's "to be with him and to be sent out to preach" (3:14)—thus describing their function—Luke declares that Jesus gave to the Twelve the title of "apostles"; it seems, however, that *apostolos* as a title was of later origin and the evangelist is reflecting Christian usage.

14f. Luke gives a list in Ac 1:13—so we have four lists altogether (cf. Mk 3:16-19; Mt 10:2-4). While no two agree on the exact order of names, all of them set out the Twelve in groups of four and the same name always appears at the head of each group: Simon Peter, Philip, and James of Alpheus. *Ioudas Iakōbou* would normally be "Judas, son of James", but "brother of

[22] M.-J. Lagrange, *op. cit.,* pp. 179f.

James" is possible (cf. Ac 1:13); by Mark and Matthew he is named "Thaddaeus". Luke alone calls Judas Iscariot "traitor".

17-19. Crowds Come to Jesus
(Mk 3:7-12; Mt 12:15-21)

17 And he came down with them and stood on a level place, with a great crowd of his disciples and a great multitude of people from all Judea and Jerusalem and the seacoast of Tyre and Sidon, who came to hear him and to be healed of their diseases; **18** and those who were troubled with unclean spirits were cured. **19** And all the crowd sought to touch him, for power came forth from him and healed them all.

Where Mark gives a summary description of the great crowds which attended the ministry of Jesus, Luke sets the stage for the Sermon. Jesus came down from the mountain—the place of prayer or revelation where he is alone or with a privileged few (cf. 9:28)—and went to meet the people (cf. 9:37). This "level place" is no longer beside the lake (cf. Mk 3:7-9). The confession of the unclean spirits and Jesus' rebuke (Mk 3:11f) have been anticipated by Luke in 4:41, since they would be out of place immediately before the Sermon. The power of God which was in Jesus (5:17) healed those who so much as touched him (cf. 8:46). At this point Luke leaves the place of Mark, which he picks up again at 8:4. The following section (6:20–8:3) is, in this respect, an insertion of Luke.

20-49. The Sermon on the Mount
(Mt 5–7)

Jesus formulated the special character of the kingdom of God [23] in a discourse which Mark has omitted and which Matthew and Luke have preserved in widely different versions. The name "Sermon on the Plain", sometimes given to the Lucan version—because of the "level plain" of v. 17—suggests that the discourse here recorded is distinct from the "Sermon on the Mount" of Matthew. In fact, because of the special symbolical value of "the mountain" in Luke—a place where the people do not come—the evangelist has changed the setting. This is entirely a literary

[23] See pp. 280ff.

device and it is best to keep the same title for both versions. The discourse in Matthew is much longer than that in Luke; but, on the other hand, many of the passages found in Mt 5–7 occur elsewhere in Luke, in chapters 11, 13, 14 and 16. It can be shown that Luke has omitted, as being of little interest to his Gentile readers, what concerned Jewish law and custom (Mt 5:17–6:18). In general, we may say that whereas Matthew, borrowing from other sayings of the Lord, has added to the original Sermon, Luke has omitted some of it.

If the additions that Matthew has made to his source can be recognized and isolated, we may get back to the original plan of the Sermon—and then see how Luke has handled it. That original plan was along the following lines—the references are to Matthew.[23a]

Introduction: the beatitudes (5:3-12)

Part I: *Perfect Justice*
General statement: Perfect justice (5:17-20)
Five concrete examples: (5:21-24, 27f, 33-37, 38-42, 43-48)

Part II: *Good Works*
General statement (6:1)
Three concrete examples (6:2-4, 5f, 16-18)

Part III: *Three Warnings*
(a) Do not judge (7:1f)
    Example: Parable of the Mote and the Beam (3-5)
(b) Beware of false prophets (15)
    Example: Parable of the Tree and Its Fruits (16-20)
(c) Practice justice (21)
    Example: Parable of the Two Builders (24-27)

The procedure of the discourse is uniform throughout: a general recommendation is illustrated by concrete examples. The first recommendation of 5:20, with five applications, is the most general, while the three sayings of chapter 7 refer directly to conduct and one example is enough to illustrate each of them. The discourse is by no means a mere collection of sayings, but has a real unity and is highly original.

[23a] J. Dupont, *Les Béatitudes* (Bruges: Abbaye de Saint-André, 1958²), pp. 43-187.

Luke, however, has done considerable editorial work on the Sermon. He set aside the section regarding our Lord's attitude to the Law (Mt 5:17-48) and the passage concerning the Jewish works of piety (Mt 6:1-18). This is quite in accordance with his method of adapting the gospel for his Gentile readers.

The discourse in Luke is introduced by the beatitudes and woes (20b-26). Only a very small part of the matter dealt with in the antitheses of the Sermon (cf. Mt 5:21-48) is included—the recommendations of the fifth and sixth antitheses of Matthew; but this is sufficient to prove that Luke had known the series of antitheses and had deliberately omitted all the rest. He has combined two sayings by introducing into the middle of the positive part of the sixth antithesis the corresponding part of the fifth:

> Mt 5:43-48 = Lk 6:27f and Lk 6:32-36
> Mt 5:39-42 = Lk 6:29f

Lk 6:27-36 then becomes an instruction on the love of enemies. The whole section, beginning with the commandment, "Love your enemies" (v. 27a)—repeated in the conclusion (v. 35a)—is a unit that is rounded off by v. 36.

Lk 6:37-42 also forms a unit. The warning not to pass judgment on others, the parable of the Mote and the Beam, and the other elements, are all linked together. Here it is no longer a question of love of enemies (as in the previous passage), but of love of the brethren. The last part of the discourse (6:43-49) regards the necessity of proving good dispositions in action and the necessity of putting into effect the teaching one has received. As a result of these changes, the plan of the discourse in Luke takes on the following form:

Introduction: Beatitudes and Woes (20b-26)
Part I: Love of Enemies (27-36)
Part II: Fraternal Charity (37-42)
Conclusion: Necessity of Good Works (43-49)

It is mainly because of his omissions that the discourse of Luke has a different character from that of Matthew, but it is also true that the omissions were motivated by Luke's outlook and, consequently, by his editorial emphasis. In this way the parable of the Two Trees (6:43f), instead of illustrating a warning against false prophets (Mt 7:15), has become a recommendation addressed to the disciples. Similarly, in Luke 6:32-34 the reference to "tax collectors" and "Gentiles" is omitted, and the conduct of Christians is opposed to that of "sinners" in general. In brief, Luke opens up a wider perspective and detaches the teaching of Jesus from its Jewish background.

This lack of emphasis on opposition to traditional Judaism characterizes Luke's version of the Sermon. It shows how Luke's purpose is different from Matthew's when both report the original discourse. We can see that the original Sermon defined Christianity in terms of perfect righteousness and in terms of a religion that is more interior and pure than that of official Judaism. The additions which Matthew makes from other discourses of our Lord serve to underline the practical consequences of this teaching. Luke is concerned rather with emphasizing the essential trait of that message—charity. It is around this theme of charity that the elements of the central section of Luke's discourse are grouped: the duty of loving one's enemies (vv. 27-36), the obligations of fraternal charity (vv. 37-42). It seems that Luke is far less interested in defining the spirit of Christianity than in pointing out the conduct which can give concrete expression to that spirit.

20-26. The Beatitudes and Woes
(Mt 5:1-12)

Matthew has nine beatitudes while Luke has four only, paralleled by four "woes". The beatitudes of Luke correspond to four of Matthew, yet with notable differences in detail. Matthew's beatitudes—except for the ninth (5:11)—are in the third person; those of Luke are in the second person. A study of macarisms (beatitudes) in the Old Testament and in Jewish literature shows that the third person is normal (cf. Pss 1:1; 32[31]:1f; 41[40]:2; Prv 3:13; 8:34; and especially Lk 1:45), while a study of Luke's style shows his preference for the second person plural—direct style (cf. Mk 2:16 and Lk 5:30; Mk 2:19 and Lk 5:34; etc.). Then, too, there is the influence of the "woes": the style of the *vae* seems to be that of apostrophe in the second person (cf. Mt 23:13-29; Lk 11:42-52); here the close parallel between woes and beatitudes is emphasized by writing the beatitudes, too, in the second person.

20b-23. THE BEATITUDES

It is felt that a comparative study of the beatitudes of Luke and Matthew will prove helpful.

1. *The Poor*

Lk 6:20b	Mt 5:3
Blessed are you poor, for yours is the kingdom of God.	Blessed are the poor in spirit, for theirs is the kingdom of heaven.

Matthew's term "kingdom of heaven" is typical of this evangelist and means just the same as Luke's "kingdom of God". The expression "poor in spirit" has been found in the Qumran texts (cf. 1Q M XIV, 7; 1Q S IV, 3); it seems unlikely that, if Luke had found it in his source, he would have dropped this qualification; we may regard "in spirit" as an addition made by Matthew in order to make more explicit the Old Testament and Jewish meaning of the word "poor" used by Jesus.

The "poor" are the literally poor, but they are not worthy of the kingdom of God by this fact alone; we must keep the context in sight. Luke is careful to point out that these are disciples (v. 20a), therefore they are poor who trust in God. Besides, one cannot overlook the fact that close behind *ptochoi*, "poor", stands the Hebrew term *anawim*, the "poor of Yahweh", with all the religious associations of the term (cf. Zech 2:3; 3:11f; Ps 131[130]). The Messiah is sent to "preach good news to the poor" (Is 61:1; cf. Lk 4:18). Jesus assures the poor who have become his disciples that their hope will not be groundless; it is already realized, for the kingdom of God is theirs. The reign of God has already begun and they participate in it—with the hope of entering into the kingdom.

2. The Hungry

Lk 6:21a	Mt 5:6
Blessed are you who hunger now for you shall be satisfied.	Blessed are those who hunger and thirst for righteousness for they shall be satisfied.

The textual differences here are notable. Matthew speaks metaphorically of hunger and thirst; Luke speaks of real hunger and omits reference to thirst, since it is implicitly contained in hunger and since the corresponding woe (v. 25) is kept in view. It seems likely that Matthew has added the precision "for righteousness" (as he had added "in spirit" in the first beatitude); he wished to emphasize the moral aspects of the beatitudes. The order of this and the next beatitude is not the same in both gospels. Matthew speaks first of the afflicted, then of the hungry; Luke has the inverse order. In Luke's thought there is a close link between poverty and hunger; therefore, he naturally cites the beatitude of the hungry after that of the poor. In view of this it is likely that Luke has changed the primitive order.

The poor who hunger in this life will be satisfied in the next—the thought of Ps 107(106):9. The beatitude is in the future tense because there is no full satisfaction in this world; the psalmist understands how and when true repletion can be found: "As for me, in my justice I shall see your face and be filled, when I awake, with the sight of your glory" (Ps 17[16]:15).

3. The Weepers

Lk 6:21b	Mt 5:5
Blessed are you that weep now, for you shall laugh.	Blessed are those who mourn, for they shall be comforted.

As in the previous beatitude, Luke has *nun* ("now"), a favorite adverb. The beatitude of Matthew is addressed to "mourners", that of Luke to "weepers"; according to Matthew the mourners will be "comforted", and according to Luke the weepers will 'laugh". The verb "to weep" is a common one in Luke (compare Mt 11:17 with Lk 7:32)—here we can suspect a stylistic touch. Besides, the verb "to mourn" occurs in the third woe (Lk 6:25) and so supports the originality of the verb in the beatitude of Matthew. The terms of Luke are more realistic, more universally human, while those of Matthew are more traditional and more biblical.

Weeping is the lot of the servants of God here below because evil is so much more in evidence than good. But they will be consoled—this promise lights up their sorrow with a ray of happiness. The promise extends to all who suffer, on condition that they are disciples of Jesus.

4. The Persecuted

(1) Persecution

Lk 6:22	Mt 5:11
Blessed are you when men hate you,	Blessed are you when men revile you
and when they exclude you and revile you, and cast out your name as evil,	and persecute you and utter all kinds of evil against you, falsely,
on account of the Son of man.	on my account.

The grades of maltreatment are better ordered in Luke: first hatred, next exclusion, then outrages and defamation; in Matthew this order is not evident (cf. Mk 12:3-5; Lk 20:10-12; Mt 21:35f). In fact, either Matthew or Luke could have changed the primitive order. In both, the beatitude is addressed directly to the disciples. Luke alone mentions hate (cf. Lk 14:26; Mt 10:37), and the presumption is that Matthew has omitted the word here. *Aphorizō*, "exclude", is a technical term meaning "excommunicate" (cf. Is 56:3; Jn 16:2; Qumran texts: 1Q S II, 16; V, 18; VI, 25; etc.); instead of hatred and exclusion Matthew speaks vaguely of "persecution". "Cast out your name as evil" means to defame, to speak falsely against (cf. Dt 22:13f,19). It is a juridical term which, like "exclude", Luke must have found in his source. Matthew ("utter all kinds of evil against you") perhaps gives the simpler equivalent of the technical term. Matthew adds "falsely"; in the light of other passages it seems certain that this is an addition of the evangelist (cf. Mk 14:55; Mt 26:59—also Mt 6:33; Lk 12:31; Mt 19:21; Mk 10:20; Lk 18:22—where Matthew makes similar additions). "On account of the Son of man" (Matthew: "on my account")—the presumption is that "Son of man" is original (cf. Lk 12:8; Mt 10:32; Mk 8:31; Lk 9:22; Mt 16:21). It would seem, in short, that Matthew has made the following changes in his source: he substituted the term "persecution" for the more descriptive expression "when men hate you and when they exclude you"; he rendered the technical expression "cast out your name" by "utter all kinds of evil"; he added that the accusations will be made "falsely"; he has substituted "on my account" for "on account of the Son of man".

(2) The Heavenly Recompense

Lk 6:23	Mt 5:12
Rejoice in that day,	Rejoice
and leap for joy,	and be glad,
for behold your reward is great	for your reward is great
in heaven;	in the heavens;
for so their fathers did	for so men persecuted
to the prophets.	the prophets
	who were before you.

In the Greek there are some stylistic changes clearly attributable to Luke. His "in that day" is related to the "now" of the second and third beatitudes; he writes "heaven" in place of the Semitic "heavens" of Matthew; the latter has "persecute" as in v. 11. On the other hand, the verb *agalliaō*, "be glad", used by Matthew, is more likely primitive; Luke shows a preference for the synonym *skirtaō*, "leap for joy" (cf. Lk 1:41, 44). The conclusion of the beatitude, as it stands, has a different meaning in each evangelist, but, from the point of view of expression, the texts are close. Matthew's "who were before you" could easily be read "your ancestors", "your fathers"; for that matter, the phrase is ambiguous. It might seem that Jesus regards his hearers too as prophets, like their ancestors; Luke has avoided the ambiguity. Besides, Luke avoids, wherever possible, the impersonal plural construction (here "men persecuted"), and he knows that, in fact, the "fathers" did persecute the prophets (cf. Lk 11:47f; Ac 7:51f). Matthew's text is to be preferred; the only retouch attributable to him is his reference to persecution. Elsewhere the differences between the two texts can be explained by the redactional changes of Luke.

This fourth beatitude is more particularly addressed to the disciples: they will not have to wait long to experience persecution and the supernatural joy which follows it (Ac 5:41). "On account of the Son of man" is the characteristic note of the beatitude: it is because they preach Christ that the disciples will be maltreated. They must rejoice not in spite of persecution but because of it; not, of course, because of persecution as such, but insofar as it is a guarantee of recompense. Jesus introduces the notion of merit, but the kingdom of God is not the reward of service rendered to God; the disciples will prepare for the heavenly reward by the practice of the humble virtues taught in the beatitudes.

Of these beatitudes Lagrange has written: "On reading the first words one would suppose that Jesus proposes a social reform which would bring about a reversal of roles: those who hunger will be filled, those who weep shall laugh. But this satisfaction and this joy are really found in heaven, in the presence of God who shares his light and his life—as all pious Jews understood. However Luke has insisted on real poverty, on real suffering, on real persecution. Those who are poor, who suffer and who are persecuted—all for the name of Jesus—have a pledge of divine life. Matthew is more spiritual, more far-reaching in outlook. His doctrine applies to all, rich and poor; it is consoling for those who possess riches without being attached to them. Luke addresses those who are really poor and suffering: when the world has no joy to offer and holds out no expectation is not one inclined to look to a heavenly hope? So this attitude, too, is penetrated by the spirit of Christianity and sees the disciples associated in the life and sufferings of their Master." [24]

The four beatitudes common to Matthew and Luke seem to presuppose the same basic source. When we have taken into account the additions and retouches made by both evangelists, we can get back to what is probably the original form of the beatitudes:

[24] *Op. cit.*, pp. 189f.

Blessed are the poor,
for theirs is the kingdom of heaven.

Blessed are those who mourn,
for they shall be consoled.

Blessed are those who hunger and thirst,
for they shall be satisfied.

Blessed are you when men hate you and exclude you,
and when they revile you and cast an evil name against you
because of the Son of man!
Rejoice and be glad,
because your reward is great in heaven,
for so men persecuted the prophets who were before you.

6:24-26. THE WOES

The four *vae* are attached to the beatitudes by the conjunction *plēn* ("however", "but") characteristic of Luke. After the *vae* the transitional phrase: "But I say to you that hear" (v. 27), brings the discourse back to the disciples; this phrase scarcely smoothes the brusque change from invective aimed at the rich to the recommendation of love of enemies (6:27-31). The difficulty seems to arise from the addition of the woes. Lagrange remarks: "V. 27 would follow better on v. 23. After saying that the disciples will be hated, Jesus teaches them to love their enemies: the context is excellent." [25] It seems impossible that Luke could have meant the woes to take the place of the beatitudes of Matthew which he himself does not have. It seems unlikely that the woes were found in the Sermon source of either evangelist. Hence, the simplest solution is that the woes are Luke's own composition and that he has inserted them here.

It is clear that the beatitudes of Luke's version should be interpreted in close relationship to the woes. The "poor" of the first beatitude must be understood of people who find themselves in a situation diametrically opposed to that of the rich of the first woe. Similarly, in the following beatitude the "hungry" must be contrasted with the "full" of the second woe, and so on. It is also evident that the point of view of the beatitudes of Luke—and this

[25] *Ibid.*, p. 192.

is emphasized by the woes—is quite different from that of Matthew, who regards the "poor in spirit" and the "hungry for righteousness". Luke's perspective is social, that of Matthew moral. And so Luke, friend of the poor and foe of wealth, presents the woes as the reverse of the beatitudes in order to underline the message of the beatitudes.

BEATITUDES AND WOES

Lk 6:20b	Mt 6:24
Blessed are you poor, for yours is the kingdom of God.	But woe to you that are rich, for you have received your consolation.

The woe is addressed to the rich who enjoy their riches and aspire to nothing else. Absorbed in the pleasures which this wealth procures, they have no desire for the kingdom of God.

Lk 6:21	Mt 6:25
Blessed are you that hunger now, for you shall be satisfied.	Woe to you that are full now, for you shall hunger.
Blessed are you that weep now, for you shall laugh.	Woe to you that laugh now, for you shall mourn and weep.

V. 25 is the antithesis of v. 21 with the same contrast between the present age and the time when each will be treated according to his deserts. It is clear that in v. 25a Luke is thinking of real hunger (and of real poverty in the previous woe) and is not speaking metaphorically (cf. Jas 4:9; 5:1).

Lk 6:22f	Mt 6:26
Blessed are you when men revile you . . . for so their fathers did to the prophets.	Woe to you when all men speak well of you, for so their fathers did to the false prophets.

While shorter than the corresponding beatitude, v. 26 is still parallel to it. The end of the verse is the exact counterpart of

v. 23, except for the qualification "false" prophets demanded by the context. It forms an *inclusion* which rounds off and relates the series of beatitudes and woes.

27-36. Love of Enemies
(Mt 5:38-48)

27 "But I say to you that hear, Love your enemies, do good to those who hate you, 28 bless those who curse you, pray for those who abuse you. 29 To him who strikes you on the cheek, offer the other also; and from him who takes away your cloak do not withhold your coat as well. 30 Give to every one who begs from you; and of him who takes away your goods do not ask them again. 31 And as you wish that men would do to you, do so to them.

32 "If you love those who love you, what credit is that to you? For even sinners love those who love them. 33 And if you do good to those who do good to you, what credit is that to you? For even sinners do the same. 34 And if you lend to those from whom you hope to receive, what credit is that to you? Even sinners lend to sinners, to receive as much again. 35 But love your enemies, and do good, and lend, expecting nothing in return; and your reward will be great, and you will be sons of the Most High; for he is kind to the ungrateful and the selfish. 36 Be merciful, even as your Father is merciful.

Of the six antitheses of Mt 5:21-48, Luke has preserved only the last two (in part). He has built a new unit by combining two sayings, and in doing so he has even reproduced the difference in person of these sayings: Lk 6:27f,32-36 = Mt 5:43-48 (second person plural); Lk 6:29f = Mt 5:39-42 (second person singular). The inspiration behind Lk 6:27-36 is clear from the admonition "Love your enemies" (v. 27a)—repeated in the conclusion (v. 35a). It is an instruction on the love of enemies, finely rounded off by v. 36.

27f. The enemies are those who injure by thought (hate), word (curse) or deed (abuse); the Christian reaction is *agapē*, a love that manifests itself in action, as the context shows.

29. The parallel (Mt 5:39-41) is more developed and more biblical in style (cf. Ex 22:25f; Dt 24:13); besides, Matthew refers to juridical action and Luke to aggression. The striking on the cheek (Mt 5:39—*right* cheek) is a calculated insult; Jesus is referring to insults suffered by his disciples *precisely as disciples*. As Luke understands this saying, its message, couched in typically hyperbolic Semitic terms, is that the most precious and most indispensable earthly things, such as honor and clothing, are nothing when balanced against the claims of *agapē*. "Each of us must be disposed to renounce his rights; and if we do uphold them in view of the common good, it should not be in a vengeful frame of mind. A detached spirit has no place for revenge." [26]

30. Characteristically, Luke adds "everyone", and his reference to the "taking away" of goods (instead of Matthew's "borrow") sustains the idea of aggression (cf. v. 29); here is the positive side of love.

31. The golden rule—much later in Matthew (7:12)—sums up the true disciple's attitude to all men at all times.

32-35. In place of the "tax collectors" and "Gentiles" of Mt 5:46f, Luke, more delicately, has "sinners"; v. 34 is a third example added by Luke. Love must be universal and disinterested.

36. In Mt 5:48 the perfection of the heavenly Father is somewhat intimidating; characteristically, Luke stresses the *mercy* of "your Father".

37-42. Fraternal Charity
(Mt 7:1-5; cf. Mt 10:27f; 15:14)

37 "Judge not, and you will not be judged; condemn not, and you will not be condemned; forgive, and you will be forgiven; **38** give, and it will be given to you; good measure, pressed down, shaken together, running over, will be put into your lap. For the measure you give will be the measure you get back."

39 He also told them a parable: "Can a blind man lead a blind man? Will they not both fall into a pit? **40** A disciple is not above his teacher, but every one when he is fully taught will be like his teacher. **41** Why do you see the speck that is in your brother's eye, but do not notice the log that is in your own eye? **42** Or how can you say to your brother, 'Brother, let me take out the speck that is in your eye,' when you yourself do not see the log that is in your own eye? You hypocrite, first take the log out of your own eye, and then you will see clearly to take out the speck that is in your brother's eye."

This passage does not have the structural coherence of the previous one; the warning not to pass judgment on others, the parable of the Mote and the Beam, and the remaining elements are rather superficially linked—Luke must have found them so

[26] M.-J. Lagrange, *op. cit.*, p. 193.

joined in his source. It is no longer a question of love of enemies but of love of the brethren; the passage brings out the concern of each for the welfare of all—a Christian is his brother's keeper.

37f. It is clear that 6:38b follows logically after v. 37 (cf. Mt 7:1f); v. 38a, an independent logion peculiar to Luke, has been added by means of the catchword "measure" and is not really at home in its new context. The passive ("it will be given") and the third person plural ("they will put"—rather than "will be put" [RSV]) are both circumlocutions or substitutes for the divine name. Thus the verse might be rendered: "Give and God will give to you; good measure . . . will God put into your lap." *Kolpos* (RSV "lap") is the fold formed by a loose garment above a retaining belt; this was often used as a pocket. The teaching is that we ought not to pass judgment on the motives or actions of others; and when we are injured by others, we ought to maintain a spirit of forgiveness.

39f. In Matthew the warning not to judge others (7:1f) is followed, logically, by the parable of the Mote and the Beam (7:3-5); Luke, however, has found two sayings inserted between them and, consequently, these sayings (Lk 6:39f) must seem somewhat out of place. Mt 15:14 gives the true context of Lk 6:39 (it refers to the Pharisees); it has been added in Luke's source through a certain rather vague association of ideas: blindness = mote or beam in the eye. The saying in v. 40b has two parts, clearly distinguished in Mt 10:24-25a. It was inserted in Luke's source because of the vague link with v. 39; a teacher is one who leads the blind (cf. Mt 15:14; 23:16,24). Luke, seemingly, understands it to mean that one cannot undertake to guide others until one has a good grasp of the Christian way of life.

41f. To avoid being a blind guide one must exercise self-criticism. "This is a parable about personal relationships. Pseudoreligion, which Jesus calls hypocrisy, is forever trying to make other people better; and the cure for it is a mirror."[27] The following passage shows that the true Christian teacher must be a genuinely good man.

[27] G. B. Caird, *op. cit.*, p. 106.

43-49. Necessity of Good Works
(Mt 7:15-27; cf. 12:23-35)

43 "For no good tree bears bad fruit, nor again does a bad tree bear good fruit; 44 for each tree is known by its own fruit. For figs are not gathered from thorns, nor are grapes picked from a bramble bush. 45 The good man out of the good treasure of his heart produces good, and the evil man out of his evil treasure produces evil; for out of the abundance of the heart his mouth speaks.

46 "Why do you call me 'Lord, Lord,' and not do what I tell you? 47 Every one who comes to me and hears my words and does them, I will show you what he is like: 48 he is like a man building a house, who dug deep, and laid the foundation upon rock; and when a flood arose, the stream broke against that house, and could not shake it, because it had been well built. 49 But he who hears and does not do them is like a man who built a house on the ground without a foundation; against which the stream broke, and immediately it fell, and the ruin of that house was great.

43f. The saying about the two trees, instead of illustrating a warning against false prophets (Mt 7:15), has become a recommendation addressed to the disciples: a man is known by the fruit he bears. With the preceding passage in mind this may mean that only a good disciple can win good converts.

45. We have here two sayings which are found, in inverse order but in a similar context, in Mt 12:34f. While the fruits of Lk 6:43f are "good works", those of v. 45 are "words"; the addition was made on the ground of the recurrence of "good" and "evil". Luke draws attention to good words (authentic and sound teaching) as to a special type of "good fruit".

46. Cf. Mt 7:21. No one can be a true disciple of Christ—no matter how much he may protest that he is one—unless he is obedient to the Lord (cf. Jn 15:14; Heb 5:9), for only so will he bear fruit (Jn 15:8).

47-49. Cf. Mt 7:24-27. Both evangelists have explicitly presented the parable as a commentary on the foregoing saying (Lk 6:46; Mt 7:21). The opening phrase of v. 47 is reminiscent of John (cf. Jn 5:40; 6:35,37,44f,65; 7:37). In Matthew the contrast is between a house built on rock and one built on sand, and the causes of destruction are heavy rain, which brings torrents of water beating against the house, and a violent wind. These conditions are typically Palestinian: the heavy winter rains are always accompanied by a gale and often by thunder and lightning. As a result, floods of water rush along the *wadi*-beds (a *wadi* is a watercourse which is dry except after heavy rain); the "sand" on which the house was built is the floor of such a *wadi,* and the man who built there was asking for trouble. Luke has changed the details so that the parable might be more readily understood by his non-Palestinian readers. He is not concerned with the situation of the house, but describes whether or not it was given a sound foundation—the wise man "dug deep". The flooding is not caused by torrential rain but by an overflowing river. With a few simple strokes he has given the parable a more general coloring; but, from a literary point of view, he has not improved on it. Matthew's version, with its balanced parallelism, its rhythm and its local color, is manifestly a faithful rendering of the Aramaic original spoken by the Lord. However, Luke's variations, readily understandable, have not at all affected the meaning of the parable. The wise man and the foolish man are alike disciples; both of them have heard the words of Jesus, but only one of them does the words of Christ. At the last judgment the doers of the word, and they alone, will stand firm. Probably, the floodwaters may equally well stand for any severe trial, and in such a time the price of security will be a life built on active obedience to the teaching of Christ.

Lagrange thus sums up the message of the Sermon in Luke: "The disciple, detached from all earthly goods, comforted in distress and sorrow by the hope of future blessings, will, in the face of a hostile world, maintain boundless charity, goodness, indulgence, liberality, and, at the same time, he will take good care not to believe himself better than others and will not pass judgment on others. It is his duty to help his brethren and so he must be their guide and be able to bring them to an awareness of their shortcomings. But he has to begin by reforming himself; he must be genuinely good if his words are to be efficacious. He must really face up to his task; it is not enough that he hear Jesus, that he follow him and call him Master, he must do what Jesus asks." [28]

[28] *Op. cit.,* p. 184.

7:1-10. Cure of a Centurion's Servant
(Mt 8:5-13)

1 After he had ended all his sayings in the hearing of the people he entered Capernaum. 2 Now a centurion had a slave who was dear to him, who was sick and at the point of death. 3 When he heard of Jesus, he sent to him elders of the Jews, asking him to come and heal his slave. 4 And when they came to Jesus, they besought him earnestly, saying, "He is worthy to have you do this for him, 5 for he loves our nation, and he built us our synagogue." 6 And Jesus went with them. When he was not far from the house, the centurion sent friends to him, saying to him, "Lord, do not trouble yourself, for I am not worthy to have you come under my roof; 7 therefore I did not presume to come to you. But say the word, and let my servant be healed. 8 For I am a man set under authority, with soldiers under me; and I say to one, 'Go,' and he goes; and to another, 'Come,' and he comes; and to my slave, 'Do this,' and he does it." 9 When Jesus heard this he marvelled at him, and turned and said to the multitude that followed him, "I tell you, not even in Israel have I found such faith." 10 And when those who had been sent returned to the house, they found the slave well.

It is sufficiently clear that Luke and Matthew have not followed an identical source but have found different versions of the incident; however, Luke's editorial hand is also in evidence.

1f. The Sermon on the Mount had been spoken in the hearing of Israel ("the people"); it may be that in turning immediately to the episode of the centurion Luke wishes to foreshadow the Gentile mission. This may explain why (unlike Matthew) Jesus does not meet the centurion: according to the plan of Luke in Acts, the Gentile mission is to follow the Ascension. The centurion (certainly a Gentile, v. 5) may be an officer of Herod Antipas; he could also have been a Roman centurion in charge of a small post at Capernaum.

3-5. The centurion sent "elders", distinguished members of the Jewish community of Capernaum, to Jesus (cf. Mt 8:5f); it was a service he could have made bold to ask and which they would have been glad to perform because of what he had done for them. He is, obviously, like Cornelius, a "God-fearer" (Ac 10:1f), one of the numerous class of Gentiles attracted to Judaism, but distinct from the proselytes who took on full Jewish observance. These "God-fearers" were freely admitted to the synagogue worship; they came to know and appreciate the main tenets of the religion and began to observe certain Jewish practices.

6f. The man is aware that Jesus, as a Jew, might be loath to incur the ritual defilement involved in entering a Gentile house (cf. Ac 10:28; 11:4); but his words, together with his action in sending an embassy rather than directly approaching Jesus, serve to emphasize the man's humility—a theme dear to Luke (cf. 1:48, 51-53; 14:11; 16:15; 18:9-14; 20:46f).

8. The centurion is confident that Jesus can heal by a word: as a soldier, and subject to authority himself, he knew how a word of command could bring results.

9f. Jesus' declaration that the faith of this Gentile is greater than Israel's prepares the reader for the later acceptance of the gospel by the Gentiles (cf. Ac 28:28). The saying of Mt 8:11f is given by Luke in another context (13:28f).

11-17. Raising of the Widow's Son

11 Soon afterward he went to a city called Nain, and his disciples and a great crowd went with him. **12** As he drew near to the gate of the city, behold, a man who had died was being carried out, the only son of his mother, and she was a widow; and a large crowd from the city was with her. **13** And when the Lord saw her, he had compassion on her and said to her, "Do not weep." **14** And he came and touched the bier, and the bearers stood still. And he said, "Young man, I say to you, arise." **15** And the dead man sat up, and began to speak. And he gave him to his mother. **16** Fear seized them all; and they glorified God, saying, "A great prophet has arisen among us!" and "God has visited his people!" **17** And this report concerning him spread through the whole of Judea and all the surrounding country.

This is a passage peculiar to Luke who has inserted the miracle here as a preparation for the reply to the Baptist ("the dead are raised up", v. 22).

11. Nain lies about 8 miles southeast of Nazareth, on the slope of the Little Hermon.

12f. The added poignancy of the death of a widow's only son moves Jesus to compassion; here only is this sentiment attributed to him by Luke. *Ho Kyrios* ("the Lord") henceforth appears regularly as a title of Jesus: 7:19; 10:1,39,41; 11:39; 12:42; 13:15; 16:18; 17:5f; 18:6; 19:8; 22:61; 24:34 (but once only in a parallel passage of Mark and Matthew: Mk 11:3; Mt 21:3). It is a Christian title (cf. Rm 10:9; Phil 2:11), implying divinity, and Jesus was not addressed as "Lord", in this full sense, during his ministry.

14f. The body, wrapped in a shroud, lay on a stretcher without a coffin; life was restored by the mere word of Jesus (cf. 1 Kg 17:23).

16. "Fear" is the normal reaction to a manifestation of divine power (cf. Lk 1:12,65; 2:9; 5:26; 8:25,37), quickly followed by praise of God (cf. 2:20; 5:25f; 9:43; 13:13; etc.). The people see in Jesus a great prophet (cf. 24:19) like Elijah or Elisha, who also raised people from the dead (1 Kg 17:17-24; 2 Kg 4:18-37); his deed is a merciful intervention of God in favor of his people (cf. Lk 1:68,78).

17. "Judea" is used in its wide sense of the land of the Jews— Palestine.

18-23. The Baptist's Question
(Mt 11:2-6)

18 The disciples of John told him of all these things. **19** And John, calling to him two of his disciples, sent them to the Lord, saying, "Are you he who is to come, or shall we look for another?" **20** And when the men had come to him, they said, "John the Baptist has sent us to you, saying, 'Are you he who is to come, or shall we look for another?'" **21** In that hour he cured many of diseases and plagues and evil spirits, and on many that were blind he bestowed sight. **22** And he answered them, "Go and tell John what you have seen and heard: the blind receive their sight, the lame walk, lepers are cleansed, and the deaf hear, the dead are raised up, the poor have good news preached to them. **23** And blessed is he who takes no offense at me."

18-20. Luke does not have to explain that John is in prison (cf. 3:19f). The Baptist's question was prompted by the fact that, in his eyes, the coming Messiah was the awesome judge of the end-time (cf. 3:9,16f); Jesus' approach was so different from anything he had expected.

21. Proper to Luke; it is a preparation for v. 22, but superfluous after v. 18.

22. These are the works of the Messianic age (cf. Is 26:19; 29:18f; 35:5f; 61:1)—John can draw his own conclusions.

23. The Baptist is the object of this blessing: Jesus understands John's perplexity and appreciates the sincere motive that urged him to seek clarification.

24-30. Panegyric of John
(Mt 11:7-15)

24 When the messengers of John had gone, he began to speak to the crowds concerning John: "What did you go out into the wilderness to behold? A reed shaken by the wind? 25 What then did you go out to see? A man clothed in soft raiment? Behold, those who are gorgeously apparelled and live in luxury are in kings' courts. 26 What then did you go out to see? A prophet? Yes, I tell you, and more than a prophet. 27 This is he of whom it is written,

> 'Behold, I send my messenger before thy face,
> who shall prepare thy way before thee.'

28 I tell you, among those born of women none is greater than John; yet he who is least in the kingdom of God is greater than he." 29 (When they heard this all the people and the tax collectors justified God, having been baptized with the baptism of John; 30 but the Pharisees and the lawyers rejected the purpose of God for themselves, not having been baptized by him.)

24-28. Almost identical with Mt 11:7-11.

24f. The precise meaning is not certain. What is clear is that the first two questions lead up to that of v. 26 and its answer. Thus we may understand: the crowds that flocked to the desert certainly did not go to look at a reed on the Jordan bank stirring in the wind, and did not expect to be greeted by a dandified courtier in that unlikely place! Only the presence of a prophet could have drawn those crowds. Alternatively, the meaning may be that John is no sycophant—no reed—but a man who boldly took issue with Herod Agrippa (3:19) and no sensual courtier, but an ascetic (7:33).

26f. The prophet whom they had gone to see was, in reality, more than a prophet: he is the messenger of Mal 3:1 (cf. Lk 1:17,76).

28. John belonged to the "time of Israel"—the greatest figure of that epoch, because he had immediately prepared the way for the Messiah. Now was the "time of Christ", the time of the present kingdom which had arrived with Jesus; men entered this kingdom by becoming disciples of Jesus. John remained the Precursor—that was his role—and so he stood on the threshold of the new era of salvation, but did not enter. The personal sanctity of the Baptist is not in question, nor is it suggested that he will have no place in the ultimate kingdom (cf. 13:28f); this is a statement of historical fact. The kingdom inaugurated by Jesus, and more firmly established by his death, Resurrection and sending of the Spirit, is later than the Baptist's time; those who belong to the new order are more privileged than he (cf. Heb 11:39f).

29f. Luke has omitted Mt 11:12f (he has the sayings in another context—11:16) and Mt 11:14 (he has already dealt with the return of Elijah—1:17). Instead, he has inserted vv. 29f—found in a different context in Mt 21:32—which prepare the way for v. 35. The despised common people (cf. Jn 7:49), and even the tax collectors (regarded as "sinners"), recognized John's baptism of repentance as being of God and availed themselves of it; the Pharisees and lawyers, by rejecting his baptism, placed themselves outside God's plan.

31-35. Judgment of Jesus on His Generation
(Mt 11:16-19)

31 "To what then shall I compare the men of this generation, and what are they like? 32 They are like children sitting in the market-place and calling to one another,

'We piped to you, and you did not dance;
we wailed, and you did not weep.'

33 For John the Baptist has come eating no bread and drinking no wine; and you say, 'He has a demon.' 34 The Son of man has come eating and drinking; and you say, 'Behold, a glutton and a drunkard, a friend of tax collectors and sinners!' 35 Yet wisdom is justified by all her children."

31-34. The parable of the Capricious Children is set squarely in its context by Luke (vv. 29f)—the attitude of the Pharisees and lawyers is criticized. We can more accurately picture the little scene that Jesus describes if, with Matthew (11:16), we take it that the children are "shouting to their playmates" and not "shouting to one another" (Lk 7:32)—there is a difference. The children in question, *sitting* in the marketplace—the boys playing the flute and the girls chanting a funeral dirge—form part of a game. The remaining boys are expected to dance the wedding dance (the round dance at weddings was performed by men), and the rest of the girls ought to have formed a funeral procession. Since they

have failed to do so, the others loudly complain that they are
spoilsports. The point of the parable, then, is the frivolous cap-
tiousness of these children and the thrust of it is obvious: the
conduct of the scribes and Pharisees is no better. At this moment
of crisis when the last messengers of God had appeared, they
hearkened neither to the preaching of repentance nor to the
preaching of the Good News, but criticized and sulked.

35. Luke's "by all her children" (and not Matthew's "by her
deeds"—11:19b) would seem to be the original text. The "children
of Wisdom (God)", the wise ones, are the people and the tax collectors (vv. 29f) who have recognized and accepted the word of
God; they have heard both John and Jesus and have heeded
them.

36-50. The Pardoned Sinner

36 One of the Pharisees asked him to eat with him, and he went
into the Pharisee's house, and sat at table. 37 And behold, a woman
of the city, who was a sinner, when she learned that he was sitting at
table in the Pharisee's house, brought an alabaster flask of ointment,
38 and standing behind him at his feet, weeping, she began to wet
his feet with her tears, and wiped them with the hair of her head, and
kissed his feet, and anointed them with the ointment. 39 Now when
the Pharisee who had invited him saw it, he said to himself, "If this
man were a prophet, he would have known who and what sort of
woman this is who is touching him, for she is a sinner." 40 And Jesus
answering said to him, "Simon, I have something to say to you." And
he answered, "What is it, Teacher?" 41 "A certain creditor had two
debtors; one owed five hundred denarii, and the other fifty. 42 When
they could not pay, he forgave them both. Now which of them will
love him more?" 43 Simon answered, "The one, I suppose, to whom
he forgave more." And he said to him, "You have judged rightly."
44 Then turning toward the woman he said to Simon, "Do you see this
woman? I entered your house, you gave me no water for my feet, but
she has wet my feet with her tears and wiped them with her hair.
45 You gave me no kiss, but from the time I came in she has not
ceased to kiss my feet. 46 You did not anoint my head with oil, but
she has anointed my feet with ointment. 47 Therefore I tell you, her
sins, which are many, are forgiven, for she loved much; but he who
is forgiven little, loves little." 48 And he said to her, "Your sins are
forgiven." 49 Then those who were at table with him began to say
among themselves, "Who is this, who even forgives sins?" 50 And he
said to the woman, "Your faith has saved you; go in peace."

These verses are proper to Luke. Nowhere more clearly than in this passage, the story of the "woman of the city who was a sinner", do we see Jesus as Luke saw him. The context, too, is admirable: here indeed is the "friend of sinners" (v. 34). Despite certain resemblances in detail, it is not possible to identify this anointing with that at Bethany (Mk 14:3-9; Mt 26:6-13; Jn 12: 1-8). At Bethany the host is "Simon *the leper*"—John would suggest Lazarus—and there is no suggestion at all that the woman was a sinner. There are no tears, her motive is not gratitude, and the disciples grumble at her prodigality, while Jesus points to the symbolic nature of the anointing.

36. The Pharisee (Simon, v. 40), though he had invited Jesus to dine with him, had been coldly formal in his reception of his guest (vv. 44-46). Jesus, in the Oriental manner, would have left his sandals at the door and, at table, would have reclined on a low couch with his feet behind him.

37f. Though "sinner" is of wider connotation, the impression is that this was a woman of loose morals and was well known as such. Luke has courteously refrained from naming her and she must remain anonymous; there are no grounds for identifying her with Mary Magdalen (8:2), while her identification with Mary the sister of Martha (10:38-42) is entirely out of the question. Obviously, she had known that Jesus would be present and had come prepared to anoint his feet; she also knew who he was and had already turned from her sinful ways (v. 47). Her action was an extraordinary display of gratitude for the mercy she had already received (v. 47) and her tears, too, were tears of thankfulness.

39. Simon's reasoning was: if Jesus was so unaware of the character of the woman that he had now incurred the ritual uncleanness of contact with a sinner, then he could not be the prophet that many believed him to be.

41-43. The money-lender of the parable, who remits the debt simply because his debtors are unable to pay, is hardly typical of his calling. It is manifest that close behind him stands a God who is ready to forgive any debt; such is God, Jesus says, so infinitely good and merciful. In the parable, and throughout the narrative, "love" means "thankful love", "gratitude"; so the question of Jesus would run: "Which of them would be the more grateful?"

44-47. While Simon has omitted those gestures of affection

and esteem with which an honored guest was received, the woman has so prodigally supplied them. What Simon is told is the application of the parable: This woman, despite her sinful past, is nearer to God than you, for she has what you lack, gratitude.

47. While v. 47a, by itself, could mean that her sins were forgiven as a result of her love, the context (the parable and v. 47f) exclude this sense. It must be taken the other way about: her loving gratitude is a consequence of forgiveness: "For this reason I tell you that her sins, her many sins, must have been forgiven her, or she would not have shown such great love." [29]

48f. These verses do not quite fit the context, since only now does Jesus declare the woman free from sin. They form a literary doublet (cf. 5:20f) and have been added here, doubtless in Luke's source, by association with the idea of forgiveness of sins.

50. Similarly this saying, really in place in 8:48, is loosely attached here; hence, the sudden switch to "faith" from the "love" theme of the whole passage is no longer a problem.

8:1-3. Women Disciples of Jesus

1 Soon afterward he went on through cities and villages, preaching and bringing the good news of the kingdom of God. And the twelve were with him, 2 and also some women who had been healed of evil spirits and infirmities: Mary, called Magdalene, from whom seven demons had gone out, 3 and Joanna, the wife of Chuza, Herod's steward, and Susanna, and many others, who provided for them out of their means.

These verses are peculiar to Luke.

1. Jesus is fulfilling the declaration of 4:43.

2f. It is typical of Luke that he took care to introduce these women disciples of Jesus. Faithful to the end, they were present at the foot of the cross (23:49) and at the burial (23:55f) and became witnesses of the Resurrection (24:1-11). Mary Magdalen (from Magdala on the western shore of the lake of Gennesaret) had been possessed by many ("seven") demons; this has to be understood in the same way as other cases of possession related in the gospels—most likely what was involved in her case was severe mental illness. It does not follow that Mary had lived an immoral life—a conclusion reached only by means of a mistaken

[29] *The Jerusalem Bible*, p. 104.

identification with the anonymous woman of 7:36-50. Joanna, named only by Luke, is mentioned again in 24:10; her husband, Chuza, steward of Herod Antipas, and Susanna, are named nowhere else. Though their role was restricted to ministering to the needs of Jesus and his disciples, the presence of these women among the group of disciples meant a break with Jewish practice (especially in religious matters women were firmly relegated to the background) and prepared the way for the service of women in the early Church (cf. Rm 16:1,3,6,12f; 1 Cor 16:19).

4-8. The Sower
(Mk 4:1-9; Mt 13:1-9)

4 And when a great crowd came together and people from town after town came to him, he said in a parable: **5** "A sower went out to sow his seed; and as he sowed, some fell along the path, and was trodden under foot, and the birds of the air devoured it. **6** And some fell on the rock; and as it grew up, it withered away, because it had no moisture. **7** And some fell among thorns; and the thorns grew with it and choked it. **8** And some fell into good soil and grew, and yielded a hundredfold." As he said this, he called out, "He who has ears to hear, let him hear."

At this point Luke resumes contact with Mark.

4. A vague description replaces the picturesque setting of Mk 4:1; we are just somewhere in Galilee (Lk 8:1) as Jesus speaks the parable to an assembled crowd.

5-8. In v. 5 Luke has "his seed" and the observation that the seed "was trodden upon". The second detail betrays the evangelist's concern to make the parable more intelligible to his Greek readers who would, of course, have been unfamiliar with Palestinian agricultural conditions. And unless we are, to some extent, aware of these conditions, the action of the sower must seem strange. In Palestine, sowing precedes plowing and the sower strides over the unplowed stubble. He sows intentionally on the casual path because it is going to be plowed up, as are the withered thorns; he cannot avoid the rocks that jut through the thin soil. Luke's *rock,* for Mark's *rocky ground,* again abstracts from local conditions. He depicts the seed as falling on a roadway or on rocks bordering a field; it is surely the manner in which we tend to visualize the situation. It would seem that Luke's desire for simplification has led him too far because it is hard to see how seed fallen on a rock can grow or even sprout! (The "rocky ground" of Mark raises no such difficulty, but, of course, the idea remains perfectly clear). Luke underlines the astonishing abundance of the harvest, omitting the thirtyfold and sixtyfold of Mark. If we take the parable just as it is, keeping in mind the Palestinian background and realizing that it was spoken by Jesus in the early enthusiastic period of the Galilean ministry, the original meaning of it must surely be obvious. On the one hand, we have a description of the difficulties and frustration that must meet the sower: poor land, thieving birds, scorching sun, and thorns. On the other hand we are assured that, despite all this, the seed ripens to the harvest, a harvest abundant beyond expectation. In spite of everything, we are taught, in the face of every failure and of every hindrance, the kingdom of God will grow and develop. But though the idea of growth is certainly present, it does not come to the forefront; the emphasis is on the harvest. The perspective is eschatological, for the harvest is the full flowering of the kingdom.

9-15. Explanation of the Sower
(Mk 4:10-20; Mt 13:10-23)

9 And when his disciples asked him what this parable meant, he said, "To you it has been given to know the secrets of the kingdom of God; but for others they are in parables, so that seeing they may not see, and hearing they may not understand. **11** Now the parable is this: The seed is the word of God. **12** The ones along the path are those who have heard; then the devil comes and takes away the word from their hearts, that they may not believe and be saved. **13** And the ones on the rock are those who, when they hear the word, receive it with joy; but these have no root, they believe for a while and in time of temptation fall away. **14** And as for what fell among the thorns, they are those who hear, but as they go on their way they are choked by the cares and riches and pleasures of life, and their fruit does not mature. **15** And as for that in the good soil, they are those who, hearing the word, hold it fast in an honest and good heart, and bring forth fruit with patience.

9f. In Mk 4:10 Jesus is asked, privately, why he speaks in parables; here he is asked openly for the meaning of "this parable". Luke has somewhat softened the impact by cutting short the text of Is 6:9 (cf. Mk 4:12). The saying of v. 10 originally referred not to the parables, but to the Lord's teaching in general. It concerned the "secrets (Mark—'secret') of the kingdom" which is revealed to the disciples and not to all: that the kingdom of God is already present in Jesus and in his works. By dint of patient teaching, the disciples have arrived at a realization of this truth, but the people had quite failed to recognize the signs of the times (Lk 12:54-59). In its present context the saying reflects the truth that not even the parables have won over the hearers to faith.

11-15. We have noted that the message of the parable, in its original *Sitz im Leben,* has to do with the development of the kingdom: the emphasis is on the abundant harvest. But, like many of the parables, the Sower found a new setting in the life of the early Church. The point of interest now is rather the word, and the hearers' reception of the word, for the Christians have applied the parable to themselves; it has become an exhortation to converts to examine themselves and to test the sincerity of their conversion. In order to do this the parable has been allegorized. When we look at it squarely, it is obvious that the explanation of the Sower is somewhat forced. It seems clear that Luke is aware that the traditional interpretation does not quite fit the parable and he does attempt to overcome the difficulty, but he can succeed only to a limited extent. However, when we compare his text with that of Mark we realize that Luke has gone a long way towards making the explanation easier to grasp.

11. By "word of God" Luke understands the preaching of Jesus —the seed is the gospel preaching.

12. In the parable the seed (that is, the kingdom) held the center of interest throughout; in the explanation the emphasis is on the reaction of men to the gospel preaching, and the seed has to represent *both* the word *and* the hearers of the word. But though the details of the explanation must, in the circumstances, be strained, the explanation itself is readily understandable. *Ho logos* ("the word"), used absolutely, is a technical term for the gospel current in the primitive Church (cf. Ac 4:4; 6:4; 8:4; 10:36,44; etc.); it is significant that "the word" is found in the mouth of Jesus *only* in the interpretation of the Sower (8 times in Mark, 5 times in Matthew and 3 times in Luke)—and, apart from Mk 2:2, the designation occurs nowhere else in the Synoptics. In the original parable the details were not significant but filled in the rural background of the story, but in the allegorical application they have a symbolical value. The thieving birds represent Satan ready to snatch away the word before it can take root. In v. 10 Luke has left aside the conclusion of the citation from Isaiah (6:10): "lest they should turn again and be forgiven", read in Mk 4:12—yet he keeps it in mind, for his addition in v. 12 "that they may not believe and be saved" is patently an echo of it.

13f. The seed represents the hearers of the word (though we have to recall that in v. 11 "the seed is the word"). Those standing on the rock have no root, they are hearers who will not persevere; the thorns symbolize the cares, riches and pleasures of life which eventually overcome those who try to grow amid them. It is to be noted that the explanation, so far, has considered only the obstacles in the way of the fruition of the word or, perhaps more accurately, the failure of those who hear it. We have seen, on the other hand, that the parable envisages the kingdom triumphing over all difficulties: the parable is optimistic, full of hope, but the commentary is more aware of the dangers and strikes a note of warning.

15. However, it too closes on an encouraging note, for the hearers standing on good ground hold the word fast. Once again, Luke has an eye to his Gentile readers for the "noble and good" heart reflects the "beautiful and good", the moral ideal of the Greeks. These last hearers bring forth fruit "with endurance" or "in patience": their endurance contrasts with the fickleness and apostasy of the others.

The explanation of the Sower looks to the individual and is, indeed, a psychological study. Every man who has heard the gospel message is challenged to examine himself seriously and to weigh up his reactions; for the word will find obstacles both outside a man and within. And he who will boldly face up to those difficulties, the generous and virtuous man, he alone will be a disciple because he alone will bring forth the lasting fruit of the Christian life. But has the interpretation wandered too far from the import of the parable? If the description of seed growing to the harvest depicts the irresistible development of the kingdom, how can it come to mean anything else? Yet we may reflect that the gospel of Jesus and the hearers of the gospel are the constituents of the kingdom. We may reflect, too, that the triumph of the kingdom is the triumph of the word of Jesus over the hearts of men. So, if the explanation does go beyond the obvious meaning of the parable, it is still true to the ultimate meaning of the parable.

We may conclude that the interpretation of the Sower—at least in the form in which it has been transmitted—is a product of the primitive Church. However, the fact that all three synoptists have attributed it to Jesus is not without significance. It is reasonable to believe that they did sometimes explain his parables; this is suggested by Mt 15:15-20 (cf. 13:36-43) and was, besides, the practice of the rabbis. If, as is likely, the explanation of the Sower now found in our gospels does go back to an interpretation of Jesus, we do, however, find that the first Christians and the evangelists, who have commonly adapted and applied his parables, have here gone a step further and have adapted his commentary on a parable.

16-18. On Hearing the Word
(Mk 4:21-25; cf. Mt 13:12)

16 "No one after lighting a lamp covers it with a vessel, or puts it under a bed, but puts it on a stand, that those who enter may see the light. 17 For nothing is hid that shall not be made manifest, nor anything secret that shall not be known and come to light. 18 Take heed then how you hear; for to him who has will more be given, and from him who has not, even what he thinks that he has will be taken away."

The fact that these sayings are doublets—they occur in another version and context elsewhere in the gospel—is sufficient indication that they were originally isolated logia. Following on the explanation of the Sower, they apply to the disciples as hearers of the word; they must shed abroad the enlightenment which they have won, for the teaching of Jesus is not an esoteric doctrine to be kept carefully hidden.

16. Repeated in 11:33; cf. Mt 5:15.

17. Repeated in 12:12; cf. Mt 10:26. Luke omits Mk 4:23-24b.

18. Hearing is not enough (cf. v. 21). The saying of 18b is repeated in 19:26; cf. Mt 13:12; 25:29. By writing "what he thinks

he has" instead of "what he has" (Mk 4:25), Luke has softened the paradox.

19-21. True Kindred of Jesus
(Mk 3:31-35; Mt 12:46-50)

19 Then his mother and his brothers came to him, but they could not reach him for the crowd. **20** And he was told, "Your mother and your brothers are standing outside, desiring to see you." **21** But he said to them, "My mother and my brothers are those who hear the word of God and do it."

Luke has judged that the passage will form an excellent conclusion to his short treatment of the parabolic teaching of Jesus, and so he has changed it from its Markan context. However, he has omitted Mk 3:33f. It is clear that Luke is chiefly interested in the saying of v. 21; this is a typical pronouncement story: the visit of the family of Jesus is the occasion of this declaration.

21. In Mark and Matthew the kindred of Jesus are those who "do the will of God"; in Luke they are those "who hear the word of God", recalling the parable of the Sower. Those who listen to the preaching of Jesus and live accordingly enter into a real relationship with him; they belong to the family of God.

22-25. The Stilling of a Storm
(Mk 4:35-41; Mt 8:18, 23-27)

22 One day he got into a boat with his disciples, and he said to them, "Let us go across to the other side of the lake." So they set out, **23** and as they sailed he fell asleep. And a storm of wind came down on the lake, and they were filling with water, and were in danger. **24** And they went and woke him, saying, "Master, Master, we are perishing!" And he awoke and rebuked the wind and the raging waves; and they ceased, and there was a calm. **25** He said to them, "Where is your faith?" And they were afraid, and they marvelled, saying to one another, "Who then is this, that he commands even wind and water, and they obey him?"

In Mark the incident occurred on the evening of the day of parable teaching; Luke has simply "one day". Throughout, he has improved the style, but he has sacrificed the picturesque touches of Mark. The "power of the Lord" that was in Jesus to heal (5:17;

6:19) also gave him authority over nature: it is God who "stills the roaring of the seas, the roaring of their waves" (Ps 65[64]:7).

24. Jesus "rebuked" the rebellious force of wind and waves just as he rebuked demonic spirits (4:35f).

25. In their panic they had not quite lived up to that trust and confidence in Jesus which had made them his disciples, although they did turn to him for help. Their awe and wonder reflect the reaction of 4:36.

26-39. The Gerasene Demoniac
(Mk 5:1-20; Mt 8:28-34)

26 Then they arrived at the country of the Gerasenes, which is opposite Galilee. **27** And as he stepped out on land, there met him a man from the city who had demons; for a long time he had worn no clothes, and he lived not in a house but among the tombs. **28** When he saw Jesus, he cried out and fell down before him, and said with a loud voice, "What have you to do with me, Jesus, Son of the Most High God? I beseech you, do not torment me." **29** For he had commanded the unclean spirit to come out of the man. (For many a time it had seized him; he was kept under guard, and bound with chains and fetters, but he broke the bonds and was driven by the demon into the desert.) **30** Jesus then asked him, "What is your name?" And he said, "Legion"; for many demons had entered him. **31** And they begged him not to command them to depart into the abyss. **32** Now a large herd of swine was feeding there on the hillside; and they begged him to let them enter these. So he gave them leave. **33** Then the demons came out of the man and entered the swine, and the herd rushed down the steep bank into the lake and were drowned.

34 When the herdsmen saw what had happened, they fled, and told it in the city and in the country. **35** Then people went out to see what had happened, and they came to Jesus, and found the man from whom the demons had gone, sitting at the feet of Jesus, clothed and in his right mind; and they were afraid. **36** And those who had seen it told them how he who had been possessed with demons was healed. **37** Then all the people of the surrounding country of the Gerasenes asked him to depart from them; for they were seized with great fear; so he got into the boat and returned. **38** The man from whom the demons had gone begged that he might be with him; but he sent him away, saying, **39** "Return to your home, and declare how much God has done for you." And he went away, proclaiming throughout the whole city how much Jesus had done for him.

Luke has stylistically improved, and abbreviated, Mark's version. In vv. 26 and 37 some manuscripts give the variant readings

"Gadarenes" and "Gergesenes", but Gerasenes is to be preferred. The "country of the Gerasenes": perhaps a district named from the town of Gerasa (Jerash) in Transjordan some 30 miles from the lake; or, perhaps, the lakeside village of *el-Korsi* may be meant. On this occasion only, in Luke, does Jesus cross to the eastern shore of the lake and leave Jewish territory.

24f. On hearing Jesus' command (v. 29) the possessing spirits made the customary adjuration (cf. 4:34,41). It would not be unusual for a pagan to name the God of the Jews "God Most High"; "Son of the Most High God" is simply an acknowledgment of the Messiahship of Jesus as in 4:3,34,41.

29f. This was a particularly severe case of possession involving a whole regiment of devils (the Roman legion numbered about 6,000 men).

31. Whereas in Mk 5:10 the demons begged not to be sent "out of the country", in Luke they ask not to be sent "into the abyss", their normal habitat (Ap 9:1f,11; 11:7; 17:8; 20:1,3).

32f. The presence of a large herd of swine again suggests Gentile territory; for Jews the pig was an unclean animal (Lv 11:7f). This new earthly habitat of the demons was quickly lost to them.

34-36. It is not surprising that the herdsmen fled the scene, nor that people quickly came to verify their extraordinary story.

37. The presence of a man enjoying such power over evil spirits was potentially dangerous and demonstrably costly!

38f. The man who had been exorcized wished to join the band of disciples, but his mission lay elsewhere. He is bidden to return to his home—Decapolis (cf. Mk 5:20) is not named in this gospel. Instead of an admonition to silence customary on similar occasions (cf. Lk 4:41; 5:14), we find a command to proclaim the event: in a Gentile setting there is no danger that the work of Jesus will be misunderstood in terms of popular Jewish Messianism. "It must be admitted that nothing seems stranger to the modern outlook than this episode. But it is a fact that in the time of Jesus all men, even the Greeks, were convinced of the evil role of demons, and it is also a fact that Jesus had proclaimed the end of the reign of Satan (Lk 10:18)." [30]

[30] M.-J. Lagrange, *op. cit.*, p. 251.

40-56. The Daughter of Jairus and the Woman with the Flow of Blood

(Mk 5:21-43; Mt 9:18-26)

40 Now when Jesus returned, the crowd welcomed him, for they were all waiting for him. 41 And there came a man named Jairus, who was a ruler of the synagogue; and falling at Jesus' feet he besought him to come to his house, 42 for he had an only daughter, about twelve years of age, and she was dying.

As he went, the people pressed round him. 43 And a woman who had a flow of blood for twelve years and could not be healed by any one, 44 came up behind him, and touched the fringe of his garment; and immediately her flow of blood ceased. 45 And Jesus said, "Who was it that touched me?" When all denied it, Peter said, "Master, the multitudes surround you and press upon you!" 46 But Jesus said, "Some one touched me; for I perceive that power has gone forth from me." 47 And when the woman saw that she was not hidden, she came trembling, and falling down before him declared in the presence of all the people why she had touched him, and how she had been immediately healed. 48 And he said to her, "Daughter, your faith has made you well; go in peace."

49 While he was still speaking, a man from the ruler's house came and said, "Your daughter is dead; do not trouble the Teacher any more." 50 But Jesus on hearing this answered him, "Do not fear; only believe, and she shall be well." 51 And when he came to the house, he permitted no one to enter with him, except Peter and John and James, and the father and mother of the child. 52 And all were weeping and bewailing her; but he said, "Do not weep; for she is not dead but sleeping." 53 And they laughed at him, knowing that she was dead. 54 But taking her by the hand he called, saying, "Child, arise." 55 And her spirit returned, and she got up at once; and he directed that something should be given her to eat. 56 And her parents were amazed; but he charged them to tell no one what had happened.

Luke improves the style of Mark but notably abbreviates his source.

40. When Jesus had crossed to the western shore of the lake he was met by a sympathetic crowd.

41f. Jairus was an *archisynagogos* (v. 49), the director of the synagogue worship. Luke adds that this was his only daughter and mentions her age at the beginning of the story; Mark has it almost as an afterthought (Mk 5:42).

43. The majority of manuscripts add: "and had spent all her money upon physicians"—better omitted with Codex Vaticanus and Codex Bezae (and others) as due to harmonization with Mk 5:26.

44. Luke has "the fringe of" his garment, a detail not in Mark. Natural embarrassment and the fact that she was ritually unclean (cf. Lv 15:25) kept the woman from openly seeking a cure.

45f. Peter is the spokesman; cf. Mk 5:31—"his disciples". Jesus was conscious that his miraculous power had been called into play.

47. Luke insists that the woman's admission was made in the presence of "all the people" (cf. Mk 5:33); the healing was witnessed (symbolically) by the whole people of Israel.

48. Her faith, that is, her trust and confidence in the goodness and power of Jesus, had occasioned her cure.

49f. A like faith is demanded of the messenger bringing news of the girl's death; more probably it is Jairus who is being asked to maintain his confidence.

51. The order of the privileged disciples is changed: John precedes James (cf. Mk 5:37), the same order as in Lk 9:28; Ac 1:13. John has special prominence for Luke—22:8; Ac 3:1,3,11; 4:13,19; 8:14 (for the theme of the companionship of Peter and John, cf. Lk 22:8).

52f. These verses form a sort of parenthesis; Luke has used the same technique in 8:38f.

54. Luke omits the Aramaic phrase of Mk 5:41. There are affinities with the raising of Tabitha, Ac 9:40f.

55. "Her spirit returned"—raising from the dead is not the granting of new life but the restoring of the former life principle. Immediately, and not a little later as in Mk 5:43, Jesus directs that the girl should be given something to eat.

56. In contrast to the commission to the exorcized Gerasene (Lk 8:39), here, back in a Jewish environment, we find a command to preserve secrecy. In the circumstances of this miracle—which cannot be kept from the crowd—there is something stylized about the "Messianic secret" motif.

9:1-6. The Mission of the Twelve
(Mk 6:7-13; Mt 10:5,8-14)

1 And he called the twelve together and gave them power and authority over all demons and to cure diseases, 2 and he sent them out

to preach the kingdom of God and to heal. 3 And he said to them, "Take nothing for your journey, no staff, nor bag, nor bread, nor money; and do not have two tunics. 4 And whatever house you enter, stay there, and from there depart. 5 And wherever they do not receive you, when you leave that town shake off the dust from your feet as a testimony against them." 6 And they departed and went through the villages, preaching the gospel and healing everywhere.

Luke leaves aside the passage of Mk 6:1-6 (Jesus in Nazareth) because he has already (4:16-30) dealt with the reception of Jesus there. Otherwise he follows Mark closely.

1f. Jesus gives the Twelve authority to preach the Good News of the kingdom of God and power like his own over demons and disease; they are associates in his mission.

3. Whereas Mk 6:8 permits the carrying of a staff, Luke agrees with Mt 10:10 on its prohibition. The Twelve can go out without preparation, confident of being well received by the people in this early enthusiastic period of Jesus' ministry; but changed circumstances will radically alter this easy abandon (cf. 22:35f).

4f. One household in each district will become the center of apostolic ministry—thus saving time and avoiding rivalry between contending hosts; later the apostolic Church will adhere to this recommendation by its practice of establishing the Christian assembly in a given house (cf. Rm 16:5; 1 Cor 16:19; Col 4:15; Phm 2). They are not to waste time on villages where they are refused a hearing. The symbolic gesture of shaking off the dust of such a place (which reflects the practice of Jews on leaving Gentile soil) is a declaration that they have no fellowship with such people who reject the proclamation of the Good News.

6. Luke has "preaching the gospel" for Mark's "preached that men should repent", and with his "healing everywhere" sums up Mk 6:13.

7-9. Herod and Jesus
(Mk 6:14-16; Mt 14:1f)

7 Now Herod the tetrarch heard of all that was done, and he was perplexed, because it was said by some that John had been raised from the dead, 8 by some that Elijah had appeared, and by others that one of the old prophets had risen. 9 Herod said, "John I be-

headed; but who is this about whom I hear such things?" And he
sought to see him.

An excellent example of Luke's editorial liberty. Herod (Antipas) the tetrarch (Mark: "king") is skeptical on the subject of
prophets coming back from the dead: "John I beheaded", i.e. that
accounts for him (cf. "John, whom I beheaded, has been raised",
Mk 6:16). His express wish to see Jesus (v. 9) prepares the way
for the meeting of 23:8. Luke omits the account of John's execution (Mk 6:17-29)—it would have interrupted the flow of events.

10-17. Return of the Twelve; Multiplication of Loaves
(Mk 6:30-44; Mt 14:13-21; Jn 6:1-13)

10 On their return the apostles told him what they had done. And
he took them and withdrew apart to a city called Bethsaida. 11 When
the crowds learned it, they followed him; and he welcomed them and
spoke to them of the kingdom of God, and cured those who had need
of healing. 12 Now the day began to wear away; and the twelve came
and said to him, "Send the crowd away, to go into the villages and
country round about, to lodge and get provisions; for we are here in
a lonely place." 13 But he said to them, "You give them something to
eat." They said, "We have no more than five loaves and two fish—
unless we are to go and buy food for all these people." 14 For there
were about five thousand men. And he said to his disciples, "Make
them sit down in companies, about fifty each." 15 And they did so,
and made them all sit down. 16 And taking the five loaves and the
two fish he looked up to heaven, and blessed and broke them, and
gave them to the disciples to set before the crowd. 17 And all ate and
were satisfied. And they took up what was left over, twelve baskets of
broken pieces.

10. In Mark (6:31) Jesus took the returned Apostles to a
"lonely place", and only after the multiplication of loaves did they
cross to Bethsaida (6:45)—Bethsaida Julias on the northeast of
the lake. Luke has taken the place-name from the Markan incident of the walking on the waters (Mk 6:45-52) which he has
omitted (probably because the passage is so like Lk 8:22-25).

11. Jesus spoke to the crowd about the kingdom of God, and
healed—just as he had empowered the Twelve to do on their mission (9:2). In 9:12-17 Luke follows, and rewrites to a certain
extent, Mk 6:35-44.

12. As Jesus continued to teach and heal, and the hours passed, the Twelve grew restive: what was to become of this crowd?

13. Luke has given a humorous turn to the querulous question of the Twelve in Mk 6:37.

14f. The number is given at once (cf. 8:42), not, as in Mk 6:44, almost as an afterthought; Luke's careful "about" is characteristic.

16. Jesus took, looked up to heaven, blessed, broke—the language is liturgical, with the Eucharist in mind. In his ch. 6 John develops the eucharistic symbolism of the multiplication of loaves.

17. All four evangelists draw attention not only to the full satisfaction of the people's hunger, but to the superabundance provided by Jesus: twelve baskets of fragments were collected. There may be a symbolism in the fact and number: "Basketfuls, corresponding in number to all Israel, and to the number of the Apostles by whom the spiritual food of Christ is later on to be distributed, are left over after all are fed."[31]

After 9:17 Luke omits Mk 6:45–8:26—the so-called "great omission". He may have done so in order to keep his work within definite limits. It is noteworthy that the first and last episodes of the Markan section are set at Bethsaida (6:45-52; 8:22-26); we might say that Luke has omitted a journey of Jesus which began and ended at Bethsaida. The omission has the effect of making the feeding of the multitude the immediate prelude to his instruction of the Twelve on the meaning of his suffering and death (cf. Jn 6).

18-22. Peter's Profession of Faith and the First Prediction of the Passion
(Mk 8:27-33; Mt 16:13-23)

18 Now it happened that as he was praying alone the disciples were with him; and he asked them, "Who do the people say that I am?" **19** And they answered, "John the Baptist; but others say, Elijah; and others, that one of the old prophets has risen." **20** And he said to them, "But who do you say that I am?" And Peter answered, "The Christ of God." **21** But he charged and commanded them to tell this to no one, **22** saying, "The Son of man must suffer many things, and be rejected by the elders and chief priests and scribes, and be killed, and on the third day be raised."

[31] G. W. H. Lampe, *op. cit.*, 726i.

Luke gives no indication of the setting of this incident; he has deliberately avoided mentioning Caesarea Philippi (Mk 8:27) lest it might detract from the central place of Jerusalem in his gospel, and also because Galilee is the scene of the first part of his mission. The sequence—multiplication of loaves, Peter's confession of faith (Lk 9:10-20)—is found also in Jn 6:1-69.

18f. Typically, Luke refers to the prayer of Jesus (cf. 3:21; 5:16; 6:12). Even after the multiplication of loaves the people still think of Jesus in the same terms as before; cf. the rumors which Herod Antipas had heard (9:7f).

20. Peter's "the Christ of God" (cf. 2:26)—in place of Mark's "the Christ"—is an Old Testament expression (cf. 1 Sm 24:7,11; 26:9): the one whom God has anointed, his Messiah.

21f. The "Messianic secret" is not something peculiar to Mark. With Matthew (16:21) Luke changes Mark's "after three days" to "on the third day". Luke has omitted the intervention of Peter and the rebuke of Jesus (Mk 8:32f)—he has spared the Apostle. In Mark's gospel, Peter's profession of faith, followed by the prediction of the Passion, marks a turning point: the public ministry is over, Jesus goes to his death; in Luke's literary plan the ministry goes on.

23-27. The Following of Jesus
(Mk 8:34–9:1; Mt 16:24-28)

23 And he said to all, "If any man would come after me, let him deny himself and take up his cross daily and follow me. 24 For whoever would save his life will lose it; and whoever loses his life for my sake, he will save it. 25 For what does it profit a man if he gains the whole world and loses or forfeits himself? 26 For whoever is ashamed of me and of my words, of him will the Son of man be ashamed when he comes in his glory and the glory of the Father and of the holy angels. 27 But I tell you truly, there are some standing here who will not taste death before they see the kingdom of God."

As in Mark, the invitation is addressed not only to the disciples but to all who would be disciples.

23. Three conditions are listed: denying oneself, that is to say, not to be preoccupied with oneself and one's personal interests, but to have in mind only him whose disciple one would be; taking up one's cross daily by patiently bearing trials and so dying to the world (cf. 1 Cor 15:31)—the "daily" taking up of the cross indicates a spiritual interpretation (by the early Church) of a saying of Jesus which originally pointed to martyrdom (cf. Mk 8:34; Lk 9:23); these conditions prepare the way for the third—the following of Jesus by the acceptance of his way of life.

24f. The Markan phrase "and the gospel's sake" (Mk 8:35) is omitted. In the spiritual sense of the context, *psyche*, "soul", is to be understood in the Aramaic sense of "person": hence to "save one's person" is the opposite of the "denying oneself" (cf. v. 23) while "losing one's person" means just that—Luke has explained what the renunciation demanded of a disciple of Jesus entails. The obstacle to self-denial (a necessary condition for following Jesus) is the attraction of the world; in other words, one must choose between Jesus and the world. Luke omits Mk 8:37.

26f. These verses are distinct sayings linked by the common idea of a coming of the kingdom. The first (v. 26) refers to the final coming of the Son of man; the other concerns the establishment of the kingdom of God on earth (by the establishment of the Church after the Ascension), marked unmistakably by the destruction of Jerusalem in 70 A.D.—an event which underlined the passing of the old dispensation; "some standing here" could well be witnesses of that event. The kingdom comes through the glorification of Christ by his death and Resurrection—the Transfiguration is a foretaste of his glorification.

28-36. The Transfiguration
(Mk 9:2-8; Mt 17:1-8)

28 Now about eight days after these sayings he took with him Peter and John and James, and went up on the mountain to pray. 29 And as he was praying, the appearance of his countenance was altered, and his raiment became dazzling white. 30 And behold, two men talked with him, Moses and Elijah, 31 who appeared in glory and spoke of his departure, which he was to acomplish at Jerusalem. 32 Now Peter and those who were with him were heavy with sleep but kept awake, and they saw his glory and the two men who stood with him. 33 And as the men were parting from him, Peter said to Jesus, "Master, it is well that we are here; let us make three booths, one for you and one for Moses and one for Elijah"—not knowing what he said. 34 As he said this, a cloud came and overshadowed them; and they were afraid as they entered the cloud. 35 And a voice came out of the cloud, saying, "This is my Son, my Chosen; listen to him!" 36 And when the

voice had spoken Jesus was found alone. And they kept silence and told no one in those days anything of what they had seen.

The Transfiguration has greater significance for Luke than for Mark, and he departs rather freely from the latter. It is a typical mountain scene, where Jesus is separated from the people (vv. 28,37), involving a special manifestation; the geographical situation (Tabor, southwest of the lake of Gennesaret or—more likely —Hermon, northeast of Caesarea Philippi, cf. Mk 8:27) has no relevance for Luke. The purpose of the heavenly revelation is to show that the Passion is something decreed by God; it also serves to corroborate Peter's profession of faith and is a means of strengthening the disciples for the road that lies ahead.

28. "About eight days": in place of Mark's (and Matthew's) "after six days". Jesus prays as on other major occasions (3:21; 6:12; 9:18; 22:41).

29. Luke avoids the term *metemorphōthē*, "transfigured" (Mk 9:2), which might be misunderstood by his Gentile readers in the sense of the metamorphosis of a pagan deity.

30f. Moses and Elijah represent the Law and the prophets: the Old Testament bears witness to Christ (cf. 24:27,44). Luke gives the theme of the consecration: the "departure" (*exodus*—Wis 3:2; 7:6; 2 Pet 1:12 = "death") of Jesus at Jerusalem. The Transfiguration is at once a preparation for the Passion and the authentication of Jesus' claim to glory (Lk 9:26).

32f. Peter's offer of three booths is meant to prolong the moment ("as the men were parting from him"). Luke gives a psychological explanation of this unthinking suggestion: Peter is overwrought by sleepiness and awed by the glory of Jesus (as at his Second Coming, 9:26). It is likely that the Transfiguration took place at night (9:28,32,37).

34f. Luke specifies that the disciples "entered into the cloud"; their fear is due to their recognition of the Old Testament value of the "cloud"—the accompaniment of a theophany (cf. Ex 16:10; 19:9,16; 24:15f; Lv 16:2; Num 11:25); "overshadowed" recalls Ex 40:29. Though attested by a greater number of manuscripts than "my Chosen", the variant reading "my Beloved" is almost certainly due to harmonization with Mark and Matthew. "Listen to him" is an application of what was said of the "prophet like

Moses" (Dt 18:15). Jesus is God's Elect (cf. Jn 1:34 where the better, if less widely attested, reading is "Elect of God"), a heavenly confirmation of Peter's profession of faith (9:20).

36. The "Messianic secret" is implied. Luke omits Mark's passage on the coming of Elijah (Mk 9:11-13). The following four incidents show how very much the disciples have yet to learn and, by contrast, emphasize how radical was the change wrought in them by the Resurrection and the gift of the Spirit. Now, in rapid order, we see their weak faith, slow comprehension, self-seeking and intolerance.

37-43a. Cure of an Epileptic
(Mk 9:14-29; Mt 17:14-21)

37 On the next day, when they had come down from the mountain, a great crowd met him. 38 And behold, a man from the crowd cried, "Teacher, I beg you to look upon my son, for he is my only child; 39 and behold, a spirit seizes him, and he suddenly cries out; it convulses him till he foams, and shatters him, and will hardly leave him. 40 And I begged your disciples to cast it out, but they could not." 41 Jesus answered, "O faithless and perverse generation, how long am I to be with you and bear with you? Bring your son here." 42 While he was coming, the demon tore him and convulsed him. But Jesus rebuked the unclean spirit, and healed the boy, and gave him back to his father. 43 And all were astonished at the majesty of God.

Luke drastically shortens Mark; he has altogether omitted: Mk 9:14b-16, 20b-24, 25b-26, 28f. On the other hand, he adds that the child was an only son (v. 38) and describes the impression of the crowd (v. 43).

40f. The failure of the disciples is connected with their lack of faith. Jesus' exasperated exclamation seems to be addressed principally to the disciples and to the father of the boy: to the disciples because they lacked the proper dispositions and to the father because his confidence had been shaken. Jesus, who had just discoursed with Moses and Elijah on his rendezvous with death in Jerusalem (9:31), is keenly aware of the urgency of the hour; he is disappointed at the slowness of his disciples.

43b-45. Second Prediction of the Passion
(Mk 9:30-32; Mt 17:22f)

But while they were all marvelling at everything he did, he said to his disciples, **44** "Let these words sink into your ears; for the Son of man is to be delivered into the hands of men." **45** But they did not understand this saying, and it was concealed from them, that they should not perceive it; and they were afraid to ask him about this saying.

Luke departs from Mark in many respects. He says nothing of a rather furtive journey through Galilee (Mk 9:30) but, instead, emphasizes the wonder of the people at the deeds of Jesus. The difference of approach is explained by the place which the passage occupies in each gospel. For Luke, Jesus, though conscious of his goal, is still busily teaching and healing; but in Mark the Galilean ministry is over and Jesus, accompanied only by his disciples, is journeying to his death.

44. The disciples are warned that they must not be led astray by the momentary enthusiasm of the crowds; they are to bear well in mind that he, by God's design (cf. Ac 2:23), will be handed over to the power of his enemies.

45. Their total failure to understand is emphatically stated; in Luke's view it is the risen Christ alone who can and will enlighten them (24:25-27,44-46). Yet the next passage suggests that their obtuseness is, in some measure, due to their failure to recognize true greatness in the Person of Jesus.

46-50. Dispute about Precedence; The Strange Exorcist
(Mk 9:33-50; Mt 18:1-35)

46 And an argument arose among them as to which of them was the greatest. **47** But when Jesus perceived the thought of their hearts, he took a child and put him by his side, **48** and said to them, "Whoever receives this child in my name receives me, and whoever receives me receives him who sent me; for he who is least among you all is the one who is great."

49 John answered, "Master, we saw a man casting out demons in your name, and we forbade him, because he does not follow with us." **50** But Jesus said to him, "Do not forbid him; for he that is not against you is for you."

This passage is all that Luke has preserved of the original

ecclesiastical discourse underlying the parallel passages of Mark and Matthew. Luke has omitted any indication of place, and also the question of Jesus (Mk 9:34).

47f. A parable in action. There is no place for degrees of greatness among the disciples of Jesus; the least disciple of Jesus possesses greatness. Whoever receives a child for the sake of Jesus receives Jesus, and in turn receives God who sent him; the greatness that comes from belonging to Jesus, from being his disciple, can be enjoyed by a child. Jesus is not establishing the authority of his disciples over others but is pointing out the greatness of discipleship—there is no greater dignity (cf. Mk 10:44f; Jn 13:12-17). It follows that ecclesiastical office is, above all, a *service*. This is seen more clearly in Mk 9:35—"If anyone would be first, he must be the last of all and the servant of all." "Effectively Jesus says that there is no 'first' in the reign of God. If you want to be first, become every man's lackey; return to your childhood and then you will be fit for the first place. Jesus leaves little room for ambition; and he leaves no more room for the exercise of power. Lackeys and children are not the bearers of power." [32]

49f. Luke abbreviates Mark, omitting Mk 9:39b,41. Vv. 48 and 49 are linked by the catchwords "in my name", "in your name". Here is an attitude that did not cease with John, and these again are words of Jesus which might have been taken more effectively to heart. In our present atmosphere of ecumenism we are, at last, better disposed to take them seriously. The true disciple of Jesus will always regard as an ally one who is obviously doing God's work. Here ends the Galilean ministry in Luke.

[32] J. L. McKenzie, *The Power and the Wisdom* (Milwaukee: Bruce, 1965), p. 184.

B. Journey from Galilee
to Jerusalem

IV. THE JOURNEY TO JERUSALEM 9:51–19:27

The long section (9:51–18:14) has been inserted by Luke into the plan of Mark. The sayings and narratives of this section are grouped together and the whole is fitted into the framework of a journey to Jerusalem (a journey which ends at 19:46). On examination it can be seen that the arrangement is artificial. It is a striking fact, for instance, that though the chapters are supposed to describe a journey from Galilee, all topographical reference to any place other than Jerusalem is suppressed. The journey is explicitly indicated in 9:51: "When the days drew near for him to be received up, he set his face to go to Jerusalem." The Samaritans [33] would not receive him "because his face was set toward Jerusalem" (9:53), and so he went on to "another village" (9:56). In 10:1 there is reference to "every town and place" where he was to go and, in 10:38, while on his way he entered "a village". In 11:1 he prayed "in a certain place". In short, we may say with Lagrange: "In vain do we try to discover where he is; we know only that he is still in the land of Israel because there is no indication that he has left it. Apart from references to Jerusalem there is no indication of place; the scene is always just 'somewhere'." [34]

In 13:22 we are again reminded of the goal: "He went on his way through towns and villages, teaching, and journeying towards Jerusalem." When he was warned to get away "from here" (13:31) he replied: "I must go on my way today and tomorrow and the day following; for it cannot be that a prophet should perish away from Jerusalem" (13:33)—and he apostrophized the city (13:34f). In 14:25 we read that "great multitudes" accompanied him; it is like a solemn procession.

A reference in 17:11 removes any doubt that the framework is

[33] See pp. 291f.
[34] *Op. cit.*, p. xxxviii.

artificial. Though he had begun his journey from Galilee in 9:51, and had been on his way ever since, we are now told: "On the way to Jerusalem he was passing along between Samaria and Galilee"—he is still at the starting place. In 18:31-33 he tells his Apostles plainly that the journey to Jerusalem is a journey to his death, and from now on the tempo speeds up remarkably and other place-names appear to mark the final stages of the journey. He drew near to Jericho (18:35) and entered the town (19:1). This was near the holy city (19:11) and he went on ahead of the others "going up to Jerusalem" (19:28). He drew near to Bethphage and Bethany (19:29) and came to the Mount of Olives (19:37). He wept over the city that now at last lay before him (19:41) and, finally, he entered the Temple, his Father's house (19:45; cf. 2:49).

The intention of the evangelist is manifest: to present dramatically the last journey of our Lord to Jerusalem. The overall effect is striking, especially the mounting tension of the final chapters. But he has obviously used this same journey to frame, and give a certain unity to, an important collection of sayings and parables; and the framework does set these sayings of Jesus in relief and gives them an added solemnity. The plan of this long section is only one expression among many of a constant preoccupation of the evangelist—to center his whole gospel around Jerusalem.

51-56. Unfriendly Samaritans

51 When the days drew near for him to be received up, he set his face to go to Jerusalem. 52 And he sent messengers ahead of him, who went and entered a village of the Samaritans to make ready for him; 53 but the people would not receive him, because his face was set toward Jerusalem. 54 And when his disciples James and John saw it, they said, "Lord, do you want us to bid fire come down from heaven and consume them?" 55 But he turned and rebuked them. 56 And they went on to another village.

51. This verse is the title of the journey section. The "receiving up" of Jesus comprises his death, Resurrection, and Ascension as one event in the same way as do the Johannine terms "glorification" (Jn 7:39; 12:16; 13:31f) and "elevation" (3:14; 8:28; 12:32,34); he returns to his Father (cf. 2:49).

53. The Samaritans, always hostile to the Jews (Jn 4:9), abso-

lutely refuse to receive one who is apparently going on pilgrimage to Jerusalem.

54. James and John, living up to their reputation as "sons of thunder" (Mk 3:17), expect Jesus to act like Elijah (2 Kg 1:10-12); indeed many manuscripts add: "as Elijah did".

55. Jesus rebukes them: his way is one of mercy, not destruction. Many manuscripts have the Marcionate addition: "You do not know what manner of spirit you are of; for the Son of man came not to destroy men's lives but to save them."

56. Most likely this was another Samaritan village.

57-62. The Demands of Discipleship
(Mt 8:19-22)

57 As they were going along the road, a man said to him, "I will follow you wherever you go." And Jesus said to him, "Foxes have holes, and birds of the air have nests; but the Son of man has nowhere to lay his head." **59** To another he said, "Follow me." But he said, "Lord, let me first go and bury my father." **60** But he said to him, "Leave the dead to bury their own dead; but as for you, go and proclaim the kingdom of God." **61** Another said, "I will follow you, Lord; but let me first say farewell to those at my home." **62** Jesus said to him, "No one who puts his hand to the plow and looks back is fit for the kingdom of God."

The first two sayings are common to Matthew and Luke, the third is proper to Luke.

57f. According to Matthew the man is a scribe. The disciples of Jesus must be, like him, a homeless wanderer.

59f. In Matthew the second questioner is a disciple. It is not implied, of course, that the father has just died: the man's excuse is that he must wait until his father has died before he can become a disciple—he appeals to the demands of the fourth commandment. Others who are "dead", insensible to the call of Jesus, will take care of the man's obligation to his father (cf. 14:26). Luke adds the commission to proclaim the kingdom of God (cf. 4:43; 8:1; 9:2; 16:16)—discipleship implies missionary activity.

61f. Like Elijah (1 Kg 19:19-21) this man wants to return to take leave of his people; Jesus is more demanding than Elijah. His reply is in proverbial form: the man who is suitable for the proclaiming of the kingdom is one who gives himself to it without reserve like a plowman who must give his whole attention to plowing a straight furrow. The sayings teach, in forthright language, that sacrifice and total self-commitment are demanded of a disciple of Jesus; and they suggest that "the most difficult choices in life are not between the good and the evil, but between the good and the best".[35]

10:1-16. Mission of the Seventy-Two

1 After this the Lord appointed seventy others, and sent them on ahead of him, two by two, into every town and place where he himself was about to come. **2** And he said to them, "The harvest is plentiful, but the laborers are few; pray therefore the Lord of the harvest to send out laborers into his harvest. **3** Go your way; behold, I send you out as lambs in the midst of wolves. **4** Carry no purse, no bag, no sandals; and salute no one on the road. **5** Whatever house you enter, first say "Peace be to this house!" **6** And if a son of peace is there, your peace shall rest upon him; but if not, it shall return to you. **7** And remain in the same house, eating and drinking what they provide, for the laborer deserves his wages; do not go from house to house. **8** Whenever you enter a town and they receive you, eat what is set before you; **9** heal the sick in it and say to them, 'The kingdom of God has come near to you.' **10** But whenever you enter a town and they do not receive you, go into its streets and say, **11** 'Even the dust of your town that clings to our feet, we wipe off against you; nevertheless know this, that the kingdom of God has come near.' **12** I tell you, it shall be more tolerable on that day for Sodom than for that town.

13 "Woe to you, Chorazin! woe to you, Bethsaida! for if the mighty works done in you had been done in Tyre and Sidon, they would have repented long ago, sitting in sackcloth and ashes. **14** But it shall be more tolerable in the judgment for Tyre and Sidon than for you. **15** And you, Capernaum, will you be exalted to heaven? You shall be brought down to Hades.

16 "He who hears you hears me, and he who rejects you rejects me, and he who rejects me rejects him who sent me."

A discourse parallel to that of 9:1-6. Matthew has (9:35–10:16) combined elements of both discourses—though he does not mention the seventy-two. It does not seem that the sending of the seventy-two foreshadows the universal mission of the disciples (as has been suggested); in 24:47 the Gentile mission is entrusted to the Twelve. It seems best to regard 9:1-6 and 10:1-16 as *one*

[35] G. B. Caird, *op. cit.*, p. 141.

sending: Jesus addressed not only the Twelve but a wider circle of disciples. It is understandable that the emphasis should have been brought to bear on the mission of the Twelve.

1. "Seventy-two" (Codex Vaticanus, Codex Bezae, Old Latin, Syriac) is preferable to "seventy" (the majority)—a change to a round number. Their office is not that of the messengers of 9:52, a material one, but a mission of preaching.

2f. Cf. Mt 9:37f; 10:16—obviously distinct sayings; taken together they reflect the experience of the first missionaries: their own zeal and the opposition they encountered.

4. Cf. 9:3 = Mk 6:8f; Mt 10:9f. The warning not to waste time on civilities (elaborate, in the Oriental manner) (cf. 2 Kg 4:29) underlines the urgency of the mission.

5f. Cf. Mt 10:12f. Luke gives the Jewish greeting: "Peace"; Matthew has "salute it". "Son of peace" is a Hebraism = one worthy of peace. Clearly, the greeting is meaningful, a blessing.

7. Cf. 9:4; Mk 6:10; Mt 10:11. Food and shelter are not alms but wages (cf. 1 Cor 9:14; 1 Tm 5:18).

8f. Cf. Mt 10:7. The mission is not private but is a public proclamation of the kingdom.

10f. Cf. 9:5; Mk 6:11; Mt 10:14. The kingdom is near, so they are not to waste time on those who will not receive them; the message must be brought to others.

12. Cf. Mt 10:15. The unreceptive town will not go unpunished; "on that day" = on the day of judgment (cf. Mk 13:32).

13-15. Cf. Mt 11:21-24. In Matthew the saying refers to the rejection of the preaching of Jesus; here it is added because of the similar theme of v. 12. Chorazin lay about two miles north of Capernaum; for Bethsaida cf. 9:10. Tyre and Sidon, in Phoenicia, are typical Gentile towns. Truly, he had not found in Israel the faith he sought.

16. Cf. Mt 10:40. Jesus, sent by the Father, has sent the disciples; rejection of them is the rejection of God (cf. 9:48; Mk 9:37; Jn 13:20).

17-20. Return of the Seventy-Two

17 The seventy returned with joy, saying, "Lord, even the demons are subject to us in your name!" **18** And he said to them, "I saw Satan fall like lightning from heaven. **19** Behold, I have given you authority to tread upon serpents and scorpions, and over all the power of the enemy; and nothing shall hurt you. **20** Nevertheless do not rejoice in this, that the spirits are subject to you; but rejoice that your names are written in heaven."

Proper to Luke. **17.** The ability to cast out demons had, understandably, made a deep impression on the disciples. The power had come to them from Jesus (v. 19; cf. 9:1) and it is by their faith in him that they have succeeded.

18. The real cause for rejoicing is that the kingdom has come (cf. 11:20; Mt 12:28); for Satan it is the beginning of the end— his fall will be lightning fast (cf. Jn 12:31).

19. The disciples have received power over the enemy of mankind in all fields; serpents and scorpions (though these may have a spiritual sense, cf. Ps 91[90]:13) exemplify evils in nature, the works of Satan (cf. Ac 28:3-6).

20. The assurance of being numbered among the elect is the ultimate reason for rejoicing. The image of the "book of life" is a common Old Testament one: Ex 32:32f; Is 4:3; Dn 12:1; Mal 3:16; Ps 69(68):29; Ap 3:5; 13:8; 17:8; 20:12,15.

21-24. The Thanksgiving of Jesus
(Mt 11:25-27)

21 In that same hour he rejoiced in the Holy Spirit and said, "I thank thee, Father, Lord of heaven and earth, that thou hast hidden these things from the wise and understanding and revealed them to babes; yea, Father, for such was thy gracious will. **22** All things have been delivered to me by my Father; and no one knows who the Son is except the Father, or who the Father is except the Son and any one to whom the Son chooses to reveal him."

23 Then turning to the disciples he said privately, "Blessed are the eyes which see what you see! **24** For I tell you that many prophets and kings desired to see what you see, and did not see it, and to hear what you hear, and did not hear it."

21f. "In that same hour"—Luke, unlike Matthew, gives an excellent psychological explanation of the joy of Jesus: he had just witnessed the power of God at work through his disciples. "Rejoicing in the Holy Spirit" is characteristic of Luke (cf. 4:1, 14,18). For the rest, the saying, so reminiscent of John, and so clearly expressing the unique relationship of Father and Son, is the same as Matthew. The "wise" are the leaders of Israel; the "babes" are the simple folk (whom the "wise" regarded as little more than children)—the disciples who hear and do (cf. 1:51f). The secret that the Father has confided to the humble is the mutual knowledge of Father and Son, revealed to those whom the Son chooses: the disciples. For v. 22 cf. Jn 1:18; 3:35; 10:15; 13:3; 17:25.

23f. Cf. Mt 13:16f. The saying is in a better context in Matthew: the revelation of the "secret of the kingdom" to the disciples, that is, that the kingdom is present in the Person of Jesus. Yet, for all that, in Luke's context, the words have even greater depth: what the disciples see is the secret of the Son—his unique relationship to his Father; the whole history of Israel converged on this mystery.

Lagrange thus sums up the passage 10:1-24: "Jesus sends his disciples to proclaim that the kingdom of God is near. In fact it has arrived because their preaching occasions the fall of Satan. However, the Master expressly confirms their power because they will have need of it in that struggle with the forces of evil which they must face before taking their place in heaven. Then he thanks his Father for having revealed his secret to the humble, not a secret pertaining to the close of the age but the mutual knowledge of Father and Son, revealed to those whom the Son has chosen, his disciples. They see and hear, already, what the prophets had so desired to see and hear: that the Messianic age has been inaugurated by Jesus and his disciples, that it is a reality. Already the Son is here. The glorification of the Son of man can add nothing to the relationship between Son and Father because, already, all things have been delivered to the Son. This is indeed the theology of the Incarnation, attached to the expectation of Israel, a hope now realized. It is theology, but free of metaphysical language, a theology that can be taught to 'babes'." [36]

25-37. The Principal Commandment; The Good Samaritan

25 And behold, a lawyer stood up to put him to the test, saying, "Teacher, what shall I do to inherit eternal life?" **26** He said to him, "What is written in the law? How do you read?" **27** And he answered,

[36] *Op. cit.*, p. 309.

"You shall love the Lord your God with all your heart, and with all your soul, and with all your strength, and with all your mind; and your neighbor as yourself." **28** And he said to him, "You have answered right; do this, and you will live."

29 But he, desiring to justify himself, said to Jesus, "And who is my neighbor?" **30** Jesus replied, "A man was going down from Jerusalem to Jericho, and he fell among robbers, who stripped him and beat him, and departed, leaving him half dead. **31** Now by chance a priest was going down that road; and when he saw him he passed by on the other side. **32** So likewise a Levite, when he came to the place and saw him, passed by on the other side. **33** But a Samaritan, as he journeyed, came to where he was; and when he saw him, he had compassion, **34** and went to him and bound up his wounds, pouring on oil and wine; then he set him on his own beast and brought him to an inn, and took care of him. **35** And the next day he took out two denarii and gave them to the innkeeper, saying, 'Take care of him; and whatever more you spend, I will repay you when I come back.' **36** Which of these three, do you think, proved neighbor to the man who fell among the robbers?" **37** He said, "The one who showed mercy on him." And Jesus said to him, "Go and do likewise."

25-29. Cf. Mk 12:28-31; Mt 22:34-40. In Mark the scribe is sincere and is praised by Jesus, and his question is about the principal commandment; in Luke he seeks to trap Jesus and asks about eternal life. While it may be that Mark's text is primitive and Luke's shows a development in the tradition, it is, on the whole, more reasonable to suppose that in the passage 10:25-37 Luke follows a distinct source. The original question was meant to embarrass Jesus; but he, adroitly, put the onus on his questioner, who found his reply (from Dt 6:5 and Lev 19:18) winning the approval of Jesus. So the lawyer tried again and asked for a definition of "neighbor". This time he must have felt that the "Master" would have been hard put to reply for it was, in fact, a much discussed problem. The Pharisees would have excluded all non-Pharisees, while the Essenes of Qumran would go even further and declare that all the "sons of darkness", i.e. all who did not belong to the sect, should be hated. All would agree that, even in the broadest interpretation, the term should be limited to Jews and proselytes. It is expected that Jesus, too, will respect these limits; it remains to be seen whether he will narrow them appreciably.

The story that Jesus proceeds to tell illustrates at once the working of the Semitic mind and the purpose of a parable. A question has been asked which, to one of Greek culture, begs for a clear-cut definition. The approach of Jesus is very different but his method is perfectly acceptable to the lawyer who unerringly grasps the point of the parable (v. 37). Though the story does not concern an historical incident its setting is credible. The road from Jerusalem to Jericho was, until recent times, a dangerous one for lone travelers. The brigands were members of local Bedouin tribes who knew the wild country inside out and were practically immune from effective pursuit. But in this all too familiar background the parable Jesus relates is highly distinctive.

30. Though it is not explicitly stated, it is certainly implied that the man who was waylaid on the road was a Jew. His nationality is not expressly mentioned because the very point of the parable is that the lawyer's problem is not going to be solved in terms of nationality or race.

31f. The priest chanced to be going along the same road and carefully avoided the wounded man. A suggestion that he took him to be dead and did not wish to incur ritual impurity by contact with a corpse is foreign to the perspective of the parable; besides, he was coming from Jerusalem; his period of Temple service was over. We are to take it quite simply that he did not want to get involved in what, one way or another, was sure to be a messy business. The Levite took the same selfish course. Jesus does not accuse them of callousness, he does not pass judgment on their conduct. They are men who lack the courage to love; dare we say that they represent the average man?

33-35. After the priest and Levite, it might have been expected that the third traveler—a series of three is typical of the popular story—would turn out to be a Jewish layman; the bias would be in some way anti-clerical. The drama is that the third man, and the hero of the story, is one of the hated Samaritans. He has been designedly chosen to bring out the essential unselfishness of love. This man applied first aid to the wounded traveler and, curiously, in v. 34, Luke has put the ministrations in inverse order, for the wounds would have been first washed with wine and then dressed with oil and bandaged. His beast was almost certainly a donkey, so the Samaritan would have walked beside the animal, supporting the injured man. And when he came to the inn he did not feel that his obligations had ended. Whatever a cynic might have thought of his conduct so far, the man turns out to be very much a realist. He did not naïvely presume on the charity of the inn-keeper, but payed him two denarii (a denarius represented a day's wages) and assured him that he would settle any further accounts when he returned by that way. It seems that the Samaritan was a merchant—on a very modest scale no doubt—who plied between his own country and Jerusalem.

36. At the end, Jesus got the lawyer to answer his own question. Yet, did he really answer the original question? In v. 29 he asked: "Who is my neighbor?" while the question that Jesus put in v. 36 is rather: "To whom am I neighbor?" The very question indicates the difference there is between the Jewish outlook and Christian charity. The lawyer was concerned with the object of love and his question implied a limitation: my neighbor is one who belongs to such and such a group. Jesus looked to the subject of love: which of the three had acted as neighbor? The lawyer's question was not answered because it was a mistaken question. A man cannot determine theoretically who his neighbor is, because love is not theory but practice. A man's neighbor is any man who needs his help, says the parable; the wounded man was neighbor to the priest and Levite just as much as he was to the Samaritan, but while they would have theorized in the manner of the lawyer, he acted. The traveler was neighbor to all three; the Samaritan alone was neighbor in return.

37. And the lawyer had learned his lesson and answered correctly. A frequent suggestion that he deliberately avoided pronouncing the hated name "Samaritan" is doubtless unfair to him; in fact his answer does underline the message of the Savior—"he who performed the work of mercy on him." Significantly, Jesus bids him *act* accordingly (cf. 1 Jn 3:18). Though the final recommendation of Christ was addressed to the lawyer it holds a message and a warning for all Christians. We must not pause to ask ourselves: "Is this man really my neighbor?" Such a question has no place in the Christian life. Christian charity knows no bounds and oversteps all man-made limits. The pity is that there are so few Samaritans among us.

38-42. Martha and Mary

38 Now as they went on their way, he entered a village; and a woman named Martha received him into her house. 39 And she had a sister called Mary, who sat at the Lord's feet and listened to his teaching. 40 But Martha was distracted with much serving; and she went to him and said, "Lord, do you not care that my sister has left me to serve alone? Tell her then to help me." 41 But the Lord answered her, "Martha, Martha, you are anxious and troubled about many things; 42 one thing is needful. Mary has chosen the good portion, which shall not be taken away from her."

Proper to Luke. 38f. From Jn 11:1 we know that the village was Bethany, on the eastern slope of the Mount of Olives—so much for Luke's "journey" to Jerusalem! In Jn 11:1-44 the sisters have the same contrasting temperaments.

40. The familiar relationship between Jesus and the family of Bethany, explicitly indicated in Jn 11:5, is here strikingly exemplified: the exasperated Martha does not hesitate to point out that it is partly Jesus' fault that she is left on her own to make all the preparations.

41f. He gently chides her for her agitation. There is textual confusion with regard to 42a. The longer reading, impressively attested ("few things are needful, or only one"), refers to the needless preparation of Martha—one dish will suffice. The shorter reading ("one thing is needful"), however, may well be authentic: Martha is told that the one thing necessary is the seeking of the kingdom (cf. 12:29-41)—Mary, drinking in the words of Jesus, has chosen the good portion ("undivided devotion to the Lord", 1 Cor 7:35). In support of this interpretation is the fact that v. 42b must be understood in a spiritual sense.

11:1-4. The Lord's Prayer
(Mt 6:9-13)

1 He was praying in a certain place, and when he ceased, one of his disciples said to him, "Lord, teach us to pray, as John taught his disciples." 2 And he said to them, "When you pray, say:
"Father, hallowed be thy name. Thy kingdom come. 3 Give us each day our daily bread; 4 and forgive us our sins, for we ourselves forgive every one who is indebted to us; and lead us not into temptation."

In 11:1-13 Luke has a short treatise on prayer, comparable to that of Mt 6:5-12. The catechesis of Matthew is addressed to men who, from youth, have been accustomed to pray but who may fall victim to routine: it is a catechesis for converts from Judaism. Luke has in mind men who have to be taught to pray and who need encouragement: it is a catechesis for Gentile converts. But, in both cases, the Lord's Prayer is a prayer that the Christian *must* know.

1-2a. Luke informs us that it was the sight of Jesus in prayer, alone in an unspecified place, that moved the disciples to ask him to teach them to pray; in this Luke has surely given us the circumstances in which the Savior spoke the prayer. This request of the disciples is significant: it is an acknowledgment of the distinctiveness of Jesus—he stands apart from Judaism and even from John. He shows a new way of approaching God and this calls for a new form of prayer; the Our Father is a prayer for the Christian community. Matthew has placed the prayer in the context of the Sermon on the Mount, but this is clearly secondary. It is now generally held that Luke's shorter version more closely represents, in the number of its petitions, the prayer as historically spoken by Jesus. Matthew's version could have been developed by the evangelist (like his beatitudes and his whole Sermon on the Mount); or, more likely, attained its fuller form in the liturgy. Thus we find that the version of the prayer found in the first-century Didachē is almost identical with Matthew's version— and carries the liturgical conclusion: "For thine is the power and the glory forever." On the other hand, the wording of the Lucan petitions, in the interest of Greek style, departs somewhat from the Aramaic flavor of the original, more noticeable in Matthew. As in the case of the beatitudes, a comparative treatment seems indicated.

1. *The Address*

Lk 11:2b	Mt 6:9b
Father	Our Father who art in heaven

It is altogether probable that Luke's "Father" is primitive. The expression "Father in heaven" is typical of Matthew: it occurs twenty times in Matthew, once in Mark (11:25), never in Luke.

(Cf. Mt 5:48 = Lk 6:36; Mt 6:26,32 = Lk 12:24,30; Mt 10:32f = Lk 12:8f; Mt 12:50 = Mk 3:35.) Besides, in the other prayers of Jesus recorded in the gospels, he addresses God simply as "Father" (cf. Mt 11:25f = Lk 10:21f; Mk 14:36; Lk 23:34; Jn 17:1-26). *Pater* stands for the Aramaic *Abba*. The title *Abba*, given to his Father by Jesus (cf. Mk 14:36), is intimate, familiar, and was never used, with reference to God, by the Jews. In the Old Testament God is not often called Father, but the occurrence of the title is noteworthy. He is the Father of Israel who has delivered, saved, and chosen his people by his interventions in history (Hos 11: 1-4). The prophets could accuse the people of failing to honor their Father (cf. Mal 1:6); yet the people, too, repentant, could acknowledge the relationship: "Thou, O Lord, art our Father" (Is 63:16); and God's pardon would follow their change of heart (cf. Jer 21:20). In the post-exilic period the notion of a personal relationship between God and individuals became prevalent; yet God still remained, in the first place, the Father of Israel. Palestinian Jews, when addressing God as "Father", used the Hebrew noun *ab*, or, more generally, they addressed "our Father" (*abinu*). It was usual, too, among the Jews to specify Father "in heaven" in order to emphasize the unique Fatherhood of God. It seems clear that Matthew has added "in heaven" (or had found it in his source) and that behind Luke's "Father" is the Aramaic *Abba* spoken by our Lord; "Abba" is the *ipsissima vox* of Jesus. This intimate title expressed his unique knowledge of the Father and his own standing as Son (Lk 10:22); it contains within itself the affirmation of his mission and the heart of his message. And now, in the Our Father, Jesus grants to his own the right to address God as Abba, as he himself did. We know that the first Christians did take him at his word (Gal 4:6; Rom 8:15).

2. *The Petitions*

The address to the Father is followed by a number of petitions, six in Matthew, five in Luke.

(1) Sanctification of the Name

Hallowed be thy name—Lk 11:2b; Mt 6:9c.

The precise meaning of this petition is disputed; it is not immediately clear whether the subject of it is God or men. It may mean that God is sanctified or glorified, by the conduct of men; the sanctifying of God's name implied that men revere and praise him and lead good lives according to his commands. There is, of course, no question of "sanctifying" God in any active sense, but only of making his holiness known in and through themselves (cf. Lv 22:32; Sir 33:4). But, so understood, this first petition is no real prayer but rather a wish.

In the Old Testament it is God who sanctifies himself, who glorifies his name: "I will sanctify my great name" (Ezek 36:23); and the notion that the name of God is glorified by men is secondary. The passive, here and in the third petition, is a circumlocution or substitute for the divine name ("Father, sanctify thy name"); from a sense of reverence Jews avoided the divine name (cf. Lk 6:38). It is God, then, who sanctifies his name, who glorifies himself. In Ezekiel especially (20:41; 28:22-26; 36:20f; 38:16-23; 39:21-29) the sanctifying of God's name signifies an eschatological action of God which is clearly connected with the coming of the kingdom of God. It is only when the reign of God is manifest and his power and holiness are fully revealed that the first petition will be fully answered. Jesus himself, when the hour of return to his Father was at hand, could pray: "Father, glorify thy name," and the Father could answer: "I have glorified it [i.e. in and through the ministry of Jesus] and will glorify it again [i.e. in Jesus' return and the sending of the Spirit, cf. Jn 16:14]" (Jn 12:28).

We are not asking, primarily, that more and more men should acknowledge God and worship him—though this has its place too. No, we are asking first of all that God should glorify his own name, that he should glorify himself. We pray God, confidently and humbly, that he will openly manifest his glory.

(2) The Kingdom

Thy kingdom come—Lk 11:2c; Mt 6:10a

This is the primary and central petition of the prayer. Desire for the prompt coming of the kingdom of God is a leading feature of Jewish piety, but this longing always includes the restoration of Israel and her deliverance from the power of her enemies, a nationalistic outlook that is here surpassed. The aorist verb form of the Greek text indicates that the coming of the kingdom is a single act by which God will bring this age to an end and establish his kingship over the world; then God will be all in all (1 Cor 15:28). Only God knows the day and the hour of this happening (Mt 24:36); yet we can and must pray for the final coming of God's reign for, by so doing, we enter into God's plan and, so to say, make God's business our concern too. Both petitions echo the *Qaddish*, the Aramaic concluding doxology of the synagogue service—a prayer that must have been very familiar to Jesus.

(3) The Will of God

> Thy will be done,
> on earth as it is in heaven—Mt 6:10b

This petition is not found in Luke; the first part of it occurs again in Matthew's version of Jesus' prayer in Gethsemane (26:42). It is impossible to decide, with certainty, whether Matthew found the petition in his source of the Pater Noster or whether he has himself inserted it here. The petition is not a wish that the will of God should, in this world, be better known and followed by men—the will of God being the sum of his commandments. Indeed, the aorist passive *genēthētō* is best rendered: "May (your will) come about", that is, may God bring his own will to pass. This "will" of God is his plan of salvation effective through his Son (cf. Eph 1:5-12). It is this will that Jesus had come to do (Jn 6:38); this same salvific plan of God he accepted in Gethsemane (Mk 14:36); it will be complete when all things are subject to the Father, in Christ (Eph 1:20-22). Like the other two, this third petition must also be understood in an eschatological sense. When the Kingship of God will be finally manifest, then, throughout the whole of creation, all things will be entirely subject to God and his reign will be fully acknowledged, as it now is in heaven.

The first three petitions thus form a close unity. They are, fundamentally, a threefold development of *one* petition: that the kingdom of God may come. This is the chief object of the prayer as it also is the central point of the whole teaching of Jesus. These petitions are not concerned with the present circumstances

of men but look to the world that is to come. But this sets things
in proper perspective because this life should be a striving after
the kingdom (Mt 6:33). Moreover, these petitions are the expression of a sure confidence, of total abandonment to God.

(4) Our Daily Bread

Lk 11:3	Mt 6:11
Give us each day	Give us today
our daily bread	our bread of the morrow

The wording of both petitions is quite notably different in the
Greek. Matthew has the aorist imperative *dos*, "give (once)", and
sēmeron, "today"; Luke has the present imperative *didou*, "give
(continually)", and *to kath' hēmeran*, "daily". Whereas Luke's
version is manifestly non-eschatological (in the strict sense), it
can be maintained that this text of Matthew, like all the others,
is to be understood in an eschatological sense.

A real crux is provided by the word *epiousios* common to both
versions; the etymology of this term is uncertain.

(a) From *epi + ousia*, "substance", "subsistence"—the bread "necessary for subsistence"; hence the *supersubstantialis* of the Vulgate, though this goes beyond the meaning of the Greek term.

(b) It may be an equivalent form of *epi tēn ousan* (*hēmeran*),
"of the present day", "daily"—hence *quotidianus*.

(c) From *hē epiousa* (*hēmera*)—"the following (day)" (cf. Ac
16:11).

This could mean the bread for the coming day, for the future.
St. Jerome [*In Matth* 6, 11] says that the gospel of the Hebrews
—an Aramaic apocryphal gospel based on our Matthew—read
mahar = "tomorrow"—and so it is a question of bread for the morrow. This is a weighty argument despite the secondary character
of the gospel of the Hebrews. "Because, in Palestine, the recita-
tion of the Our Father in Aramaic had been the practice throughout the first century, the translator of Matthew into that language
had not translated the Our Father like the rest of the gospel but
had simply written down the Lord's Prayer just he he was accustomed to recite it each day."[37] In other words, the Aramaic-

[37] J. Jeremias, *Paroles de Jésus* (Paris: Cerf, 1963), p. 72.

speaking Jewish Christians, who clung to the original tenor of the prayer, used the formula: "Give us today our bread of the morrow", i.e. our future bread—the bread of eternal life. It would seem that in Matthew's context the future meaning is more in place; this bread is the bread of the heavenly banquet (cf. Mt 8:11; Lk 6:21; 14:29f), it is the yearning of Christians. In Luke, however, the eschatological interpretation has yielded to the more pressing daily outlook: "Keep on giving us our daily bread"—cf. Lk 9:23, "to take up the cross *daily*". We pray for our daily bread, that God may continue to give us the necessaries of life; we do not pray for wealth and opulence, for these things might more easily be a hindrance than a help.

(5) Forgiveness

Lk 11:4a	Mt 6:12
And forgive us our sins,	And forgive us our debts
for we ourselves forgive	as we also forgive
every one who is	our debtors
indebted to us	
(our debtor)	

It is sufficiently clear that Luke has substituted the more precise *tas hamartias*, "sins" (cf. 5:20; 7:47), for the *opheilēmata*, "debts", of Matthew—he has retained *opheilonti*, "debtor", in the second part of his own petition. Matthew's "as we have forgiven" expresses the singleness of the action, an action before God's judgment seat. In this petition Christians stand by anticipation before God's throne: their forgiveness of one another as brothers and their own final and complete forgiveness by their Father are parts of the one great gift. Luke's "we forgive"—like the request for bread "each day"—is a tendency away from eschatology. It would seem to be the result of later experience or of further reflection: we need each day the necessities of life, and the obligation of forgiveness holds good at all times. And even if eschatology does, strictly speaking, refer to the period of the last days, the end of this world, we already do, in a real if broader sense, live in the last age; God's kingdom has come in the Person of Jesus. Hence, "for the disciples of Jesus to be ready to forgive is, in its own way, to reach out the hand towards God's forgiveness. We live, they say, in the Messianic times, in the era of mercy; that pardon which we ourselves receive we are willing to extend to others. And so, loving Father, grant us your own forgiveness which is the grace of the time of salvation, grant it to us now, today, here below!" [38]

(6) The Trial

Lk 11:4b	Mt 6:13
And lead us not into temptation	And lead us not into temptation but deliver us from the Evil One (or, from evil)

If this petition is to fit into context, we ask not to be delivered from daily temptation (which is the lot of the Christian, Jas 1:2,12), but from the final battle between God and Satan (cf. Mk 14:38; Apoc 3:10); it is a prayer to be preserved from the final onslaught of Satan. This meaning is emphasized by the *apo tou ponērou* of Mt 6:13b which is better rendered "from the Evil One" (cf. Mt 13:19,38; Jn 17:15; 1 Jn 5:18; 2 Thes 3:3). The Christian asks his Father not only to spare him in the trial of the terrible final struggle, but to set him free from the power of Satan. Again, in Luke's version, *peirmasmos* may well be taken in the sense of daily trial (cf. Jas 1:2) and his saying might be paraphrased: "Do not allow us to succumb to temptation!"

In conclusion we may quote a rather long, but highly relevant, passage from an important study on the Lord's Prayer:

"We can see how coherently the eschatological viewpoint binds together the petition into one picture. The Christian community of the first century, anxiously expecting the Second Coming, prays that God will completely glorify his name by establishing his kingdom, which represents the fulfillment of the plan he has willed for both earth and heaven. For its portion in this consummation of time, the community asks a place at the heavenly banquet table to break bread with Christ, and a forgiveness of its sins. A titanic struggle with Satan stands between the community and the realization of its prayer, and from this it asks to be delivered.

"Already in the Lucan form of the Pater Noster, the intensity

[38] *Ibid.*, p. 75.

of eschatological aspiration has begun to yield to the hard facts of daily Christian living. It is a sign of the genius of this prayer, taught by the divine Master, that it could serve to express such different aspirations. Nevertheless, as we say the prayer nineteen centuries later, now completely enmeshed in the temporal aspect of the Christian life, it would, perhaps, profit us to revive, in part, some of its original eschatological yearning. Even if we choose to relegate the last things to a minor tract in theology, the return of Christ comes persistently closer each day. The Pater Noster, said as a fervent *maranatha,* 'Our Lord, come!', would not be an inappropriate welcome." [39]

5-8. The Friend at Midnight

5 And he said to them, "Which of you who has a friend will go to him at midnight and say to him, 'Friend, lend me three loaves; **6** for a friend of mine has arrived on a journey, and I have nothing to set before him'; **7** and he will answer from within, 'Do not bother me; the door is now shut, and my children are with me in bed; I cannot get up and give you anything'? **8** I tell you, though he will not get up and give him anything because he is his friend, yet because of his importunity he will rise and give him whatever he needs."

Peculiar to Luke. In the context of Lk 11:1-13, a synthesis of Jesus' teaching on prayer, the parable has to do with persevering prayer, although we shall see that originally it did not have precisely this meaning.

5f. We must imagine a small village without shops. Bread was baked in the early morning so that the man who had lent the loaves was not seriously inconvenienced—fresh bread would be available for the morning meal. Three of the flat round loaves were regarded as a meal for one man; the reception of the guest must be measured by the Oriental code of hospitality. The phrase *tis ex humōn* regularly, in the New Testament, introduces questions which invite the emphatic answer: "Impossible! Nobody!" or "Of course! Everybody!" (cf. Mt 6:27; 7:9; 12:11; Lk 11:11; 12:25; 14:5,28; 15:4; 17:7; etc.). The phrase may best be rendered, "Can you imagine that any of you would . . .?" Here vv. 5-7 should be regarded as one rhetorical question: "Can you im-

[39] R. E. Brown, *New Testament Essays* (Milwaukee: Bruce, 1965), p. 253.

agine that if one of you had a friend, and he should come to you
at midnight and say to you, 'Friend, lend me three loaves, for a
friend of mine on a journey has come to me and I have nothing
to set before him,' that you would answer, 'Go away and leave
me in peace'—can you imagine that?" The answer must be an
indignant denial: "Impossible! Of course not!"

7. The house consisted of a single room and the "bed" was a
mat, laid on the floor, on which the whole family slept—the opening of the door would involve disturbing the children stretched
on the floor.

8. Though the refusal of the request is regarded as unthink-
able—a blatant breach of the code of hospitality—yet, for the sake
of argument, Jesus supposes that if the man is to be moved
neither by friendship nor by the demand of hospitality, he will
at least grant the request in order to be rid of the other. The
lesson is obvious: if this man acts so, how much more will God
hearken to those who call upon him. Jesus insists that prayer
must be *trustful*—one must have unshaken confidence in the
goodness of God; and if Luke finds in the parable a teaching on
perseverance in prayer, is not perseverance the consequence of
trust?

9-13. The Efficacy of Prayer
(Mt 7:7-11)

9 "And I tell you, ask, and it will be given you; seek, and you will
find; knock, and it will be opened to you. 10 For everyone who asks
receives, and he who seeks finds, and to him who knocks it will be
opened. 11 What father among you, if his son asks for a fish, will
instead of a fish give him a serpent; 12 or if he asks for an egg, will
give him a scorpion? 13 If you then, who are evil, know how to give
good gifts to your children, how much more will the heavenly Father
give the Holy Spirit to those who ask him!"

These sayings of Jesus—placed in the Sermon on the Mount
by Matthew—were not originally a sequel to the parable; their
present position is due to Luke (or to his source). The introduction, "I tell you" is emphatic—Jesus speaks in his own name and
with authority.

9f. The passive form stands in place of the divine name (a
reverential circumlocution): "Ask and God will give you. . . .

God will open to you." Normally one receives only when one has asked, one finds only when one has sought, one enters a house only when one has knocked on the door—all this could have been suggested by the preceding parable. And if these actions do not always, on the human level, meet with success, the disciples are assured that God will not fail them.

11f. In v. 11 it seems preferable to accept the longer reading, "What father among you, if his son asks for *a loaf, will give him a stone; or if he asks for* a fish, will instead of a fish give him a serpent", although it is possible that the words in italics may have been inserted here from Mt 7:9. Where Matthew (7:9f) has "stone" and "serpent" Luke has "serpent" and "scorpion", showing a development in the direction of the unlikely (cf. 5:36) for, though stone and serpent might be mistaken for loaf and fish respectively, the scorpion can only be the black Palestinian species which no one could mistake for an egg.

13. A typical argument *a minore ad maiorem*. Luke has "Holy Spirit" in place of "good gifts" (Mt 7:11): the Holy Spirit is, therefore, the gift *par excellence*.

14-23. Jesus and Beelzebul
(Mt 12:22-30; 9:32-34; Mk 3:22-30)

14 Now he was casting out a demon that was dumb; when the demon had gone out, the dumb man spoke, and the people marvelled. **15** But some of them said, "He casts out demons by Beelzebul, the prince of demons"; **16** while others, to test him, sought from him a sign from heaven. **17** But he, knowing their thoughts, said to them, "Every kingdom divided against itself is laid waste, and house falls upon house. **18** And if Satan also is divided against himself, how will his kingdom stand? For you say that I cast out demons by Beelzebul. **19** And if I cast out demons by Beelzebul, by whom do your sons cast them out? Therefore they shall be your judges. **20** But if it is by the finger of God that I cast out demons, then the kingdom of God has come upon you. **21** When a strong man, fully armed, guards his own palace, his goods are in peace; **22** but when one stronger than he assails him and overcomes him, he takes away his armor in which he trusted, and divides his spoil. **23** He who is not with me is against me, and he who does not gather with me scatters."

14-16. Jesus casts out a "dumb demon", that is, a demon causing dumbness (cf. Mt 9:32f); in Matthew's parallel passage

(12:22) a blind and dumb demoniac is healed. Some of the witnesses—Pharisees (Mt 12:24); scribes from Jerusalem (Mk 3:22)—accuse him of having made a pact with Beelzebul. In 2 Kg 1:2-16 Beelzebul appears as a god of the Philistinian town of Ekron; the meaning of the Hebrew term is "lord of flies", probably a contemptuous corruption of the god's name; in the gospels the name is applied to a prince of demons (Mk 3:22; Mt 10:25; 12:24,27; Lk 11:15-19). Luke (Matthew also) avoids the suggestion that Jesus himself was possessed (cf. Mk 3:22). V. 16 anticipates 11:29-32 (cf. Mt 12:38).

17-20. Cf. Mt 12:25-28; Mk 3:24-26. Internal strife can bring about the fall of a kingdom or dynasty; Satan would be undermining his own kingdom if he were to grant the power of exorcism. Logically, too, the accusation against Jesus would have to be leveled at recognized Jewish exorcists (cf. Ac 19:13). Here it is the good faith of the Jewish exorcists that is in question, not the efficacy of their exorcisms. But Jesus' *power* over the devils is manifest: he casts them out "by the finger of God" (Mt 12:28—"Spirit of God")—an echo of Ex 8:19. In him and in his works the kingdom of God is present and the power of Satan is broken (10:18).

21f. The figure is that of a duel; in Mk 3:27 and Mt 12:29 it is a case of armed robbery. The "strong man" is Satan (the "ruler of this world", Jn 12:31); the contest is decisive: Satan has been overcome by a mightier than he.

23. Cf. Mt 12:20. In the context this is a warning to the adversaries of Jesus: they cannot avoid becoming supporters of Satan if they refuse to side with Jesus—there is no possibility of neutrality in this war. The apparently contradictory saying of Lk 9:50 is explained by its different setting.

24-26. Counteroffensive of Satan
(Mt 12:43-45)

24 "When the unclean spirit has gone out of a man, he passes through waterless places seeking rest; and finding none he says, 'I will return to my house from which I came.' 25 And when he comes he finds it swept and put in order. 26 Then he goes and brings seven other spirits more evil than himself, and they enter and dwell there; and the last state of that man becomes worse than the first."

This passage in Luke's source would have been attached to the foregoing passage by the catchwords "unclean spirit", "demon".

24f. "Unclean spirit", in Palestinian idiom, means simply "demon". He finds no rest in the desert places, the habitat of demons, because he desires to harm men. A possessed man was frequently described as the "house" of a devil. Now that house is "swept and put in order", ready for the reception of a guest.

26. "Seven other spirits"—seven stands for totality, therefore complete possession. It seems that v. 25 represents a Semitic conditional clause: "And if he comes and finds it swept. . . ." The house should not have remained empty—a new Master should have been installed there; it should have become a dwelling place of God in the Spirit (Eph 2:22). However, Luke understands the parable in the light of the warning of v. 23. The contemporaries of Jesus, in their refusal to recognize the coming of the kingdom of God and the victory of Jesus, have exposed themselves to a religious situation that is much worse than their state before they had been witnesses of these miracles: instead of gathering they scatter—two situations stand contrasted. The parable may also be read as a warning that the victory won by Jesus over Satan will not avail those who do not acknowledge the victor.

27-28. The True Blessedness

27 As he said this, a woman in the crowd raised her voice and said to him, "Blessed is the womb that bore you and the breasts that you sucked!" **28** But he said, "Blessed rather are those who hear the word of God and keep it!"

Proper to Luke (but cf. Mk 3:31-35). The episode is admirably in place after the malicious charge against Jesus and his defense: *une femme lui donne raison avec son coeur de mère.*[40] The idea is Jewish: a woman's joy in her son, especially a distinguished son (Gen 30:13; Prov 23:25). For v. 28, cf. 8:21— those who live according to the preaching of Jesus truly belong to the family of God. "Jesus did not reject this compliment to himself and to his mother but he drew attention to another

[40] M.-J. Lagrange, *op. cit.,* p. 335.

order, to a sphere in which Mary herself has excelled all women, she who must be blessed by all generations. Luke could not have forgotten what he had written in 1:42,45,48 and he doubtless regarded the cry of this unknown woman as the first accomplishment of those words." [41]

29-32. Seeking for Signs
(Mt 12:38-42; cf. Mt 16:1-4; Mk 8:11-13)

29 When the crowds were increasing, he began to say, "This generation is an evil generation; it seeks a sign, but no sign shall be given to it except the sign of Jonah. **30** For as Jonah became a sign to the men of Nineveh, so will the Son of man be to this generation. **31** The queen of the South will arise at the judgment with the men of this generation and condemn them; for she came from the ends of the earth to hear the wisdom of Solomon, and behold, something greater than Solomon is here. **32** The men of Nineveh will arise at the judgment with this generation and condemn it; for they repented at the preaching of Jonah, and behold, something greater than Jonah is here."

Already introduced in 11:16, this passage, except for v. 30, is textually very close to Mt 12:39-42.

30. In Mt 12:40 the Resurrection of Jesus, typified by the miracle of Jonah (Jon 1:17), will be the only sign he will give, but a decisive one. Luke gives an early Christian adaptation of the same saying, which now refers to the Parousia: Jonah had been a warning of ruin to the Ninevites; Jesus at his coming will be a sign to those who have rejected him, a sign *ad condemnandum*. On the other hand, the meaning may be that just as Jonah had pointed out to the Ninevites the way of salvation, so Jesus has shown it to his contemporaries who, less generous than the Ninevites, have refused to follow it.

31f. The verses occur in reverse order in Matthew: these are two scriptural examples which underline the incredulity of Jesus' contemporaries. The queen of Saba (1 Kg 10:1) undertook a long journey to hear the wisdom of Solomon; the Jews have turned a deaf ear to the greater than Solomon who stands in their midst. The pagan Ninevites repented at the call of an insignificant Jewish prophet (Jon 3:4-10); the Jews will not listen to a far greater prophet than Jonah.

[41] *Ibid.*, p. 336.

33-36. The Light
(Mt 5:15; 6:22f; Mk 4:21 = Lk 8:16)

33 "No one after lighting a lamp puts it in a cellar or under a bushel, but on a stand, that those who enter may see the light. 34 Your eye is the lamp of your body; when your eye is sound, your whole body is full of light; but when it is not sound, your body is full of darkness. 35 Therefore be careful lest the light in you be darkness. 36 If then your whole body is full of light, having no part dark, it will be wholly bright, as when a lamp with its rays gives you light."

33. This verse is found essentially the same in the parallel texts; the "cellar" (here only) reflects a departure from the Palestinian background—there houses did not have cellars. In its Lucan context the light is Jesus himself (cf. Jn 1:5; 8:12); no further sign is necessary.

34f. In another context by Matthew, these sayings are superficially linked to v. 33. Here they imply that undistorted vision is required to see the light of Jesus. Those who seek signs, or perversely misrepresent his works (vv. 15f), are, in fact, blind.

36. This saying, not in Matthew, is related to v. 34. Its meaning would seem to be: "When a man, through the *inner* light of sound eyes is full of light and has no trace of darkness (evil), then and only then will the light *from without,* the God-enkindled light of Jesus, enlighten him wholly." [42]

37-54. The Pharisees and Lawyers Denounced
(Mt 23:1-36)

37 While he was speaking, a Pharisee asked him to dine with him; so he went in and sat at table. 38 The Pharisee was astonished to see that he did not first wash before dinner. 39 And the Lord said to him, "Now you Pharisees cleanse the outside of the cup and of the dish, but inside you are full of extortion and wickedness. 40 You fools! Did not he who made the outside make the inside also? 41 But give for alms those things which are within; and behold, everything is clean for you.

42 "But woe to you Pharisees! for you tithe mint and rue and every herb, and neglect justice and the love of God; these you ought to have done, without neglecting the others. 43 Woe to you Pharisees! for you love the best seat in the synagogues and salutations in the market

[42] J. Schmid, *Das Evangelium nach Lukas* (Regensburg: Pustet, 1960⁴), p. 209.

places. **44** Woe to you! for you are like graves which are not seen, and men walk over them without knowing it."

45 One of the lawyers answered him, "Teacher, in saying this you reproach us also." **46** And he said, "Woe to you lawyers also! for you load men with burdens hard to bear, and you yourselves do not touch the burdens with one of your fingers. **47** Woe to you! for you build the tombs of the prophets whom your fathers killed. **48** So you are witnesses and consent to the deeds of your fathers; for they killed them, and you build their tombs. **49** Therefore also the Wisdom of God said, 'I will send them prophets and apostles, some of whom they will kill and persecute,' **50** that the blood of all the prophets, shed from the foundation of the world, may be required of this generation, **51** from the blood of Abel to the blood of Zechariah, who perished between the altar and the sanctuary. Yes, I tell you, it shall be required of this generation. **52** Woe to you lawyers! for you have taken away the key of knowledge; you did not enter yourselves and you hindered those who were entering."

53 As he went away from there, the scribes and Pharisees began to press him hard, and to provoke him to speak of many things, **54** lying in wait for him, to catch at something he might say.

Luke only mentions invitations to dine with Pharisees (3:36; 11:37; 14:1) and each time there is a controversy of some sort during the meal. This fact would seem to indicate that the setting of this denunciation is redactional. While Luke places the denunciation as a climax to the discussion on signs, Matthew puts it, more suitably, at the close of the Jerusalem ministry. The two versions differ widely; Matthew, as might be expected, is longer.

37f. Jesus did not observe the extreme punctiliousness of the Pharisees in the matter of ritual purification before meals (cf. Mk 7:2-4).

39. Cf. Mt 23:25f. At first, the Pharisees only are addressed. This verse does not reply to the unspoken criticism of the Pharisee; Luke, using his setting of a meal, refers to the cleansing of tableware; i.e. the link with v. 38 is redactional only.

40. Not in Matthew. The sense of this apparently banal question would seem to be: Because God is not only the Creator of "outer" visible things but also of the things within, i.e. the heart of man from which good and bad ("clean" and "unclean") come (Mk 7:15), it is a grave error to set store by ritual cleanliness to the neglect of moral cleanness.

41. Cf. Mt. 23:26. The verse might be rendered: "Give alms according to your resources"; in the light of v. 40 the sense is that true cleansing is effected by almsgiving.

42-44. Three "woes" are addressed to the Pharisees—all paralleled in Matthew, with some differences. In v. 42 Luke has "rue and every herb" instead of the "dill and cummin" of Mt 23:23, and "justice and the love of God" in place of "justice and mercy and faith". The idea of v. 43, not in *vae* form, is found at the beginning of Matthew's discourse (23:6) and, closer to Matthew's form, in Lk 20:46. For v. 44, cf. Mt 23:27; both sayings depict the hypocrisy of the Pharisees—the whitewashed tombs (Matthew) and the hidden graves (Luke) which can occasion ritual impurity (Nm 19:16).

45-52. Three "woes" are addressed to the lawyers. In Matthew the series of woes is addressed to the "scribes and Pharisees"; in Luke the doctors of the Law feel themselves particularly affronted by the reproaches against pharisaism in general (v. 45). V. 46 is paralleled by Mt 23:4 (though not in *vae* form). Where Mt 23:29-31 is straightforward, Lk vv. 47f is ironical: by building the tombs of the prophets the lawyers imagine that they can repair the crimes of their ancestors—while all the while they are disposed to kill the prophet *par excellence*.

49. Cf. Mt 23:34—the "Wisdom of God": perhaps "God in his Wisdom"; or the plan of God revealed by Jesus. Luke has "apostles" instead of "wise men and scribes" (Mt).

50f. The position of Chronicles as the last book of the Hebrew Bible is indicated: the murder of Zechariah (2 Chr 24:20-22) is the last recorded in Scripture as that of Abel is the first. Luke does not state that Zechariah was "son of Barachiah" (Mt 23:35) and so avoids the difficulty raised by that detail. The warning is addressed not to the lawyers only but to "this generation".

52. Cf. Mt 23:13. Where Matthew has "kingdom of heaven" Luke has "knowledge". The lawyers have appropriated the key which opens the door of knowledge: they will permit none except themselves to explain the Scriptures. Yet they have not entered themselves, that is, they do not possess that true understanding of the Scriptures which would reveal to them the plan of God. Worse still, they, by their authority, prevent others from professing faith in Jesus.

53f. From now on the opposition against Jesus hardens: 19:47; 30:19f; 22:2. The text of these verses exhibits an unusual number of variations; the RSV rendering is supported by Codex Sinaiticus and Codex Vaticanus among others.

12:1-12. Exhortation to Fearless Preaching
(Mt 10:26-33; 12:32; 10:19f)

1 In the meantime, when so many thousands of the multitude had gathered together that they trod upon one another, he began to say to his disciples first, "Beware of the leaven of the Pharisees, which is hypocrisy. 2 Nothing is covered up that will not be revealed, or hidden that will not be known. 3 Whatever you have said in the dark shall be heard in the light, and what you have whispered in private rooms shall be proclaimed upon the housetops.

4 "I tell you, my friends, do not fear those who kill the body, and after that have no more that they can do. 5 But I will warn you whom to fear: fear him who, after he has killed, has power to cast into hell; yes, I tell you, fear him! 6 Are not five sparrows sold for two pennies? And not one of them is forgotten before God. 7 Why, even the hairs of your head are all numbered. Fear not; you are of more value than many sparrows.

8 "And I tell you, every one who acknowledges me before men, the Son of man also will acknowledge before the angels of God; 9 but he who denies me before men will be denied before the angels of God. 10 And every one who speaks a word against the Son of man will be forgiven; but he who blasphemes against the Holy Spirit will not be forgiven. 11 And when they bring you before the synagogues and the rulers and the authorities, do not be anxious how or what you are to answer or what you are to say; 12 for the Holy Spirit will teach you in that very hour what you ought to say."

The passage is composed of various sayings loosely linked; almost all occur in Matthew, in a different context.

1. Though surrounded by a multitude (a Lucan touch, cf. 14:25; 18:36; 19:3; 20:45; 21:38), Jesus first addresses his disciples. He bids them avoid the hypocrisy of the Pharisees which is a pervasive evil influence. In Mk 8:15 their "leaven" is contrasted with the bread given by Jesus; in Mt 16:12 "leaven" stands for the teaching of the Pharisees and Sadducees.

2f. These verses serve to explain v. 1 though, in fact, they are only loosely attached to it. In Mt 10:26f (cf. Mk 4:22 = Lk 8:17) the sayings refer to the gospel preaching; but the sense here is that a man's true disposition cannot remain hidden forever. Even the most confidential words that men speak will one day be made public.

4f. An admonition to fearless profession of faith and to readiness for martyrdom; Luke develops the lapidary saying of Mt 10:28. Jesus addresses his disciples as "my friends" as in Jn 15:14f. The best comment is the statement of Peter (Ac 5:29): "We must obey God rather than men." Here only in Luke is Gehenna named: the abode of the godless in the intermediate state and after the judgment.

6f. If men are not to be feared neither are they to be one's support; and God, who is judge, is also the God of mercy whose provident care extends to the least of his creatures; the disciples are especially dear to him. Five sparrows for twopence (cf. Mt 10:29) is a typical Lucan development of detail (cf. Lk 5:36; 11:12).

8f. The disciples bear testimony to Christ: he will acknowledge them as his own, before God, when as glorified Son of man he comes as judge. But those who deny him by failing to recognize him despite his works and words, or who have turned aside from following him, will also encounter him as judge. In both verses "angels" is a periphrasis for "God"; originally the phrase would have run: "before the angels" and the added "of God" is redundant (cf. Mt 10:32f; Mk 8:38; Lk 9:26).

10. Cf. Mt 12:32; Mk 3:28f. Linked to the foregoing by the catchword "Son of man". Vv. 9 and 10 were originally distinct sayings, and the apparent discrepancy between v. 9 and v. 10a is due solely to their artificial juxtaposition. Where v. 9 envisages disciples only, v. 10 contrasts those who do not know Jesus for what he is and may be excused with disciples who deny Christ and so, sinning against the light, blaspheme the Holy Spirit.

11f. Mt 10:17-20; Mk 13:11 = Lk 21:12-15. This saying has been added here by the catchword "Holy Spirit". In its present context it would seem to reassure the disciples: "There is no need to be afraid of committing this unpardonable blasphemy by ill-advised language before a prosecuting tribunal; for the Holy Spirit himself will direct their words." [43]

---

[43] A. Plummer, *The Gospel according to St. Luke* (Edinburgh: Clark, 1922[5]), p. 321.

13-21. The Rich Fool

13 One of the multitude said to him, "Teacher, bid my brother divide the inheritance with me." **14** But he said to him, "Man, who made me a judge or divider over you?" **15** And he said to them, "Take heed, and beware of all covetousness; for a man's life does not consist in the abundance of his possessions." **16** And he told them a parable, saying, "The land of a rich man brought forth plentifully; **17** and he thought to himself, 'What shall I do, for I have nowhere to store my crops?' **18** And he said, 'I will do this: I will pull down my barns, and build larger ones; and there I will store all my grain and my goods. **19** And I will say to my soul, Soul, you have ample goods laid up for many years; take your ease, eat, drink, be merry.' **20** But God said to him, 'Fool! This night your soul is required of you; and the things you have prepared, whose will they be?' **21** So is he who lays up treasure for himself, and is not rich toward God."

Proper to Luke. Though the parable begins at v. 16 the immediate context is necessary for an understanding of it.

13-16a. The Jews were accustomed to submit similar questions to their rabbis for a practical decision. The presentation of the case, and the title of *didaskale*, "Teacher", strikingly indicate the standing Jesus had won with the people. He formally declined to arbitrate; he will not seem to condone an attitude of absorption in this world's goods. With the phrase, "And he said to them", Luke links a saying which fits the incident since it warns against avarice and points out that riches will not guarantee a long life. Next, by means of another link-formula: "he told them a parable", the evangelist fits in the Rich Fool; in this setting it illustrates the previous passage and serves as a warning against greed.

16b-19. The rich man is providing for the coming years when his crops may not be so abundant; he can then sit back and enjoy himself—the future is secure. "Soul" has the biblical meaning of the seat of desire and satisfaction, the principle of life; and at the moment that the rich man's plans are laid God will take away his life.

20. Rightly is the man called "fool"—in Old Testament usage one who, in practice, denies God (cf. Ps 13:1)—for he had forgotten God, so absorbed in his possessions had he become. The climax of the parable is the man's confrontation by God in his moment of security. In his utter self-confidence he is unaware of the crisis which looms immediately ahead. One thing at least is sure: Jesus did not speak this parable to illustrate the truism that death can come to a man at any time; the Rich Fool finds its proper place among the parables of crisis.

21. This verse has all the appearances of a generalizing conclusion and is, in fact, omitted by some manuscripts; it serves to underline the truth that the man is indeed a "fool" and to emphasize the worthlessness of worldly possessions.

22-34. Trust in Providence
(Mt 6:25-33)

22 And he said to his disciples, "Therefore I tell you, do not be anxious about your life, what you shall eat, nor about your body, what you shall put on. 23 For life is more than food, and the body more than clothing. 24 Consider the ravens: they neither sow nor reap, they have neither storehouse nor barn, and yet God feeds them. Of how much more value are you than the birds! 25 And which of you by being anxious can add a cubit to his span of life? 26 If then you are not able to do as small a thing as that, why are you anxious about the rest? 27 Consider the lilies, how they grow; they neither toil nor spin; yet I tell you, even Solomon in all his glory was not arrayed like one of these. 28 But if God so clothes the grass which is alive in the field today and tomorrow is thrown into the oven, how much more will he clothe you, O men of little faith! 29 And do not seek what you are to eat and what you are to drink, nor be of anxious mind. 30 For all the nations of the world seek these things; and your Father knows that you need them. 31 Instead, seek his kingdom, and these things shall be yours as well.

32 "Fear not, little flock, for it is your Father's good pleasure to give you the kingdom. 33 Sell your possessions, and give alms; provide yourselves with purses that do not grow old, with a treasure in the heavens that does not fail, where no thief approaches and no moth destroys. 34 For where your treasure is, there will your heart be also."

The passage 12:22-31 is very like Mt 6:25-33, but the context is different: Matthew has it in the Sermon; in Luke it is addressed to the disciples as a development of the previous parable's message.

22f. Food and clothing are the most pressing needs of man, but they ought not become all-absorbing cares; at any rate, disciples should trust in God's providence. Several examples of God's care encourage them to do so. But these examples are meant to emphasize God's solicitude for his creatures. Men are not animals and plants—in God's plan they must work for their material needs (cf. 2 Thes 3:10); at the same time, man is destined for the kingdom.

24. "Ravens" ("unclean" birds, Lv 11:15; Dt 14:14; cf. Job 38:41; Ps 147[146]:9) is more likely to be original than Matthew's "birds of the air".

25f. The parable has reminded us that man's life span is in the hands of God; no one can add a single instant to his length of days. For "cubit" (a measure of length) referred to duration of days; cf. Ps 39(38):5—"Thou hast made my days a few hand-breadths".

27f. "Consider the lilies; they neither spin nor weave" is preferable to: "Consider the lilies, how they grow; they neither toil nor spin", a majority reading, but suspect of harmonization with Mt 6:28.

29f. The disciples—unlike others—must not be "of anxious mind" with regard to material needs; that is, they must not be unreasonably preoccupied with these cares and they must not worry over them; after all, their *Father* is aware of his children's needs.

31. The seeking of God's kingdom (cf. 11:2) should be the primary concern of the disciple. "The real cure for worry is to put first things first, to care more about God's kingdom than about personal needs. Those who do so find that God provides for his servants, but they also find that the necessities of life are fewer and simpler than selfishness supposes." [44] All of this teaching has been explicitly addressed to disciples; it contrasts "anxious care" for the things of this life with the "seeking" of the kingdom of God. The lesson is not that material goods are to be despised, but that the Christian should be serenely conscious of the solicitude of his heavenly Father who has called him to a place in his kingdom.

32. This verse has been added by means of the catchword "kingdom". A "little flock" (cf. Jn 10:2,11f,14,16; 21:16,18) in a hostile world, the disciples must not be discouraged but must look with confidence to a Father who has chosen them for his kingdom.

[44] G. B. Caird, *op. cit.*, p. 163.

33f. Cf. Mt 6:20f. In v. 33 Luke has rewritten a saying that may have originally been close to Matthew's version; the danger of riches and the value of almsgiving are favorite themes of Luke.

The following passage, 12:35-48—on watchfulness and faithfulness—is a compilation of parables and sayings on the common theme of judgment; Matthew has much of the same material in his Parousia discourse (Mt 24:43-51).

35-38. The Waiting Servants

35 "Let your loins be girded and your lamps burning, 36 and be like men who are waiting for their master to come home from the marriage feast, so that they may open to him at once when he comes and knocks. 37 Blessed are those servants whom the master finds awake when he comes; truly, I say to you, he will gird himself and have them sit at table, and he will come and serve them. 38 If he comes in the second watch, or in the third, and finds them so, blessed are those servants!"

This is best regarded as another version of Mk 13:33-37 (cf. Mt 25:1-13); both evangelists have understood it in terms of the Parousia and allegorical additions in Luke have heightened the application.

35. This verse, Luke's introduction to the series of parables (12:36-48), is an exhortation to constant vigilance. The skirts of the long outer garment were tucked into the cincture for freedom of movement; the lamp must be ready and lighted—the ancient oil lamp cannot be lighted by pressing a switch!

36-38. The servants are expected to sit up for their master who is returning from a wedding—in Mark he has been on a journey. Mark (13:35) follows the Roman fourfold division of the night, while Luke (v. 37) gives the three Jewish watches. In 37b Luke has an addition which points to the identity of the master: unlike any earthly master (cf. 17:7f) he himself will serve the faithful servants. Two texts spring to mind: Lk 22:27 and Jn 13:14; this "master" is manifestly the Lord who welcomes his faithful servants to the Messianic feast. By this allegorical detail the message of the parable has been underlined. From v. 22 of the chapter onward Jesus had been speaking to his disciples (cf. v. 32); it is to them that the Waiting Servants is addressed, one of his frequent warnings to vigilance. The coming of the Son of man will be unexpected and watchfulness must characterize the attitude of the disciples who wait for his return.

39-40. The Thief at Night
(Mt 24:43f)

39 "But know this, that if the householder had known at what hour the thief was coming, he would have been awake and would not have left his house to be broken into. **40** You also must be ready; for the Son of man is coming at an hour you do not expect."

This little parable points to the uncertainty of the hour at which the Lord will return—he will come "like a thief in the night" (1 Thes 5:2; Lk 17:24; 21:34f). The householder is not in the same situation as the servants of the previous parable. They knew the night of their master's return—though not the precise hour—and so they could keep watch; but the householder has no idea when his house is going to be burglarized. Therefore the moral, expressed in v. 40, is not so much vigilance, as before, but preparedness: the Son of man will appear as judge at an unexpected moment. It is by association of ideas that the parable has been inserted here—the reference to watching in v. 39 and the mention of the coming of the Son of man in v. 40 match the theme of 12:35-38.

41-48. The Servant: Faithful or Unfaithful
(Mt 24:45-51)

41 Peter said, "Lord, are you telling this parable for us or for all?" **42** And the Lord said, "Who then is the faithful and wise steward, whom his master will set over his household, to give them their portion of food at the proper time? **43** Blessed is that servant whom his master when he comes will find so doing. **44** Truly I tell you, he will set him over all his possessions. **45** But if that servant says to himself, 'My master is delayed in coming,' and begins to beat the menservants and the maidservants, and to eat and drink and get drunk, **46** the master of that servant will come on a day when he does not expect him and at an hour he does not know, and will punish him, and put him with the unfaithful. **47** And that servant who knew his master's will, but did not make ready or act according to his will, shall receive a severe beating. **48** But he who did not know, and did what deserved a beating, shall receive a light beating. Every one to whom much is given, of him will much be required; and of him to whom men commit much they will demand the more."

41. The question is absent from Matthew and its style betrays the hand of Luke: it refers to the preceding parable of the Waiting Servants (12:36-38).

42-46. The parable deals with the alternative conduct of a servant whom his master would place in charge of his affairs while he himself was absent on a long journey. If he were to prove faithful he would be richly rewarded, but if he abused his authority he would be severely punished when the master had come and taken him by surprise. At v. 46b the parable has been allegorized: it is no longer an earthly master who stands there but the Son of man who has come as judge. Moreover, the parable has been reapplied. As Jesus spoke it, the servant set in authority represented Israel's leaders and perhaps, more specifically, the scribes: "The scribes and the Pharisees sit on Moses' seat" (Mt 23:2; cf. Lk 11:46-52), they are the religious leaders of the people—but they had betrayed their trust. The early Christians, however, interpreted it as a warning to the Church's leaders—a perfectly natural extension of its meaning. The new interpretation is neatly brought out by Peter's question.

47-48a. These verses (not in Matthew) have no more than a loose link with the parable; they introduce the fresh idea that the punishment of disobedience will be in proportion to knowledge of the master's will. Though now referred to the disciples, originally it would have contrasted the scribes' culpable rejection of Christ (they were the professional "searchers" of the Scripture that spoke of him, cf. Jn 5:39) with the far less culpable rejection by the ordinary people "who do not know the Law" (Jn 7:49).

48b. This saying stands on its own. The passive and the impersonal forms stand for the divine name and the verse might be rendered: "Of every one to whom God has given much will he require much; and of him to whom God has entrusted much will he demand the more." Though likely originally addressed to the religious leaders of Israel, the saying can be readily applied to the leaders of the new Israel.

49-53. The Moment of Truth
(Mt 10:34-36)

49 "I came to cast fire upon the earth; and would that it were already kindled! 50 I have a baptism to be baptized with; and how I am constrained until it is accomplished! 51 Do you think that I have come to give peace on earth? No, I tell you, but rather division; 52 for henceforth in one house there will be five divided, three against two and two against three; 53 they will be divided, father against son and son against father, mother against daughter and daughter against her mother, mother-in-law against her daughter-in-law and daughter-in-law against her mother-in-law."

The coming of Jesus marks a time of decision, a crisis in which none can be neutral.

49f. Proper to Luke, these verses may first be considered independently of their context. The fire which Jesus wishes to see kindled is that which purifies souls, a fire lighted on the Cross (cf. Jn 12:32). The "baptism" is the Passion which will "plunge" Jesus into a sea of suffering. Jesus is the bringer of salvation to men, but he is aware that the way to salvation is through suffering—through fire and water (cf. 22:41-44). But Luke has understood the saying in relation to vv. 51-53: Jesus is the "sign of contradiction" (2:34f).

51-53. Cf. Mt 10:34-36. Jesus is "set for the fall and rising of many in Israel" (2:34): men will be for or against him. The description of family dissension (a dramatic presentation of the division he brings) is based on Mi 7:6. In this passage of Luke we discern another Johannine contact, because it is a feature of the fourth gospel, to be met with again and again, that Christ, by his very presence, causes division: men must be for or against the light (cf. Jn 8:12; ch. 9).

54-59. The Signs of the Times
(Mt 16:2f; 5:25f)

54 He also said to the multitudes, "When you see a cloud rising in the west, you say at once, 'A shower is coming'; and so it happens. 55 And when you see the south wind blowing, you say, 'There will be scorching heat'; and it happens. 56 You hypocrites! You know how to interpret the appearance of earth and sky; but why do you not know how to interpret the present time?

57 "And why do you not judge for yourselves what is right? 58 As you go with your accuser before the magistrate, make an effort to settle with him on the way, lest he drag you to the judge, and the judge hand you over to the officer, and the officer put you in prison. 59 I tell you, you will never get out till you have paid the very last copper."

54-56. The images of Mt 16:2f are different but the idea is the same. In Palestine the southwest wind brings rain and the southeast wind is the *khamseen* or sirocco. The works and words of Jesus are the signs which herald a new age: the people *will not* discern these signs and they refuse to recognize the urgency of the hour.

57. This is Luke's link between the discernment of signs and the following parable.

58f. The little parable has been inserted by Matthew in the Sermon (5:25f). For Luke it is a parable of crisis: this is the judgment. The Jews who have misread the signs of the times are, whether they realize it or not, in the position of the accused: they must settle accounts with God, repent without delay. The following passage (13:1-9) sustains the thought of crisis and judgment.

13:1-9. The Call to Repentance

1 There were some present at that very time who told him of the Galileans whose blood Pilate had mingled with their sacrifices. 2 And he answered them, "Do you think that these Galileans were worse sinners than all the other Galileans, because they suffered thus? 3 I tell you, No; but unless you repent you will all likewise perish. 4 Or those eighteen upon whom the tower in Siloam fell and killed them, do you think that they were worse offenders than all the others who dwelt in Jerusalem? 5 I tell you, No; but unless you repent you will all likewise perish."

6 And he told them this parable: "A man had a fig tree planted in his vineyard; and he came seeking fruit on it and found none. 7 And he said to the vinedresser, 'Lo, these three years I have come seeking fruit on this fig tree, and I find none. Cut it down; why should it use up the ground?' 8 And he answered him, 'Let it alone, sir, this year also, till I dig about it and put on manure. 9 And if it bears fruit next year, well and good; but if not, you can cut it down.'"

The urgent need for Israel to take immediate action is illustrated by tragic incidents (vv. 1-5); a parable further emphasizes the last chance that is being proffered.

1. The episode is otherwise unknown. The Galileans, come to offer sacrifice in the Temple, had caused some disturbance; Pilate was capable of such ruthless methods (Josephus, *Ant.* XVIII, iii, 2; iv, 1).

2f. The Galileans who suffered so were not necessarily greater sinners than others; but their fate is a warning to all Jews, a call to repentance.

4f. "Tower in Siloam", that is, a tower built near the spring of Siloam in the valley southeast of Jerusalem; foundations unearthed in 1914 may be those of the tower in question. The incident is otherwise unknown. These disasters foreshadow the massacres and destruction of 70 A.D. when Jerusalem was taken by the Romans.

6-9. Luke, who has omitted the cursing of the fig tree (Mk 11:12-14; Mt 21:18-22), is alone in giving this parable of the Barren Fig Tree. The tree had come to fruit-bearing age some three years before, and since it gave every sign of remaining unfruitful the owner of the vineyard felt that it should be cut down. The vinedresser, however, pleaded for time; he would make a last supreme effort to save it—the putting on of manure was an unusual step. The fig tree symbolizes Israel (cf. Hos 9:10; Jer 8:13)—and, as in Jeremiah, a sterile Israel. Now the ax is laid to the root of the tree (Mt 3:10); this is the last chance. God's justice is tempered by his mercy, but this justice must be satisfied. If, in the short moment left, Israel does not bring forth the fruits of repentance the time of grace will have run out; the most loving patience must have an end. Throughout, the urgency of the hour is stressed and the warning is plain.

10-17. Healing of a Woman on the Sabbath

10 Now he was teaching in one of the synagogues on the sabbath. **11** And there was a woman who had had a spirit of infirmity for eighteen years; she was bent over and could not fully straighten herself. **12** And when Jesus saw her, he called her and said to her, "Woman, you are freed from your infirmity." **13** And he laid his hands upon her, and immediately she was made straight, and she praised God. **14** But the ruler of the synagogue, indignant because Jesus had healed on the sabbath, said to the people, "There are six days on which work ought to be done; come on those days and be healed, and not on the sabbath day." **15** Then the Lord answered him, "You hypocrites! Does not each of you on the sabbath untie his ox or his ass from the manger, and lead it away to water it? **16** And ought not this woman, a daughter of Abraham whom Satan bound for eighteen years, be loosed from this bond on the sabbath day?" **17** As he said this, all his adversaries were put to shame; and all the people rejoiced at all the glorious things that were done by him.

Proper to Luke. The emphasis is not on the miracle as such but on the ensuing discussion (cf. 6:9-11; 14:1-6). There is no real link between the episodes of this chapter.

10-13. The "spirit of infirmity" does not imply that the woman was possessed but, rather, attributes her disease to Satan who can afflict men (v. 16). Without being asked (cf. 6:8; 14:4) Jesus cured her.

14. The ruler of the synagogue regarded the healing as a breach of the law of sabbath rest (Dt 5:13), but instead of accusing Jesus he petulantly complained to the people.

15f. Jesus criticizes the narrow legalism and hypocrisy of the Pharisees who can make laws to safeguard their own material interest but care nothing for human suffering; they will look after animals and neglect a daughter of Abraham—one of the chosen people. "Daughter of Abraham" is a title of honor rarely attested; the use of this title is indicative of Jesus' courteous regard for women. The same legalistic and carping outlook blinds the rulers of Israel to the significance of the works of Jesus.

17. But the people rejoice over them.

18-21. The Mustard Seed and the Leaven
(Mt 13:31-33; Mk 4:30-32)

18 He said therefore, "What is the kingdom of God like? And to what shall I compare it? **19** It is like a grain of mustard seed which a man took and sowed in his garden; and it grew and became a tree, and the birds of the air made nests in its branches."

20 And again he said, "To what shall I compare the kingdom of God? **21** It is like leaven which a woman took and hid in three measures of meal, till it was all leavened."

18f. The phrase "it is like a grain of mustard seed" represents a rabbinical introduction formula which should really be rendered: it is the case with it (the kingdom) as with a grain of mustard seed. It follows that it is not the seed itself but what happens to the seed that is significant, and the kingdom is like the tree that grows out of the seed. The smallness of the mustard seed was proverbial (cf. Mk 4:31), and yet, in favorable conditions, it could grow into a shrub some ten feet high. For the nesting birds, cf. Dn 4:12; Ezek 17:23; 31:6, where a tree sheltering the birds is a symbol of a great empire embracing all peoples; it may be that for Luke the birds symbolize the Gentiles.

20f. Mark does not have the Leaven but in Matthew and Luke it is a companion parable to the Mustard Seed. Here again the kingdom is not being compared to leaven but to what happens when leaven is placed in a mass of dough prepared for baking; ultimately, the kingdom is like the leavened dough (cf. Rm 11:16). In our modern and Western way we tend to read in the Mustard Seed and in the Leaven the story of the sure growth of the kingdom from its tiny beginning, the slow but steady permeation of human society by the leaven of the gospel. At least we are prone to stress this aspect primarily and almost exclusively. It seems that those who first heard the parables would have regarded them in a different light.

The modern man, passing through the plowed field, thinks of what is going on beneath the soil, and envisages a biological development. The people of the Bible, passing through the same plow-land, look up and see miracle upon miracle, nothing less than resurrection from the dead. Thus did Jesus' audience understand the parables of the mustard seed and the leaven as parables of contrast. Their meaning is that out of the most insignificant beginnings, invisible to human eye, God creates his mighty kingdom, which embraces all the peoples of the world.[45]

Both parables would have been the answer of Jesus to an objection, latent or expressed: could the kingdom really come from such inauspicious beginnings? His reply is that the little cell of disciples will indeed become a kingdom, and the little lump of

---

[45] J. Jeremias, *The Parables of Jesus* (New York: Scribner's, 1964), p. 149.

leaven will do its work. Although, in these parables, the contrast between insignificant beginning and mighty achievement is primary, there is also present the idea of growth—the seed grows into a plant; and of permeation—the leaven does ferment the mass. Indeed, the action of the leaven has a lesson of its own: it is a hidden activity but it is not quiet—it is pervasive, resistless. Looked at in this way the growth of the seed is also irresistible; it is a miracle of God's action. For, in the last analysis, if the kingdom does reach its full dimensions it is not due to anything in the men who are the seed of the kingdom; the growth is due solely to the power of God (cf. 1 Cor 3:6-7). That is why Jesus can speak with utter confidence of the final stage of the kingdom. The finest comment on these parables, bringing out this special aspect, is another parable of his, given only by Mark, the Seed Growing Secretly.

> It is with the kingdom of God as with a man who has scattered seed upon the ground: whether he sleeps or rises, night or day, the seed sprouts and grows—he knows not how. Of itself the earth produces first the blade, then the ear, then the full grain in the ear. And when the grain is ripe, at once he puts in the sickle because the harvest has come (4:26-29).

22-30. The Closed Door
(Mt 7:13f; 25:10f; 7:22f; 8:11f)

22 He went on his way through towns and villages, teaching, and journeying toward Jerusalem. **23** And some one said to him, "Lord, will those who are saved be few?" And he said to them, **24** "Strive to enter by the narrow door; for many, I tell you, will seek to enter and will not be able. **25** When once the householder has risen up and shut the door, you will begin to stand outside and to knock at the door, saying, 'Lord, open to us.' He will answer you, 'I do not know where you come from.' **26** Then you will begin to say, 'We ate and drank in your presence, and you taught in our streets.' **27** But he will say, 'I tell you, I do not know where you come from; depart from me, all you workers of iniquity!' **28** There you will weep and gnash your teeth, when you see Abraham and Isaac and Jacob and all the prophets in the kingdom of God and you yourselves thrust out. **29** And men will come from east and west, and from north and south, and sit at table in the kingdom of God. **30** And behold, some are last who will be first, and some are first who will be last."

In this passage various sayings of Jesus—which are found isolated in Matthew—have been built into a parable. It is unlikely that the fusion is due to Luke; it is more probable that the evangelist found the passage in his source and that he reproduced it as he had found it.

22. A reminder of the journey.

23f. This question was a current one and the regular answer was that all Israel would have a place in the future kingdom; even the ordinary people, though "ignorant of the Law" (Jn 7:49), would not be excluded—only tax collectors and suchlike, "sinners", would be debarred. Though the question is concerned solely with the salvation of Israel it is still one that Jesus refused to answer directly. Instead, he warned his questioners that an effort is demanded of them: it is no easy matter to lay hold on eternal life (cf. Mt 7:13f). V. 24b is explained by the following verses.

25-27. In v. 25 we are dealing no longer with a narrow door but with a closed door, and the image is now that of the Messianic banquet. A comparison with Mt 25:10f indicates that the master here is Jesus himself. The Jews had not accepted him, they had not entered into the kingdom while they had the chance; now it is too late, the door is firmly closed. This explains, too, why those of v. 24b are unable to enter. While in Mt 7:22f the rejected ones are unworthy Christians, here (vv. 26f) they are still the Jews. It is not enough for them to have been contemporaries of Jesus, to have seen him, to have heard him, to have eaten with him; they had not accepted him and now they are cast off.

28f. Their chagrin will be all the greater when they see not only their own great ancestors but the Gentiles, too, present at the banquet. These same verses, in Mt 8:11f, conclude the account of the cure of the centurion's servant.

30. A familiar secondary conclusion (cf. Mk 10:31; Mt 19:30; 20:16) added here in view of the contrast between Gentiles and Jews (vv. 28f).

It is obvious that the greater part of this passage is in the spirit of the parables of crisis and the sayings from v. 25 onwards are so many warnings to Israel. What is not so easy to see is why the sayings should have been built into a new parable since concern with the fate of the Jews was not a prevalent preoccupation of the early Church; indeed the tendency was to give a wider interpretation to specifically Jewish parables. But the tension between Jews and Gentiles did exist and this passage reflects it. It is also, in its way, a commentary—in his own words—on Jesus' answer to the question of v. 23, an emphasizing of the warning implied in the "narrow door".

31-33. Herod

31 At that very hour some Pharisees came, and said to him, "Get away from here, for Herod wants to kill you." 32 And he said to them, "Go and tell that fox, 'Behold, I cast out demons and perform cures today and tomorrow and the third day I finish my course. 33 Nevertheless I must go on my way today and tomorrow and the day following; for it cannot be that a prophet should perish away from Jerusalem."

31. Jesus is still in the territory of Herod Antipas (cf. 3:1) and, more likely, in Galilee than in Peraea. The "warning", significantly brought by Pharisees, is more probably a ruse of "that fox" (v. 32) to get Jesus out of his territory—he did not want a disturbance sparked by Messianic hopes.

32f. Jesus will continue to do his great works for a short while yet ("today and tomorrow"); then, in due time ("the third day") he will finish his task (cf. Jn 19:30). Nevertheless, Herod need not worry, for Jesus must soon be on his way to Jerusalem—that is the fate of a prophet (cf. 2 Chr 24:20-22; Jer 26:20-23; 2 Kg 21:16). Until then, however, his hour has not come (cf. Jn 7:30; 8:30).

34-35. Lament over Jerusalem
(Mt 23:37-39)

34 "O Jerusalem, Jerusalem, killing the prophets and stoning those who are sent to you! How often would I have gathered your children together as a hen gathers her brood under her wings, and you would not! 35 Behold, your house is forsaken. And I tell you, you will not see me until you say, 'Blessed is he who comes in the name of the Lord!'"

In Matthew this apostrophe forms the conclusion of a series of "woes" against the scribes and Pharisees; here it has been added because of "Jerusalem" in v. 33.

34. Jerusalem had consistently rejected or maltreated God's representatives: cf. Jer 26:20-23; 2 Chr 24:20-22; Ac 7:52; Heb 11:32,37. Like Yahweh ("like birds hovering, so the Lord of hosts will protect Jerusalem; he will protect and deliver it, he will spare and rescue it"—Is 31:5), Jesus would save the inhabitants of the city from the ruin that threatens them—but they will not have it so.

35. Now it is too late—Jesus abandons Jerusalem to its fate (cf. Jer 22:5). Yet the prospect is not one of unrelieved gloom: Jerusalem will one day acknowledge her Messiah (in the words of Ps 118[117]:26). This verse joins Lk 21:24, Rm 11:25f, and Apoc 11:2 in heralding the salvation of Israel.

14:1-24. A MEAL IN THE HOUSE OF A PHARISEE

The following four episodes, the first three proper to Luke, are set in the context of a meal to which Jesus had been invited. This setting is editorial and the link verses betray the hand of Luke (cf. 14:7,12).

1-6. Healing of a Man with Dropsy

1 One sabbath when he went to dine at the house of a ruler who belonged to the Pharisees, they were watching him. **2** And behold, there was a man before him who had dropsy. **3** And Jesus spoke to the lawyers and Pharisees, saying, "Is it lawful to heal on the sabbath, or not?" **4** But they were silent. Then he took him and healed him, and let him go. **5** And he said to them, "Which of you, having an ass or an ox that has fallen into a well, will not immediately pull him out on a sabbath day?" And they could not reply to this.

1. Once again Jesus receives, and accepts, an invitation from a Pharisee (cf. 7:36; 11:37); his adversaries hope that they may discover grounds for further accusations against him.

2-4. Following Oriental custom the man was free to enter the house. Jesus, knowing the thoughts of those who watched him so jealously, anticipated their objection and went on the offensive (cf. 6:6-11; 13:13-17). Despite their disapproving silence he cured the man.

5f. Cf. Mt 12:11; Lk 13:15. The reading *huios,* "son", is preferable to *onos,* "ass". The implication of the question is obvious and, as in 13:17, he lawyers and Pharisees maintained an embarrassed silence. *Tinos humōn* (literally, "which of you") has its normal meaning at the head of a similitude or parable: "can you imagine that any of you . . . ?" (cf. 11:5).

7-11. Places at Table

7 Now he told a parable to those who were invited, when he marked how they chose the places of honor, saying to them, 8 "When you are invited by any one to a marriage feast, do not sit down in a place of honor, lest a more eminent man than you be invited by him; 9 and he who invited you both will come and say to you, 'Give place to this man,' and then you will begin with shame to take the lowest place. 10 But when you are invited, go and sit in the lowest place, so that when your host comes he may say to you, 'Friend, go up higher'; then you will be honored in the presence of all who sit at table with you. 11 For every one who exalts himself will be humbled, and he who humbles himself will be exalted."

At first sight this seems to be a lesson in etiquette. Luke, however, calls it a *parabolē,* and though the underlying Hebrew term *mashal* (Aramaic = *mathla*) is wide enough to include a practical rule of conduct, his meaning is more specific. Later on the scribes are characterized as those who love "the places of honor at feasts" (20:46); in our text, such conduct, presented in parabolic guise, is censured and made the object of a warning.

7-9. One who has seated himself "in a place of honor" must yield to the eminent guest for whom that place had been reserved and, since the intermediary places will have been filled, must take the lowest place.

10. Cf. Prv 25:7—"It is better to be told 'come up here', than to be put lower in the presence of the prince."

11. The key to the passage, this saying also occurs in 18:14, as a generalizing conclusion to the Pharisee and the Publican. Here, however, it is in its proper place. The passive stands for the action of God ("For everyone who exalts himself will God humble, and him who humbles himself will God exalt"), and the future tense refers to the judgment (cf. 14:14). We are taken beyond the perspective of human relations and assured that God is no respecter of persons. Now the drift of the parable is clear. If the scribes and Pharisees arrogated to themselves privileges and demanded preferential treatment, they did so on the grounds of their observance of the Law, on their standing as religious men. They took for granted that God would see things in this way too and render them the like preferential treatment, the first places in the kingdom; here they are quietly warned that they may be fortunate to get the lowest places. It is not difficult to see that the warning could with reason, if not always with profit, have sounded down the centuries, and could continue to ring, in the ears of the professed religious men of the Christian Church.

12-14. The Choice of Guests

12 He said also to the man who had invited him, "When you give a dinner or a banquet, do not invite your friends or your brothers or your kinsmen or rich neighbors, lest they also invite you in return, and you be repaid. **13** But when you give a feast, invite the poor, the maimed, the lame, the blind, **14** and you will be blessed, because they cannot repay you. You will be repaid at the resurrection of the just."

No more than the preceding parable is this passage meant as practical advice. Rather, Jesus teaches that a limited and interested love is worthless in the sight of God (cf. 6:32-34). The passage is a commentary on 6:35.

14b. Those who act from motives of disinterested charity will receive their reward at the resurrection—they will take their place at the Messianic feast. Here Luke's concern for the poor and afflicted is manifest; he sees the following parable as an illustration of vv. 12-14 (cf. v. 21).

15-24. The Great Feast
(Mt 22:1-10)

15 When one of those who sat at table with him heard this, he said to him, "Blessed is he who shall eat bread in the kingdom of God!" **16** But he said to him. "A man once gave a great banquet, and invited many; **17** and at the time for the banquet he sent his servant to say to those who had been invited, 'Come; for all is now ready.' **18** But they all alike began to make excuses. The first said to him, 'I have bought a field, and I must go out and see it; I pray you, have me excused.' **19** Another said 'I have bought five yoke of oxen, and I go to examine them; I pray you, have me excused.' **20** And another said 'I have married a wife, and therefore I cannot come.' **21** So the servant came and reported this to his master. Then the householder in anger said to his servant, 'Go out quickly to the streets and lanes of the city, and bring in the poor and maimed and blind and lame.' **22** And the servant said, 'Sir, what you commanded has been done, and still there is room.' **23** And the master said to the servant, 'Go out to the highways and hedges, and compel people to come in, that my house may be filled. **24** For I tell you, none of those men who were invited shall taste my banquet.'"

15. The exclamation follows the mention of recompense in v. 14b; the feast is a common Jewish figure for the kingdom (cf. 12:37; Mt 22:1f). Lagrange remarks somewhat acidly that though the reflection is a pious one, it seems to result from *cette piété facile qu'ont quelque personnes après un bon repas.*[46]

16-24. This is a straightforward parable and must be close to the original Aramaic form. Mt 22:1-10 represents a later version: the dinner party has become the wedding feast of a king's son; the parable has been allegorized and part of another parable has been added by way of conclusion (Mt 22:11-14).

17. The servant was sent to remind the guests of an invitation issued (and accepted) some time before—the last-minute excuses are all the more offensive.

18-20. These excuses are vain: in each case the situation could have been foreseen and, anyhow, an absence of some hours would not seriously affect these business and household affairs; v. 20 has in mind Dt 24:5.

21-23. The double summoning of the ultimate guests would seem to point to an allegorical development. Those within the city (v. 21) are doubtless the publicans and sinners, and so we have the familiar contrast between them and the rejected leaders of the people (vv. 18-20,24). Then, the invitation to those outside the city (v. 23) can refer to the Gentiles; the intention is not quite certain but a special interest in the Gentile mission does appear to indicate a Lucan touch here.

24. The essential point of the parable is, very clearly, the refusal of the invited guests and their replacement by others. Jesus addresses the parable to his critics and opponents, in defense of the gospel and of his own conduct and as a warning to them.

[46] *Op. cit.*, p. 403.

They, the scribes and Pharisees, are like the guests who made
light of the invitation and would not accept it. Hence, he tells
them, God has called the poor and outcasts and has offered them
the salvation which they had rejected. For, ultimately, the parable explains why the "poor and maimed and blind and lame"—
who stand for the tax collectors and sinners, those classes despised by the Pharisees (cf. 15:1f)—have won their way into the
kingdom. It is a parable of mercy.

25-35. The Cost of Discipleship
(Mt 10:37f; 5:13; Mk 9:50)

25 Now great multitudes accompanied him; and he turned and said
to them, 26 "If any one comes to me and does not hate his own father
and mother and wife and children and brothers and sisters, yes, and
even his own life, he cannot be my disciple. 27 Whoever does not bear
his own cross and come after me, cannot be my disciple. 28 For which
of you, desiring to build a tower, does not first sit down and count the
cost, whether he has enough to complete it? 29 Otherwise, when he
has laid a foundation, and is not able to finish, all who see it begin to
mock him, 30 saying, 'This man began to build, and was not able to
finish.' 31 Or what king, going to encounter another king in war, will
not sit down first and take counsel whether he is able with ten thousand to meet him who comes against him with twenty thousand?
32 And if not, while the other is yet a great way off, he sends an
embassy and asks terms of peace. 33 So therefore, whoever of you
does not renounce all that he has cannot be my disciple.
34 "Salt is good; but if salt has lost its taste, how shall its saltness
be restored? 35 It is fit neither for the land nor for the dunghill; men
throw it away. He who has ears to hear, let him hear."

Luke has set the two parables (vv. 28-33) in the context of
self-renunciation.

25. This link-verse is a Lucan composition (cf. 12:1).

26f. Cf. 9:23 = Mk 8:34; Mt 10:37f. The exhortation is couched
in its strongest terms ("hate" here means detachment), and the
situation envisaged is the (relatively) rare one in which a man
is called upon to choose between the following of Christ and his
own relatives; in Matthew the situation is more explicitly one of
persecution.

27. Here "to carry the cross" means to be prepared to face
death (cf. 9:23). The disciple of Jesus must be prepared to lay

down his life; he is like one condemned to death, carrying the instrument of execution (cf. Jn 19:17).

28-32. The twin parables drive home the lesson that discipleship does involve commitment; it cannot be undertaken thoughtlessly. Though the parables appear to repeat each other they are, in fact, complementary. In the first, the builder is free to undertake his construction or not; he is considering the matter in the abstract. The king, on the other hand, is already up against it: his country has been invaded (the other king is "advancing against him"), therefore he must act. "In the first parable Jesus says, 'Sit down and reckon whether you can afford to follow me.' In the second he says, 'Sit down and reckon whether you can afford to refuse my demands.'" [47] For, indeed, there are the two factors in the call to follow Christ: we have to count the cost both of accepting that invitation and of rejecting it. He who comes to Christ must come with his eyes wide open.

The parables may seem discouraging but they are to be understood in much the same way as the saying of v. 26. The following of Christ is at all times a serious business and, in certain circumstances, it can be a very serious business indeed. This is true, for instance, in time of persecution; it is scarcely less true in the modern world where the Christian is called upon to renounce so much that is taken for granted by others. If he does come after his Master he must be prepared to take up his cross and carry it (v. 27), while at the same time he cannot, without sin, fail to live up to his obligations as a Christian. The encouraging thing is that Christ who calls him knows the cost involved and knows, too, human frailty and will lavish his grace on one who really tries to answer his call.

33. This was likely added by Luke, in the light of vv. 26f, and is a practical consequence of the parables rather than their moral.

34f. Matthew has the saying in the Sermon (5:13) and Mark has a shorter form of it (9:50). Luke, in typical manner, hardens the image and accentuates the uselessness of the savorless salt. In his context the saying warns of the fate of a disciple who has lost the spirit of total commitment to his Master.

[47] A. M. Hunter, *Interpreting the Parables* (London: SCM Press, 1960), p. 84.

15:1-32. THE PARABLES OF MERCY

1-3. The Setting

1 Now the tax collectors and sinners were all drawing near to hear him. 2 And the Pharisees and the scribes murmured, saying, "This man receives sinners and eats with them."
3 So he told them this parable:

Luke has explicitly established the original *Sitz im Leben* of the three parables of this chapter. The tax collectors and sinners (people who led immoral lives or whose work was regarded as incompatible with observance of the Law) were flocking to Jesus and listening to him, and the Pharisees and scribes, who regarded such people as outcasts, were scandalized by these goings-on: "so he told them this parable" (i.e. the Lost Sheep) and followed it with the Lost Coin. Immediately after the latter we read, "And he said" (v. 11), and then comes the Prodigal Son. In other words, the parables are a reply to the charge of the Pharisees: Jesus defends his conduct. He consorts with sinners precisely because he knows that God is a loving Father who welcomes the repentant sinner. God does not regard sinners as outcasts but follows them with love and receives them tenderly when they come back to him.

4-7. The Lost Sheep
(Mt 18:12-14)

4 "What man of you, having a hundred sheep, if he has lost one of them, does not leave the ninety-nine in the wilderness, and go after the one which is lost, until he finds it? 5 And when he has found it, he lays it on his shoulders, rejoicing. 6 And when he comes home, he calls together his friends and his neighbors, saying to them, 'Rejoice with me, for I have found my sheep which was lost.' 7 Just so, I tell you there will be more joy in heaven over one sinner who repents than over ninety-nine righteous persons who need no repentance."

Jesus tells of the shepherd who went in search of the sheep that was lost and of his joy when he had found the stray. The solicitude of the man is such that he leaves the ninety-nine in the desert, that is, in the scanty pasture of the Judean hill-country, most likely in charge of a fellow shepherd, while he searches for the others. And his joy at finding the lost sheep is so great that he must tell his neighbors of it. The moral of the story is stated in emphatic terms: God will rejoice ("joy in heaven" is a circumlocution) that, together with the just, he can also welcome home the repentant sinner. Or we might render the verse: "Thus God, at the Last Judgment, will rejoice more over one sinner who has repented, than over ninety-nine respectable persons, who have not committed any gross sin." That is why Jesus seeks out sinners, while the scribes and Pharisees, by caviling at his conduct, are criticizing the divine goodness.

8-10. The Lost Coin

8 "Or what woman, having ten silver coins, if she loses one coin, does not light a lamp and sweep the house and seek diligently until she finds it? 9 And when she has found it, she calls together her friends and neighbors, saying, 'Rejoice with me, for I have found the coin which I had lost.' 10 Just so, I tell you, there is joy before the angels of God over one sinner who repents."

Peculiar to Luke. This parable is parallel to the other; it is typical of the evangelist that he has brought a woman into the picture. The drachmas ("silver coins") represent a modest sum—the drachma was about sixteen cents—but the loss of even one coin is of great concern to a woman in humble circumstances. She had to light a lamp because the small windowless house—the only opening being a low door—was in near darkness. The phrase "before the angels of God" (v. 10) is a periphrastic rendering of the divine name: "God will rejoice" (cf. v. 7; 12:8f). The two parables consider the conversion of a sinner from God's point of view: he rejoices that the lost should return home, because they are his; he rejoices because he can forgive. God has sent his Son "to seek out and to save the lost" (19:10), and Jesus' actual concern for sinners is a concrete proof that God does more than desire that sinners should repent.

11-32. The Loving Father
(The Prodigal Son)

11 And he said, "There was a man who had two sons; 12 and the younger of them said to his father, 'Father, give me the share of property that falls to me.' And he divided his living between them. 13 Not

many days later, the younger son gathered all he had and took his journey into a far country, and there he squandered his property in loose living. 14 And when he had spent everything, a great famine arose in that country, and he began to be in want. 15 So he went and joined himself to one of the citizens of that country, who sent him into his fields to feed swine. 16 And he would gladly have fed on the pods that the swine ate; and no one gave him anything. 17 But when he came to himself he said, 'How many of my father's hired servants have bread enough and to spare, but I perish here with hunger! 18 I will arise and go to my father, and I will say to him, "Father, I have sinned against heaven and before you; 19 I am no longer worthy to be called your son; treat me as one of your hired servants."' 20 And he arose and came to his father. But while he was yet at a distance, his father saw him and had compassion and ran and embraced him and kissed him. 21 And the son said to him, 'Father, I have sinned against heaven and before you; I am no longer worthy to be called your son.' 22 But the father said to his servants, 'Bring quickly the best robe, and put it on him; and put a ring on his hand, and shoes on his feet; 23 and bring the fatted calf and kill it, and let us eat and make merry; 24 for this my son was dead, and is alive again; he was lost, and is found.' And they began to make merry.

25 "Now his elder son was in the field; and as he came and drew near to the house, he heard music and dancing. 26 And he called one of the servants and asked what this meant. 27 And he said to him, 'Your brother has come, and your father has killed the fatted calf, because he has received him safe and sound.' 28 But he was angry and refused to go in. His father came out and entreated him, 29 but he answered his father, 'Lo, these many years I have served you, and I never disobeyed your command; yet you never gave me a kid, that I might make merry with my friends. 30 But when this son of yours came, who has devoured your living with harlots, you killed for him the fatted calf!' 31 And he said to him, 'Son, you are always with me, and all that is mine is yours. 32 It was fitting to make merry and be glad, for this your brother was dead, and is alive; he was lost, and is found.'"

Peculiar to Luke. This, the most widely known and best-loved parable, might be better named the "Loving Father" (instead of the familiar "Prodigal Son").

11f. The parable speaks of *two* sons, a point sometimes overlooked (cf. Mt 21:28-31). *"There was a man who had two sons, and he lost them both, one in a foreign country, the other behind a barrier of self-righteousness. The elder contrived, without leaving home, to be as far away from his father as ever his brother was in the heathen pigsty. Both brothers were selfish, though in totally different ways. The selfishness of the younger brother was a reckless love of life. . . . The selfishness of the older brother was less obvious and less vulnerable. He asked for nothing, desired nothing, enjoyed nothing. He devoted himself dutifully to his father's service, never disobeying a command of his father, and thought, no doubt, that he was the model of unselfishness; yet he himself was the center of his every thought, so that he was incapable of entering sympathetically into his father's joys and sorrows." [48] According to the prescription of Dt 21:17 the share of the younger of two sons would be one-third of his father's property.

13. "Gathered" (*synagagōn*) is better rendered "realized"— the younger son turned his portion into cash. The journey to a "far country" is not unusual for, at the time, the Jews of the Diaspora numbered about four million, against half a million in Palestine.

14-16. In famine conditions no one had any thought for an impoverished foreigner. His degradation is great: a Jew minding pigs; for that matter the pigs are better treated than he, for they at least were given something to eat.

17-19. At last he came to his senses and realized that his father's servants were infinitely better off than he was in his present state. He determined to go back home and already began to rehearse the plea he would address to his father.

20-24. The father had not forgotten his son and now ran forward to welcome him tenderly and give him the kiss of forgiveness (cf. Sm 14:33). The son could get through the first part only of his little speech, for the father hastened to clothe him in fine garments (a mark of distinction) and had a signet ring (an indication of authority—cf. 1 Mc 6:15) put on his finger (cf. Gn 41:42). Similarly, he was given shoes for he was no barefoot servant but a son of the family: he is fully reinstated. Then followed a joyful feast with song and dance.

25-28a. The elder son, a sober, industrious type, had been about his work when the other arrived, and he knew nothing of his homecoming until he heard the sounds of merry-making.

28b-30. When he found out what the rejoicing was all about,

---

[48] G. B. Caird, *op. cit.*, p. 182.

he sulked and refused to go in. His father came to plead with him but, angrily, he broke into his father's entreaties. He had slaved all his life, had always done what he was told, but nobody had ever thought of throwing a party for *him!*

31f. His father gently pointed out that he need have no fear of being displaced, for he was the heir; but he really ought to enter into the spirit of the occasion and rejoice at the return of his brother.

The parable is two-pronged (vv. 11-24, 25-32) and the emphasis falls on the second point; both parts conclude with almost identical words (vv. 24, 32). The younger son and the father thinly veil the sinner and his God. The sinner goes his unthinking way and is brought up short only when his world breaks in pieces about him; but a loving God is looking for his return. So is God, Jesus says, so incredibly good. In the context the elder son represents the scribes and Pharisees: he, stirred no doubt by jealousy, is offended by the generosity of his father; the Pharisees and scribes cavil at the goodness of God. The parable teaches not only God's love for the sinner but shows us, too, the loving condescension of Jesus who so quietly justified his conduct in the eyes of these self-righteous men. He pointed out how wrong their attitude was, but he did not condemn. They, too, even if they did not know it, were prodigal children.

The whole of the following chapter (with the exception of 16:16-18) is a collection of parables and sayings of Jesus on the use and abuse of money.

16:1-8. The Unjust Steward

1 He also said to the disciples, "There was a rich man who had a steward, and charges were brought to him that this man was wasting his goods. **2** And he called him and said to him, 'What is this that I hear about you? Turn in the account of your stewardship, for you can no longer be steward.' **3** And the steward said to himself, 'What shall I do, since my master is taking the stewardship away from me? I am not strong enough to dig, and I am ashamed to beg. **4** I have decided what to do, so that people may receive me into their house when I am put out of the stewardship.' **5** So, summoning his master's debtors one by one, he said to the first, 'How much do you owe my master?' **6** He said, 'A hundred measures of oil.' And he said to him, 'Take your bill, and sit down quickly and write fifty.' **7** Then he said to another, 'And how much do you owe?' He said, 'A hundred measures of wheat.' He

said to him, 'Take your bill, and write eighty.' 8 The master commended the dishonest steward for his prudence; for the sons of this
world are wiser in their own generation than the sons of light.

Proper to Luke. This parable has always caused grave embarrassment to commentators; indeed the inherent difficulty of interpretation is manifest in the text of Luke. We shall be content
with an outline of two interpretations.

(1) Like the unjust judge (18:1-5) the steward is called dishonest because of malpractice in the past; it does not necessarily
follow that his action in the present case is dishonest. In the
Palestinian setting of this parable, the standing of the steward
has to be measured by the Jewish law governing agency. The
agent (steward) was not a paid factor or broker, but fully represented his master to the extent that the latter must honor his
agent's business transactions. If the agent were to swindle his
master, no legal action could be taken against him to recover the
loss; his punishment would consist in reproaches, loss of character, and dismissal. After he had received notice of dismissal the
steward had to give an account of the state of the property; this
would take some time to prepare and, until he had submitted it,
he remained his master's agent, legally authorized to act in his
name.

Also of first importance here is the attitude to usury. The law
on usury forbade the taking of interest from Jews on loans of any
kind (Ex 22:25; Lv 25:36; Dt 23:19f); but ways had been found
of evading this law. It was argued that the law was meant to
protect the destitute from exploitation; if, then, it could be shown
that a prospective borrower already possessed some of the com-
modity he wished to borrow and was under no immediate necessity to borrow the object in question, a loan could be considered
unobjectionable. In this way, by a legal fiction, large commercial
transactions might be arranged, without infringing the letter of
the law. It seems that transactions in terms of oil and wheat
could be arranged, without scruple, by the pious Jew who wished
to enter into a contract which was not biblically usurious, since
a debtor would surely have enough oil to light a lamp or enough
wheat to bake a cake—and so was not destitute. Hence, in the
parable, oil and wheat have been deliberately chosen. However,

the interest on these commodities varied greatly: on wheat it was about 25%, but on olive oil (which varied considerably in quality and could be adulterated by the addition of cheaper oils) it might be 100%. Again, the parable reflects this situation. In view of the nature of such a contract there was no witness to it. The steward of the parable simply hands back to his master's debtors their promissory notes (which undertook the payment of principal plus interest) and requests them to write new ones which obliged them to repay the principal only.

For the meaning of the parable we should note that the steward seeks the approbation of public opinion—the "people" of v. 4. Hence he does what the Law of God requires: he ceases to exact usury. He need not fear his master's resentment; indeed he suspects that his master will ratify his action and will take credit for pious conduct which he did not initiate. And, in fact (v. 8a), the master, realizing the situation, turned the steward's action to his own advantage and posed as a man of piety—"giving us an impression of the pious man who somehow omits to do the right thing until the perfect opportunity is presented to him." [49]

The meaning of the parable, then, is that one who knows his moral duty and has been neglecting it for the sake of worldly advantage is forced by circumstances connected with earlier imprudence and misjudgment to reconsider his position and seek the goodwill of those whose opinion he had neglected. V. 8b is the moral of the parable: "The worldly know both when to do the right thing, why to do it, and what means to employ while doing so; we are not to imitate them and outdo them, but are to understand their conduct as proof that our scruples are on the one hand too sensitive and on the other hand not sensitive enough." [50] V. 9 is the application of the parable, a direct exhortation that "unrighteous mammon" (money legally acquired, according to the law of man, but tainted in God's sight—like the money obtained by the sharp practice explained above) must be employed in God's service; it can even win a way into the eternal tabernacles.

This study does throw light on the background of the parable

---

[49] J. D. M. Derrett, "Fresh Light on St. Luke XVI" in *New Testament Studies* 7 (1960-61), pp. 216f.

[50] *Ibid.*, p. 365.

and the interpretation offered may point to its original meaning. But this is by no means certain and, anyhow, it does not seem that Luke understands it in this way. For him, as we shall see, the *kyrios* (and this is vital for the interpretation of the parable) is more likely to be Jesus than the steward's master.

(2) It would seem that, on the whole, another interpretation of the Unjust Steward—if we try to see it from Luke's viewpoint—is preferable.

1f. Luke refers the parable to disciples, but this may not have been its original destination. The steward accused of malpractice is about to be dismissed.

3f. Rejecting honest procedure, he thinks up, with total lack of scruple, a manner of safeguarding his future—at the cost of his master. The verb *dexontai* is not impersonal ("people may receive me") but refers to the debtors of v. 5: "they may receive me".

5f. "One by one"—the business had to be done discreetly! The "measure" (v. 6) is a *bath* (about five gallons).

7. The "measure" is a *cor* (about six bushels). One *cor* = ten *baths*, but since the price of oil was much higher than the price of wheat, the value of fifty baths of oil and twenty cors of wheat (the amount the debtors gained by the transaction) would be the same.

8. The precise meaning of *kyrios* ("Lord", "master") determines the limit of the parable. The steward's master may be meant and the verse is part of the parable; in that case v. 9 brings out the moral. However, it is preferable to take *kyrios* as meaning "Lord" and so as referring to Jesus (in Luke *ho kyrios* almost always means Jesus). Especially noteworthy is 18:6-8 which has the very same pattern as 16:8f—"The Lord said" (18:6); "I tell you" (18:8). We take it, then, that the parable ends at v. 7 and describes a rascal who, suddenly faced with a crisis which may mean utter ruin, finds a drastic means of coping with the situation. The method he adopts in order to ensure his future, though unscrupulous, is manifestly resourceful. In v. 8a we have the application of the parable by Jesus: "And the Lord commended the unjust steward for his resolute action." The remainder of the verse (which must surely be a comment of Jesus himself—thus further suggesting that he is the *kyrios* of v. 8a) explains this unexpected commendation: it is restricted to the cleverness of worldly men ("the sons of this world") in their dealings with one another ("with their like" rather than "in their generation"—RSV); "sons of light" is a Johannine (and Qumran) phrase (cf. Jn 12:36). Like the unjust steward, the hearers of the parable (in v. 14 Luke reckons Pharisees among the audience) stand before a crisis—they must act resolutely or perish. In the Person of Jesus the kingdom of God has come among them; it is the decisive moment and, in effect, they are being urged to take the bold step of accepting him—before it is too late. But, as the gospel stands, the parable is addressed to the disciples (16:1), for so it was understood by the early Church. Yet, despite the change of audience, the point and message of it remain very much the same. For if Jesus could wish that Pharisees would recognize the hour of grace, he must surely also wish that his disciples would show as much resourcefulness in God's business as men of the world do in their own affairs.

9-13. The Right Use of Money

9 "And I tell you, make friends for yourselves by means of unrighteous mammon, so that when it fails they may receive you into the eternal habitations.
10 "He who is faithful in a very little is faithful also in much; and he who is dishonest in a very little is dishonest also in much. 11 If then you have not been faithful in the unrighteous mammon, who will entrust to you the true riches? 12 And if you have not been faithful in that which is another's, who will give you that which is your own? 13 No servant can serve two masters; for either he will hate the one and love the other, or he will be devoted to the one and despise the other. You cannot serve God and mammon."

The parable is difficult and these appended verses—added by the familiar technique of catchwords—show how the early Christian teachers wrestled with it. The links are "unrighteous mammon" in vv. 9 and 11, "faithful" in vv. 10-12, and "mammon" in v. 13; while verses 9-11 are further linked by the repetition of *adikos* ("unrighteous", "dishonest").

9. In v. 8 we have the original application of the parable; now we find a different application. The meaning of the verse taken by itself seems to be: "Do good works with the unjust mammon,

that when it passes away, God may receive you into eternal dwellings." In rabbinical terminology good works are "friends"— they speak on one's behalf; the impersonal "they may receive", a reverential circumlocution, avoids the divine name. The saying, added here through verbal association (the reception into eternal habitation echoes the steward's wish in v. 4), may have been originally addressed to tax collectors or others trafficking in "unjust mammon" (or "filthy lucre"). Attached to the parable, it points to a new interpretation: the steward is commended for his wise use of money and the lesson for Christians is clear—they are to use the goods of this world in view of eternal life.

10-13. These verses are meant to answer the difficulty raised by the steward's unscrupulous conduct: how can he be, in any sense, an example? V. 10 states a general principle of conduct with regard to honesty or dishonesty in unimportant matters; in vv. 11f the principle is applied to mammon and to everlasting riches. In view of the parallelism between vv. 11 and 12, it is clear that "that which is another's" and "your own" of v. 12 mean, respectively, the material wealth that must remain external to a man ("unrighteous mammon") and the true spiritual riches ("the true riches") which are his very own. The problem of the steward's conduct is solved: he is no longer an example but a warning. He has shown himself dishonest in very little, in the goods of this world; he may find shelter under the roofs of his equally unscrupulous friends, but he has no place in the eternal dwellings. V. 13 occurs in an entirely different context in Mt 6:24; it epitomizes the obligation and the unending struggle of the Christian life.

It is clear, then, that vv. 9-13 are isolated sayings joined by catchwords, and together they form an elaborate secondary ending to the parable. It is noteworthy that these additions leave the substance of the parable unchanged, but they do bear witness to a reinterpretation of a parable which is now applied by the primitive Church to the Christian community. It is, however, an application that is very much in the line of the parable as Jesus spoke it. The resolute action which he recommends does embrace the generosity of v. 9, the faithfulness of vv. 10-11, and the rejection of mammon in v. 13. The early Christians did not miss the point of the parable but, applying it to themselves, they necessarily caused a shift of emphasis. They were able to bring to bear on their daily lives a teaching that bore on the urgency of a great decision, because their day-to-day lives were lived in the atmosphere of that decision: they had accepted the kingdom.

14-15. The Pharisees and Money

14 The Pharisees, who were lovers of money, heard all this, and they scoffed at him. **15** But he said to them, "You are those who justify yourselves before men, but God knows your hearts; for what is exalted among men is an abomination in the sight of God."

The Pharisees realized that the parable had them in mind and they scoffed (literally "turned up the nose") at him. Though not alone in their love of money (cf. 20:47), they tended to regard wealth as a special blessing, a reward for their care in obeying the Law. Their piety in the eyes of men (Mt 6:1; 23:28) was a veneer; God saw beyond it (cf. Lk 18:9-14). The sayings prepare for the parable of vv. 19-31.

16-18. The Law and Divorce
(Mt 11:12f; 5:18,32)

16 "The law and the prophets were until John; since then the good news of the kingdom of God is preached, and every one enters it violently. **17** But it is easier for heaven and earth to pass away, than for one dot of the law to become void.
18 "Every one who divorces his wife and marries another commits adultery, and he who marries a woman divorced from her husband commits adultery."

These three sayings break the link between vv. 14f and the following parable. The sayings are loosely joined, perhaps by a common idea of law: the word *nomos,* "law", occurs in vv. 16 and 17, and v. 18 treats of a particular point of law; Luke is likely to have found them already grouped.

16. The saying appears, in inverse order, in a very different context of Matthew. The Old Testament ended with John; now Jesus preaches the Good News of the kingdom which is open to all who force their way into it—recalling the resolute action recommended by the parable of the Unjust Steward.

17f. The old order has come to an end and the new age has dawned, but the Law, as a norm of morality, still remains intact (cf. Mt 5:17f). V. 18 is an example which shows that the gospel has not abrogated the Law but has, instead, brought out the spirit of the Law.

19-31. The Rich Man and Lazarus

19 "There was a rich man, who was clothed in purple and fine linen and who feasted sumptuously every day. 20 And at his gate lay a poor man named Lazarus, full of sores, 21 who desired to be fed with what fell from the rich man's table; moreover the dogs came and licked his sores. 22 The poor man died and was carried by the angels to Abraham's bosom. The rich man also died and was buried; 23 and in Hades, being in torment, he lifted up his eyes, and saw Abraham far off and Lazarus in his bosom. 24 And he called out, 'Father Abraham, have mercy upon me, and send Lazarus to dip the end of his finger in water and cool my tongue; for I am in anguish in this flame.' 25 But Abraham said, 'Son, remember that you in your lifetime received your good things, and Lazarus in like manner evil things; but now he is comforted here, and you are in anguish. 26 And besides all this, between us and you a great chasm has been fixed, in order that those who would pass from here to you may not be able, and none may cross from there to us.' 27 And he said, 'Then I beg you, father, to send him to my father's house, 28 for I have five brothers, so that he may warn them, lest they also come into this place of torment.' 29 But Abraham said, 'They have Moses and the prophets; let them hear them.' 30 And he said, 'No, father Abraham; but if some one goes to them from the dead, they will repent.' 31 He said to him, 'If they do not hear Moses and the prophets, neither will they be convinced if some one should rise from the dead.' "

Proper to Luke. It is not unlikely that behind this parable stands a popular story of Egyptian origin which concerns the contrasting fate in the nether world of two men, one wealthy and one poor, who are being carried to burial at the same moment. The moral of the story is: "He who is good on earth, receives good in the underworld, but he who is evil on earth receives evil." Introduced into Palestine by Alexandrian Jews, it became the story of the poor scribe and the wealthy tax collector Bar Majan. Jesus' adaptation of the folktale would be all the more effective because the story was familiar to his hearers. However, we cannot be sure that he is, in fact, adapting this tale. The parable calls attention to the danger of wealth and the lack of sensitivity and selfishness it breeds; the saying of 16:13 is dramatically illustrated.

19. This rich man was a worldling who did not look beyond the good things of this life.

20f. In sharp contrast is the crippled ("lay") beggar Lazarus—the name means "God helps". The dogs, wild scavengers, add to his misery since he is unable to keep them at bay. He would have been glad to have—if they had been offered to him—the pieces of bread with which the guests wiped their fingers and which they then dropped on the floor. The rich man might (according to Luke's understanding of v. 9) have made of Lazarus a friend to welcome him into the eternal habitations, but he was too frivolous, or too callous, to care.

22. The contrast between the two men in the next life is much more pronounced—but they have exchanged roles. Death was currently described as "going to Abraham" or "being gathered to Abraham", a modification of the Old Testament phrase "gathered to the fathers", that is, the patriarchs (cf. Gn 15:15; 47:30). Lazarus is given the place of honor at the right hand of the patriarch; the phrase "to Abraham's bosom" is explained by Jn 13:23: "One of his disciples, whom Jesus loved, was reclining upon the bosom of Jesus", that is, at his right side and leaning backward toward him. The rich man's burial, in keeping with his wealth, merely emphasized the futility of his life, for he went to the place of torment.

23f. In speaking to Jews, Jesus followed the prevalent ideas on life beyond the grave. Throughout most of the Old Testament *Sheol*, a dark, gloomy place, is the abode of all the dead, where good and bad lead a vague, unhappy existence. When, eventually, the doctrines of resurrection, and retribution after death, had evolved—not until well into the 2nd century B.C.—this notion of Sheol necessarily underwent a change. Now, it was thought to have two compartments: in one the just quietly awaited the resurrection, while in the other the wicked were already being punished. Though these two sections were rigidly separated (v. 26), it was commonly believed that both parties were in sight of each other. The rich man begged his father Abraham for a single drop of the cool water that flowed in the abode of the just.

25f. Abraham does not disown him: as a Jew he is, according to the flesh, his son, but this is not enough to save him. The rich man realized that his present state was a punishment, not a change of fortune only, and that Lazarus was rewarded not for his poverty but for his virtue. The abyss not only divides the two compartments of Sheol but marks a definitive separation between the two classes of dead. In all this Jewish imagery we are not given anything resembling a "topography of hell"; besides, it is a description of the intermediate state, before the Last Judgment.

27f. This is one of the double-edged parables (cf. 15:11-32) and, true to form, the greater emphasis is on the second point (vv. 27-31). But, just as in the first part we are given no real description of hell, so here we can learn nothing of the psychology of the damned. The reaction of the rich man is described from an ordinary human point of view: his present sorry state has at last opened his eyes and he is understandably desirous that his brothers should escape his fate.

29. Abraham answers that the five, who evidently led much the same sort of life as their unhappy brother, have "Moses and the prophets", that is, the Old Testament (cf. Ex 22:25; Dt 24:6, 10-13; Am 6:4-7; 8:4), while a text of Isaiah meets exactly the situation of Lazarus: what God asks of his people is "to share your bread with the hungry, and bring the homeless poor into your house; when you see the naked to cover him" (58:7).

30. The man makes one more bid. Surely if Lazarus were to come back from the dead his brothers would at last be moved and repent.

31. A miracle will not help those who have made no use of the means God has put at their disposal (cf. Jn 5:46f). The burden of the second part of the parable might be put like this: "If a man (says Jesus) cannot be humane with the Old Testament in his hand and Lazarus on his doorstep, nothing—neither a visitor from the other world nor a revelation of the horrors of hell—will teach him otherwise." [51]

There can be little doubt that the parable was originally aimed at the Pharisees. Elsewhere (cf. 11:29f) Jesus had refused to grant a like request: they will receive no sign but the sign of Jonah. Any other sign would leave them unmoved and unconvinced. As it is they stand, unheeding, before a crisis. Luke, how-

---

[51] A. M. Hunter, *op. cit.*, p. 84.

ever, has taken it as addressed to the disciples (cf. 16:1; 17:1), and he sees it as a warning against the danger of riches (it is that, of course), a frequent theme of his gospel. The rich man is one who, thanks to his wealth, is immersed in worldly pleasures and is forgetful of God; all that his wealth has done for him is to make him selfish and irreligious. Lazarus is in no such danger; obviously, we must not regard him only as materially poor, for he is also "poor" in the religious sense of a virtuous, pious man (cf. 6:20). In short, we are shown the great danger of riches and we are taught that poverty need not be an obstacle, and may be a help, to eternal happiness.

17:1-6. Teaching on Scandal, Forgiveness, and Faith
(Mt 18:6f; Mk 9:42; Mt 17:20; 21:21; Mk 11:22f)

1 And he said to his disciples, "Temptations to sin are sure to come; but woe to him by whom they come! 2 It would be better for him if a millstone were hung round his neck and he were cast into the sea, than that he should cause one of these little ones to sin. 3 Take heed to yourselves; if your brother sins, rebuke him, and if he repents, forgive him; 4 and if he sins against you seven times in the day, and turns to you seven times, and says, 'I repent,' you must forgive him."

5 The apostles said to the Lord, "Increase our faith!" 6 And the Lord said, "If you had faith as a grain of mustard seed, you could say to this sycamine tree, 'Be rooted up, and be planted in the sea,' and it would obey you."

The passage 17:1-10, instruction of the disciples, is a mosaic of sayings.

1-3a. The primary meaning of *skandalon* is not "stumbling-block" but "bait", "snare"; it is a snare or a lure by which a man is liable to be led into sin. In practice, it is inevitable that there should be scandal, but the man who deliberately leads astray the "little ones" (humble believers) will be severely punished. The warning, "take heed to yourselves", puts the disciples on their guard against involuntary scandal (cf. Rm 14:21; 1 Cor 8:13; Lk 21:34).

3b-4. In Matthew these sayings frame a series of sayings on discipline (18:15-22); in Luke the fault is a personal matter involving two brethren. His emphasis on repentance is typical, as is also his "seven times *in the day*"—a spirit of forgiveness must be an unfailing attribute of a Christian (cf. 9:23; 11:3).

5f. The request of v. 5 is Luke's editorial introduction to the following saying: the Apostles ask for a greater confidence in God. It is the nature of faith that matters: a grain of authentic faith—perfect confidence in God—can achieve great things. In Matthew and Mark reference is to the removal of "this mountain"; Luke's version reflects the Greek idea that nature cannot change: trees do not grow in the sea.

7-10. Unworthy Servants

7 "Will any one of you, who has a servant plowing or keeping sheep, say to him when he has come in from the field, 'Come at once and sit down at table'? **8** Will he not rather say to him, 'Prepare supper for me, and gird yourself and serve me, till I eat and drink; and afterward you shall eat and drink'? **9** Does he thank the servant because he did what was commanded? **10** So you also, when you have done all that is commanded you, say, 'We are unworthy servants; we have only done what was our duty.'"

Peculiar to Luke. **7.** The phrase *tis ex humōn* means: "Can you imagine that . . . ?" (cf. 11:5); and expects the rejoinder: "Certainly not!" We might render v. 7: "Can you imagine that any of you would say to his slave who had come in from plowing or tending sheep: 'Come at once and sit down to table?'" The situation is quite hypothetical.

8f. The farmer of the parable is not a wealthy man; he has one slave only, who must do the farm work and also serve at table. As a slave (*doulos*) there is no question of wages for his services; the master does not see why he should thank the slave for carrying out his order.

10. Jesus draws out the moral of the parable: the disciples, God's slaves, have no claim to reward for doing what God expects of them; they must humbly acknowledge that they are but poor servants. In the context *achreios* has the meaning "poor", "humble", "unworthy" (rather than "unprofitable")—there is no suggestion that men's works are useless (cf. Mt 25:31-46). But the reward of good works is a free gift—men have no right to it. This teaching is a contrast to the views of the Pharisees, and the disciples would have recognized this.

11-19. The Healing of Ten Lepers

11 On the way to Jerusalem he was passing along between Samaria and Galilee. 12 And as he entered a village, he was met by ten lepers, who stood at a distance 13 and lifted up their voices and said, "Jesus, Master, have mercy on us." 14 When he saw them he said to them, "Go and show yourselves to the priests." And as they went they were cleansed. 15 Then one of them, when he saw that he was healed, turned back, praising God with a loud voice; 16 and he fell on his face at Jesus' feet, giving him thanks. Now he was a Samaritan. 17 Then said Jesus, "Were not ten cleansed? Where are the nine? 18 Was no one found to return and give praise to God except this foreigner?" 19 And he said to him, "Rise and go your way; your faith has made you well."

Peculiar to Luke. 11. Luke again (cf. 9:51; 13:22) reminds us that Jesus is journeying to Jerusalem; the indications of this verse (still at the starting point) prove that the journey is a literary construction. Luke perhaps means that Jesus is going down to the Jordan valley so as to make his way along it to Jericho (18:35).

12-14. The lepers remain at a distance as the Law demanded (Lv 13:45). Jesus' command (cf. Lk 5:14) implied the granting of their request—the priests would verify the cure and authorize them to return to normal life (Lv 14:1-32)—but also tested their faith.

15f. All had shown faith in the word of Jesus but one only, a Samaritan, returned to thank him (cf. 2 Kg 5:14f; Lk 4:27). By implication the others were Jews; mutual hatred (cf. 9:53) was forgotten in their common misery.

17f. The nine, sons of Abraham, had apparently accepted the miracle as a matter of course; but Jesus praises the gratitude of the "foreigner" (one of the mixed Samaritan race). Again (cf. 7:9; 10:30-37) a "stranger" puts Jews to shame, and already the contrasting attitude of Jew and Gentile to Jesus and to his gospel is foreshadowed.

19. A stereotyped phrase (cf. 7:50; 8:48; 18:42).

20f. The Coming of the Kingdom

20 Being asked by the Pharisees when the kingdom of God was coming, he answered them, "The kingdom of God is not coming with

signs to be observed; 21 nor will they say, 'Lo, here it is!' or 'There!' for behold, the kingdom of God is in the midst of you."

The rabbis frequently discussed the signs and prelude of the Messianic age; the question of the Pharisees concerns the nature of these preliminary signs rather than the hour of the kingdom's coming. Jesus replies that such speculation is vain: there are no observable signs to mark the coming of the kingdom. The phrase *entos humōn* can mean "within you", but this rendering here seems ruled out on two counts: because Jesus speaks of the coming of the kingdom as a fact of history and not as an inner, spiritual experience; and because these words are addressed to Pharisees (who have not accepted Jesus). And while *entos humōn* could be "in the midst of you", Jesus cannot here (v. 20; cf. 12:56) tell his hearers that the kingdom is in the midst of them, that in his Person it has come quietly and unnoticed (cf. Jn 1:10). Though vv. 20f are distinct from vv. 22-27 (Luke's editorial link, v. 22a, shows that), the evangelist has juxtaposed these passages; it would seem natural that he understood v. 21 as a prophecy. We may, then, treat the present *esti* ("the kingdom of God *is* in the midst of you") as a prophetic present: the kingdom, when it comes, will suddenly be in your midst; it is the final consummation of the kingdom that is announced. The sense is essentially that of v. 24.

22-37. The Day of the Son of Man

22 And he said to his disciples, "The days are coming when you will desire to see one of the days of the Son of man, and you will not see it. 23 And they will say to you, 'Lo, there!' or 'Lo, here!' Do not go, do not follow them. 24 For as the lightning flashes and lights up the sky from one side to the other, so will the Son of man be in his day. 25 But first he must suffer many things and be rejected by this generation. 26 As it was in the days of Noah, so will it be in the days of the Son of man. 27 They ate, they drank, they married, they were given in marriage, until the day when Noah entered the ark, and the flood came and destroyed them all. 28 Likewise as it was in the days of Lot—they ate, they drank, they bought, they sold, they planted, they built, 29 but on the day when Lot went out from Sodom fire and brimstone rained from heaven and destroyed them all—30 so will it be on the day when the Son of man is revealed. 31 On that day, let him who is on the housetop, with his goods in the house, not come down

to take them away; and likewise let him who is in the field not turn back. 32 Remember Lot's wife. 33 Whoever seeks to gain his life will lose it, but whoever loses his life will preserve it. 34 I tell you, in that night there will be two men in one bed; one will be taken and the other left. 35 There will be two women grinding together; one will be taken and the other left." 37 And they said to him, "Where, Lord?" He said to them, "Where the body is, there the eagles will be gathered together."

Proper to Luke, though certain passages occur in the eschatological discourse of Mt 24:1-36 and its parallel. Addressed to the disciples, the passage may be regarded as an explanation, for their benefit, of the reply of vv. 20f.

22. The Hebraism *eleusontai hēmerai* (a favorite expression of Luke, cf. 19:43; 21:6; 23:29)—it has influenced the phrasing "one of the days of the Son of man", vv. 24,30—reproduces the introductory formula of an oracle of woe (cf. 1 Sm 2:31; Am 4:2; 8:11; Jer 7:32; etc.). In their trials the disciples will long for the Second Coming of Christ—but his Parousia will be delayed.

23f. Cf. Mt 24:23-27. They must take care that their vivid desire does not lead them to give credence to false rumors of his coming; indeed, the Son of man, like lightning, will be visible everywhere at once.

25. Jesus takes care to warn his disciples that his road to glory is via suffering and rejection (cf. 9:22,44; 18:31-33).

26-30. Two examples from the Old Testament illustrate the unexpectedness of the coming and the unpreparedness of many —for such people the Parousia will be a catastrophe. Matthew has the first example (24:37-39; cf. Gn 6-8); the second is peculiar to Luke (cf. Gn 18:20-33; 19:24f).

31-33. These verses, which interrupt the link between vv. 30 and 34f, have been inserted by Luke into the original discourse; here they are not really at home, but serve to introduce a theme dear to Luke. Mk 13:15f refers to flight before the threatening disaster of 70 A.D.; here v. 31 refers to the urgency of preparation for the manifestation of the Son of man. In Luke's eyes, such preparation is found in flight from worldly goods, in detachment; one must not "turn back" to such things, as Lot's wife "looked back" (cf. Gn 19:26). Only thus can one win salvation (v. 33; cf. 9:24; Mk 8:35).

34f. Cf. Mt 24:40f. Again, two examples illustrate an idea. In v. 34 Luke suggests that the Parousia will take place at night (cf. Mt 24:43; 25:6; Mk 13:35). In both examples two persons, closely associated, are suddenly separated: one is taken for the kingdom, the other is left—the basis of distinction being the interior disposition of each. After v. 35 many manuscripts insert v. 36, borrowed from Mt 24:40. The disciples' question seems to refer to the place of judgment rather than to the place of the assembly of the elect. In Matthew the reply of Jesus is that men will gather to the Son of man as instinctively as vultures (*aetoi*) —rather than "eagles"—gather to a dead body, whereas Luke understands it to mean: wherever men (= bodies) are, there will the judgment take place; or, perhaps, the vultures are those birds which will batten on the victims of God's final judgment (cf. Ezek 39:17-20; Ap 19:17-21).

18:1-8. The Unjust Judge

1 And he told them a parable, to the effect that they ought always to pray and not lose heart. 2 He said, "In a certain city there was a judge who neither feared God nor regarded man; 3 and there was a widow in that city who kept coming to him and saying, 'Vindicate me against my adversary.' 4 For a while he refused; but afterward he said to himself, 'Though I neither fear God nor regard man, 5 yet because this widow bothers me, I will vindicate her, or she will wear me out by her continual coming.'" 6 And the Lord said, "Hear what the unrighteous judge says. 7 And will not God vindicate his elect, who cry to him day and night? Will he delay long over them? 8 I tell you, he will vindicate them speedily. Nevertheless, when the Son of man comes, will he find faith on earth?"

1. Luke makes clear his understanding of this parable (proper to him): the disciples should pray at all times and persevere in it (cf. 1 Thes 5:17). Yet he still has in mind the coming of the kingdom: it will come in response to the prayer of God's elect for vindication. In reality, like the Friend at Midnight (11:5-8), the parable originally had a different emphasis.

2f. The judge, described as unjust in v. 6, is of a type that was all too common in Israel (cf. Am 5:7,10-13; Is 1:23; 5:7-23; Jer 5:28), and the Old Testament also refers very often to the helpless widow (cf. Ex 22:21f; Dt 10:18; Is 1:17; Jer 22:3). It is implied that the widow has right on her side, but the judge is not interested in the rights of a penniless plaintiff; if he is to give a decision in favor of anybody, it has to be made worth his while to do so.

4f. But this time, in the face of continued pestering, he gives in. "Wear me out"—literally, "hit under the eye"; perhaps, "she will end by hitting me over the head"; but here better understood figuratively: "lest she should come to nag me forever."

6-8a. Jesus ("the Lord") draws attention to the words of the judge; as he spoke the parable the emphasis lay on the judge rather than on the widow's entreaties. The lesson is confidence in prayer: if so callous a man as the unjust judge is moved—if only from a selfish motive—by the entreaties of a helpless widow, how much more will God, the merciful Father, hear the cries of his elect, even if he puts their patience to the test. Unexpectedly, he will deliver them; he will even shorten the time of tribulation (Mk 13:20). The lesson of perseverance is easily drawn, but it is secondary.

8b. Spoken to the disciples (v. 1), the meaning of this obscure saying appears to be: will the Son of man, at his coming, find men like them, will he find faith on earth? The saying is an echo of Mt 24:12—"Because wickedness is multiplied, most men's love will grow cold." Though, like the Friend at Midnight, this parable, too, originally bore on the certainty of God's attention to the prayers of his elect, it is even more readily understandable that, in view of the widow's determination to keep on pestering the judge, it should have been taken by the early Christians as an admonition to perseverance in prayer.

9-14. The Pharisee and the Tax Collector

9 He also told this parable to some who trusted in themselves that they were righteous and despised others; **10** "Two men went up into the temple to pray, one a Pharisee and the other a tax collector. **11** The Pharisee stood and prayed thus with himself, 'God, I thank thee that I am not like other men, extortioners, unjust, adulterers, or even like this tax collector. **12** I fast twice a week, I give tithes of all that I get.' **13** But the tax collector, standing far off, would not even lift up his eyes to heaven, but beat his breast, saying, 'God, be merciful to me a sinner!' **14** I tell you, this man went down to his house justified rather than the other; for every one who exalts himself will be humbled, but he who humbles himself will be exalted."

This parable (like the foregoing, proper to Luke) is distinct from the other; they are set side by side because both are concerned with prayer.

9. The people so described can be none other than Pharisees.

10. From the first the parable maintains a dramatic contrast. The two men who, at the same time, pray in the Temple represent the two extreme strata of Jewish society: the Pharisee, taking his stand on minute observance of the Law, is the embodiment of Jewish faith and morality; the tax collector, by his office marked off as one who does not observe the Law, scarcely merits the name of Jew.

11f. The Pharisee comes boldly into the presence of God. He is not a hypocrite, for everything he says is true: what is wrong with his prayer is not what he says but what he does not say. Jewish prayers begin by giving praise and glory to God, but this man thanks God for what he himself is. Then he proceeds to works of supererogation. The Law knew only one day of fast in the year—the Day of Atonement (Lv 16)—but he fasts twice a week (every Monday and Thursday), and he does so for the sins of the people—not for his own sins since he is not conscious of any. Likewise his payment of tithes went far beyond the demands of the Law. He is quite convinced that he stands right with God and he feels no need to ask for forgiveness. This picture of the Pharisee is not an unjust one; an extant prayer of much the same time is a remarkably close parallel to the text of Luke:

> I thank thee, Yahweh my God, that thou hast given me my lot with those who sit in the house of learning, and not with those who sit at the street-corners. For I rise early and they rise early: I rise early to study the words of the Torah and they rise early to attend to things of no moment. I weary myself and they weary themselves: I weary myself and profit thereby while they weary themselves to no profit. I run and they run: I run toward the life of the age to come and they run toward the pit of destruction.[52]

[52] H. L. Strack and P. Billerbeck, *Kommentar zum Neuen Testament aus Talmud und Midrasch II* (Munich: Beck, 1924), p. 240.

13. The tax collector does not come boldly into the Temple but, conscious of his sins, stands at a distance from the Holy Place. But he does come into God's presence and his attitude— downcast eyes and the beating of his breast—proclaims his feelings. Like the Pharisee, he is thinking of himself; but what he contemplates is his sin and misery, and he feels no temptation to compare himself with other men. His prayer is very simple, a cry from the heart, a cry for forgiveness.

14a. The Pharisees who had listened to the parable so far would perhaps have expected to be told that God does not hear sinners (cf. Jn. 9:31). They might have been prepared to hear that God did grant pardon to the tax collector, but in virtue of the justice of the other. They were quite unprepared for the verdict of Jesus: the tax collector was justified—his sins were forgiven (cf. Ps 51[50]:19); he had asked for pardon and his prayer was heard; he had won the divine favor. (The verb *dikaiousthai* means "to obtain justice, to be acquitted, to find justice, favor, grace"; this passage shows that the Pauline doctrine of justification [cf. Gal 2:15–4:11; Rm 3:21–4:25] has its roots in the teaching of Jesus.) The Pharisee was not justified (the better rendering is: "This man was justified, the other not"), his sins were not forgiven because he had not asked for pardon. His error, his blindness, was that he did not see himself for what he was. Jesus strives to bring the Pharisees to see themselves as they really are.

14b. In view of the explicit address of the parable to the Pharisees this is manifestly a generalizing conclusion; the saying is also found in Lk 14:11 and Mt 23:12.

15-17. Jesus and Children
(Mk 10:13-16; Mt 19:13-15)

15 Now they were bringing even infants to him that he might touch them: and when the disciples saw it, they rebuked them. **16** But Jesus called them to him, saying, "Let the children come to me, and do not hinder them; for to such belongs the kingdom of God. **17** Truly, I say to you, whoever does not receive the kingdom of God like a child shall not enter it."

At this point Luke returns to the plan of Mark which he

dropped at 9:50. In Luke's context the children are contrasted with the self-righteous Pharisee; the kingdom must be accepted as a gift, not earned by works.

15f. Luke omits saying that Jesus was indignant with his disciples (cf. Mk 10:14); he has also left aside Mark's conclusion (10:16) which described Jesus embracing the children. In each case the reason is the same: he is reluctant to ascribe strong emotion to Jesus.

17. The disposition of a child—receptivity, a willingness to accept what is freely given—is necessary for all who would enter the kingdom.

18-30. The Rich Ruler
(Mk 10:17-31; Mt 19:16-30)

18 And a ruler asked him, "Good Teacher, what shall I do to inherit eternal life?" **19** And Jesus said to him, "Why do you call me good? No one is good but God alone. **20** You know the commandments: 'Do not commit adultery, Do not kill, Do not steal, Do not bear false witness, Honor your father and mother.'" **21** And he said, "All these I have observed from my youth." **22** And when Jesus heard it, he said to him, "One thing you still lack. Sell all that you have and distribute to the poor, and you will have treasure in heaven; and come, follow me." **23** But when he heard this he became sad, for he was very rich. **24** Jesus looking at him said, "How hard it is for those who have riches to enter the kingdom of God! **25** For it is easier for a camel to go through the eye of a needle than for a rich man to enter the kingdom of God." **26** Those who heard it said, "Then who can be saved?" **27** But he said, "What is impossible with men is possible with God." **28** And Peter said, "Lo, we have left our homes and followed you." **29** And he said to them, "Truly, I say to you, there is no man who has left house or wife or brothers or parents or children, for the sake of the kingdom of God, **30** who will not receive manifold more in this time, and in the age to come eternal life."

The passage differs in detail only from Mark's version.

18. The "man" of Mark has become a "ruler" (*archōn*), a favorite word of Luke (cf. 12:58; 14:1; 23:13,35). This ruler, in contrast to the children, is convinced that he can win eternal life. "He supposed that entry into the kingdom was by competitive examination: he had passed Elementary Religion to his own satisfaction and, as he believed, to the satisfaction of the Examiner; now he wished to attempt Advanced Religion." [53]

19. The question of Jesus' own relation to the Father, his divinity, does not arise here. Jesus answers the man who had addressed him simply as "Master", who saw in him a "good" man; and, placing himself on the level of his interlocutor, pointed out that human goodnes is nothing in comparison with the goodness of God.

20f. Like the Pharisee of the preceding parable, the ruler (he too, no doubt, a Pharisee) could declare that he had faithfully observed the Law.

22f. Luke, typically, insists on the completeness of the renunciation: "Sell *all*", and, no less characteristically, omits reference to the sentiments of Jesus, so sacrificing the striking observation of Mark: "And Jesus looking upon him loved him" (Mk 10:21). Here is dramatic evidence of the danger of riches, the obstacle wealth can prove to higher aspirations (cf. Lk 12:13-21; 16:19-31).

24f. The hard saying of Jesus is spoken in the presence of the ruler (cf. Mk 10:22); on the other hand, the saying is not addressed to the disciples, as in Mark. The hyperbolic image (the camel was the largest animal known to Palestinian Jews) strikingly underlines this grave warning on the danger of wealth.

26f. In reply to the disciples' surprised question, Jesus does not in any way soften the seriousness of his previous declaration; he asserts that it is thanks to God's grace alone that a man can overcome the obstacle to salvation which wealth is—"for with God nothing will be impossible" (1:37).

28. Peter hastens to point out that he and the disciples, unlike the ruler, had left their homes and followed Jesus: what is their reward?

29f. They will indeed be rewarded both in this age and in the age to come. In v. 29 Luke adds "wife" (as he has done in 14:26) and writes "for the sake of kingdom of God" instead of "for my sake and for the gospel" (Mk 10:29)—Luke never uses the word "gospel". In v. 30 he has abbreviated Mk 10:30; his omission of "persecutions" as part of the disciples' lot is rather surprising.

---

[53] G. B. Caird, *op. cit.*, pp. 204f.

31-34. Third Prediction of the Passion
(Mk 10:32-34; Mt 20:17-19)

31 And taking the twelve, he said to them, "Behold, we are going up to Jerusalem, and everything that is written of the Son of man by the prophets will be accomplished. 32 For he will be delivered to the Gentiles, and will be mocked and shamefully treated and spit upon; 33 they will scourge him and kill him, and on the third day he will rise." 34 But they understood none of these things; this saying was hid from them, and they did not grasp what was said.

31-33. Luke omits Mk 10:32 since the indication is superfluous after Lk 9:51; 17:11. He refers to the fulfillment of Scripture, thus preparing the way for the risen Christ's interpretation of the Scriptures and for the apostolic preaching (cf. 24:25,27,44; Ac 3:18; 8:32-35; 13:27; 26:23).

34. Cf. 9:45. An emphatic statement, proper to Luke, on the disciples' failure to understand. Luke has omitted Mk 10:35-45, the request of the sons of Zebedee—but uses the conclusion of the passage in 22:24-27. He thereby spares the disciples, but his narrative of the blind man comes with dramatic fitness after their blindness.

35-43. The Blind Man at Jericho
(Mk 10:46-52; Mt 20:29-34)

35 As he drew near to Jericho, a blind man was sitting by the roadside begging; 36 and hearing a multitude going by, he inquired what this meant. 37 They told him, "Jesus of Nazareth is passing by." 38 And he cried, "Jesus, Son of David, have mercy on me!" 39 And those who were in front rebuked him, telling him to be silent; but he cried out all the more, "Son of David, have mercy on me!" 40 And Jesus stopped, and commanded him to be brought to him; and when he came near, he asked him, 41 "What do you want me to do for you?" He said, "Lord, let me receive my sight." 42 And Jesus said to him, "Receive your sight; your faith has made you well." 43 And immediately he received his sight and followed him, glorifying God; and all the people, when they saw it, gave praise to God.

In Mark and Matthew the miracle takes place as Jesus is leaving Jericho (Matthew has two blind men). Luke, for purely literary reasons (cf. 4:5-12), has put it at the entry to the town because he wants to fit in the episode of Zacchaeus, which takes place at Jericho, and the parable of the Pounds, which he sets in the context of departure for Jerusalem (19:11). Luke is substantially the same as Mark.

35-37. Luke omits the name of the blind man—Bartimaeus (Mk 10:46). The "multitude" is, doubtless, a group of pilgrims on their way to Jerusalem for the Passover.

38f. In Luke, as in Mark, this is the first and only occasion on which Jesus is addressed as "Son of David". The beggar is echoing the popular hope that Jesus is the promised king of David's line, a hope which will soon find a more general and dramatic expression at the entry into Jerusalem (19:37f).

40f. Luke has omitted the touching and picturesque details of Mk 10:49f, and for the Aramaic title *rabbouni* ("Master") substitutes *Kyrie* ("Lord").

42f. The man's persistence (v. 39) was an indication of his confidence in Jesus. Characteristically, Luke introduces the note of joy and praise (cf. Mk 10:52).

19:1-10. Zacchaeus

1 He entered Jericho and was passing through. 2 And there was a man named Zacchaeus; he was a chief tax collector, and rich. 3 And he sought to see who Jesus was, but could not, on account of the crowd, because he was small of stature. 4 So he ran on ahead and climbed up into a sycamore tree to see him, for he was to pass that way. 5 And when Jesus came to the place, he looked up and said to him, "Zacchaeus, make haste and come down; for I must stay at your house today." 6 So he made haste and came down, and received him joyfully. 7 And when they saw it they all murmured, "He has gone in to be the guest of a man who is a sinner." 8 And Zacchaeus stood and said to the Lord, "Behold, Lord, the half of my goods I give to the poor; and if I have defrauded any one of anything, I restore it fourfold." 9 And Jesus said to him, "Today salvation has come to this house, since he also is a son of Abraham. 10 For the Son of man came to seek and to save the lost."

Proper to Luke. Again Jesus shows himself a friend of "tax collectors and sinners" and again his solicitude meets with criticism (cf. 15:1f).

1f. Zacchaeus held a high position at an important customs post and had turned it to good account.

3f. Curious to see a man with such a reputation, Zacchaeus forgot his dignity.

5. It was Jesus who saw Zacchaeus; he "must" come to the house of the tax collector, he who had come to seek out "the lost" (v. 10).

6f. The joy of Zacchaeus is matched by the murmuring of those who did not understand the goodness of God (cf. 5:30; 15:2).

8. Touched by the gracious approach of Jesus, the tax collector is a changed man—he is more generous than the ruler (18:23). The present tense describes not a present habit but a present resolve: henceforth he will give half of his goods in alms; moreover he will make fourfold amends (the requirement of Roman Law *in furtum manifestum*) if he can ascertain that he has defrauded anybody.

9. Jesus turns to the murmurers: Zacchaeus is a son of Abraham and has as much right to the mercy of God as any other Israelite (cf. 13:16): the visit of Jesus has brought salvation to the man and his family ("house").

10. This is very likely an independent logion which echoes the theme of the parables of ch. 15—and indeed of the whole gospel; the episode is a striking illustration of it.

11-27. The Pounds
(Mt 25:14-30)

11 As they heard these things, he proceeded to tell a parable, because he was near to Jerusalem, and because they supposed that the kingdom of God was to appear immediately. 12 He said therefore, "A nobleman went into a far country to receive kingly power and then return. 13 Calling ten of his servants, he gave them ten pounds, and said to them, 'Trade with these till I come.' 14 But his citizens hated him and sent an embassy after him, saying, 'We do not want this man to reign over us.' 15 When he returned, having received the kingly power, he commanded these servants, to whom he had given the money, to be called to him, that he might know what they had gained by trading. 16 The first came before him, saying, 'Lord, your pound has made ten pounds more.' 17 And he said to him, 'Well done, good servant! Because you have been faithful in a very little, you shall have authority over ten cities.' 18 And the second came, saying, 'Lord, your pound has made five pounds.' 19 And he said to him, 'And you are to be over five cities.' 20 Then another came, saying, 'Lord, here is your

pound, which I kept laid away in a napkin; **21** for I was afraid of you, because you are a severe man; you take up what you did not lay down, and reap what you did not sow.' **22** He said to him, 'I will condemn you out of your own mouth, you wicked servant! You knew that I was a severe man, taking up what I did not lay down and reaping what I did not sow? **23** Why then did you not put my money into the bank, and at my coming I should have collected it with interest?' **24** And he said to those who stood by, 'Take the pound from him, and give it to him who has the ten pounds.' **25** (And they said to him, 'Lord, he has ten pounds!') **26** 'I tell you, that to every one who has will more be given; but from him who has not, even what he has will be taken away. **27** But as for these enemies of mine, who did not want me to reign over them, bring these here and slay them before me.'"

Despite notable differences, the Pounds and the Talents (Matthew) are versions of the same parable. However, Matthew's merchant becomes in Luke a nobleman who went abroad in order to make sure of his right to a throne (v. 12). Though an embassy of his own people tried to forestall him (v. 14) he did return as king; he set about rewarding his supporters (vv. 17,19) and punishing his enemies (v. 27). These features, admittedly foreign to the Talents, are the bones of an originally independent parable which we might name the Pretender. If we leave aside vv. 14 and 27 and reduce the nobleman to the status of a merchant, we are left with a parable differing only in detail from Mt 25:14-30. Luke, finding the Pounds and the Pretender already fused, treated the whole as a single parable.

11. In a verse that shows manifest traces of his style, he has told us how he has understood this new (composite) parable for, by placing it in the context of the entry to Jerusalem, he related it to the Parousia. In his eyes, the return of the king and the reckoning with his servants signified the return of Christ in glory. But first Jesus must go away (17:25).

12-14. While v. 13 is part of the main parable, the other verses recall an episode of 4 B.C. when, on the death of Herod the Great, his son Archelaus went to Rome to be confirmed in his possession of Judea. A deputation of Jews attempted to block his claim (v. 14) but Archelaus won out and, on his return, took a bloody revenge on those who had opposed him (v. 27). This secondary parable, the Pretender, would have been a warning to the Jews, a parable of judgment.

13. Each of ten servants received a small sum—the *mina,* about twenty dollars—and were bidden to trade with it; Matthew (25:15) has three servants who receive much larger sums. The remainder of the parable is essentially the same as in Matthew.

15-19. On his return the nobleman called his servants to account (the detail of v. 15a, "having received the kingly power", and the reward of the servants in vv. 17 and 19—"over ten cities", "over five cities"—come from the Pretender. Two of them had a nice profit to show and were rewarded.

20. Then another came—Jesus is not going to go through all ten—who had nothing to offer but a display of remarkable carelessness. The man should have taken the elementary precaution of burying the money (cf. Mt 25:18). In rabbinical law the man who buried a deposit as soon as he received it was free of blame, but one who merely wrapped it in a cloth was held responsible for its loss.

21-23. Now he tries to brazen it out, but is condemned out of his own mouth.

24f. These verses mark the end of the parable. The seam (joining the Pounds and the Pretender), not very noticeable elsewhere, may be seen here: the pound, a relatively insignificant sum, was given, as a reward, to a man who had just become governor of ten towns!

26. This is an isolated saying of Jesus (cf. 8:18; Mk 4:25; Mt 13:12) added to widen the application of the parable; the passive is a circumlocution for the divine name: "God will give . . . will take away".

27. This verse is manifestly the conclusion of the Pretender. In its context it refers to the Jews who had refused Christ as their king.

The center of interest is the conduct of the unprofitable servant, and his sentence. Jesus had the scribes in mind and the parable was originally addressed to them: they had not traded with the treasure God had entrusted to them but had kept it for themselves (11:52); therefore it will be taken from them (cf. Mt 21:43). In Luke, however, the composite parable has taken on marked allegorical traits: the nobleman is Christ who has to leave this world before returning in glory; his own citizens who do not accept him are the Jews (cf. Jn 1:11); the servants are the disciples whom he expects to work with the "capital" he has given them. When he comes to judge there will be a reckoning and the servants will be rewarded according to their deserts; the unbelieving Jews will receive particularly severe punishment. This last point is, of course, the lesson of the Pretender. The warning that the disciples must labor diligently and make full use of the charge they have received is implicit in the Pounds.

C. Last Days of the Suffering and Risen Christ in Jerusalem

V. THE MINISTRY IN JERUSALEM 19:28–21:38

28-40. The Entry into Jerusalem
(Mk 11:1-11; Mt 21:1-11; Jn 12:12-19)

28 And when he had said this, he went on ahead, going up to Jerusalem. 29 When he drew near to Bethphage and Bethany, at the mount that is called Olivet, he sent two of the disciples, 30 saying, "Go into the village opposite, where on entering you will find a colt tied, on which no one has ever yet sat; untie it and bring it here. 31 If any one asks you, 'Why are you untying it?' you shall say this, 'The Lord has need of it.'" 32 So those who were sent went away and found it as he had told them. 33 And as they were untying the colt, its owners said to them, "Why are you untying the colt?" 34 And they said, "The Lord has need of it." 35 And they brought it to Jesus, and throwing their garments on the colt they set Jesus upon it. 36 And as he rode along, they spread their garments on the road. 37 As he was now drawing near, at the descent of the Mount of Olives, the whole multitude of the disciples began to rejoice and praise God with a loud voice for all the mighty works that they had seen, 38 saying, "Blessed is the King who comes in the name of the Lord! Peace in heaven and glory in the highest!" 39 And some of the Pharisees in the multitude said to him, "Teacher, rebuke your disciples." 40 He answered, "I tell you, if these were silent, the very stones would cry out."

Luke follows Mark, but with some omissions and additions.

28. The first part of the verse is a manifest editorial link; the rest is an adaptation of Mk 10:32.

29-35. Apart from a few changes in detail, Luke has transcribed Mk 11:1-8. Clearly, the text of Zech 9:9f is in view (as Mt 21:4f explicitly asserts): "Rejoice greatly, O daughter of Zion." Sing aloud, O daughter of Jerusalem! Lo, your king comes to you; triumphant and victorious is he, humble and riding on an ass, on a colt the foal of an ass." The Messianic king will renounce the pomp of the historical kings of Israel and will enter Jerusalem on the mount of the olden princes (Jg 5:10; 10:14)— victorious by divine help and humble—(*ani*, cf. Lk 6:20); Jesus fulfills this prophecy. His Messianic entry is in keeping with the

Messiah that he is, the Messiah whom the people find so hard to accept—so that their present enthusiasm is ephemeral.

36f. Luke omits the details of Mk 11:8b; but he names the Mount of Olives and refers to the rejoicing and praise of the "whole multitude of disciples". In Luke, the acclamation takes place "at the descent of the Mount of Olives"—again, perhaps the symbolic "mountain" of the gospel.

38. Luke, thinking of his Greek readers, omits the exclamation "Hosanna"; he has rewritten Mk 11:9b-10 on the model of the angels' canticle (2:14). The entry of Jesus into Jerusalem as Messianic King is the sign that the peace, the salvation, decreed by God ("in heaven", cf. 15:7) is at hand; by that fact God glorifies his name, that is, manifests his power (cf. Mt 6:9).

39f. Not in Mark; but cf. Mt 21:15f. The Pharisees obviously fear that the general enthusiasm may lead to a disturbance. But the moment is more significant than they suspect. If men were silent nature itself would proclaim this event (cf. Hb 2:11). The acclamation of Jesus has taken place on the Mount of Olives—the symbolic "mountain"; it is distinct from the entry, the sole purpose of which is that Jesus may take possession of the Temple (v. 45).

41-44. Lament over Jerusalem

41 And when he drew near and saw the city he wept over it, **42** saying, "Would that even today you knew the things that make for peace! But now they are hid from your eyes. **43** For the days shall come upon you, when your enemies will cast up a bank about you and surround you, and hem you in on every side, **44** and dash you to the ground, you and your children within you, and they will not leave one stone upon another in you; because you did not know the time of your visitation."

Peculiar to Luke (cf. 13:34f; 23:27-31). There is a fine dramatic contrast in the lament of Jesus over the city while he is surrounded by an enthusiastic crowd.

41. "There is nothing more touching than this sorrow and those tears in the midst of general rejoicing, nothing which shows him more clearly as the envoy of mercy." [54]

42. Unlike the disciples (vv. 37-40) the city does not recognize

[54] M.-J. Lagrange, *op. cit.*, p. 501.

the message of salvation. Because they have not accepted Jesus as Messiah (cf. 13:34), God has punished the unbelieving Jews with blindness (cf. Jn 12:37-40); the wish of Jesus will remain unfulfilled.

43f. The ultimate fate of the faithless city—which had remained unaware of the divine favors (v. 44b)—will be terrible. *Episkopē* (v. 44b) is a divine visitation, for judgment (cf. Wis 14:11) or, more often, for salvation (cf. Gn 50:24; Ex 3:16; Lk 1:68, 78); Jesus visits the city as God's last messenger, but the city fails to recognize him. The siege imagery echoes Old Testament texts (cf. Is 29:3f; Hos 14:1; Na 3:10; Ps 137[136]:9); hence, the passage was not necessarily written after 70 A.D., though it may well have been (cf. 21:20-24).

45-48. In the Temple
(Mk 11:15-19; Mt 21:12-17; Jn 2:13-17)

45 And he entered the temple and began to drive out those who sold, **46** saying to them, "It is written, 'My house shall be a house of prayer'; but you have made it a den of robbers."
47 And he was teaching daily in the temple. The chief priests and the scribes and the principal men of the people sought to destroy him; **48** but they did not find anything they could do, for all the people hung upon his words.

By his omission of the cursing of the fig tree (Mk 11:12-14) Luke is able to present the cleansing of the Temple at Jesus' first entry. "Behind this omission there is also the idea that Jesus performs no miracles in Jerusalem, the reason being that nothing should stand in the way of the Passion." [55]

45f. A very condensed version of Mark. Two ideas emerge: the Lord has taken possession of his Father's house (cf. 2:49), and Jerusalem is unready for the day of God's visit.

47f. The general statement that Jesus taught daily in the Temple is here interpolated by Luke (cf. Mk 11:18) who creates the impression of a fairly long period of activity, of a third epoch of Jesus' ministry comparable to the two earlier ones. The popularity of Jesus is such that, without endangering their own position, the leaders could neither overlook his presence nor take

[55] H. Conzelmann, *op. cit.*, p. 76.

effective action against him. Luke naturally omits Mk 11:20-25—
a discussion based on the episode of the fig tree.

20:1-8. Question about the Authority of Jesus
(Mk 11:27-33; Mt 21:23-27)

1 One day, as he was teaching the people in the temple and preaching the gospel, the chief priests and the scribes with the elders came
up 2 and said to him, "Tell us by what authority you do these things,
or who it is that gave you this authority." 3 He answered them, "I also
will ask you a question; now tell me, 4 Was the baptism of John from
heaven or from men?" 5 And they discussed it with one another, saying, "If we say, 'From heaven,' he will say, 'Why did you not believe
him?' 6 But if we say, 'From men,' all the people will stone us; for
they are convinced that John was a prophet." 7 So they answered that
they did not know whence it was. 8 And Jesus said to them, "Neither
will I tell you by what authority I do these things."

Luke has somewhat abridged Mark's version but, otherwise, he
has followed it closely.

1. The "one day" gives the impression of a notable length of
time (cf. vv. 47f) and the expression "preaching the gospel" is
distinctive.

2. The demand regards all from the Messianic entry onwards,
including the daily teaching in the Temple (cf. Jn 2:18). The question not only concerns Jesus' authorization (cf. Ac 4:7) but also
is meant to trap him into a declaration of his Messianic authority
which would incriminate him with the Roman authorities.

3f. "Heaven" is a circumlocution for "God"; the question is:
was John an authentic prophet sent by God or was he no more
than a self-styled prophet? This is not intended as a trick question—though it does turn the tables on its hearers and embar-
rasses them. Jesus had been baptized by John whom he regarded
as his Precursor; it was right that the question of John's authority
should be faced before the question of his own authority was
raised.

5-7. The religious leaders face a dilemma. They had not supported John (7:30) and cannot now acknowledge the divine
origin of his mission; they also saw that such an acknowledgment
would involve accepting Jesus whom he had announced; while,
if they try to make out that John was a false prophet, they will

invite a sharp reaction from the people. They are driven to admit that they, the religious leaders of the nation, had formed no opinion about John and his movement.

8. Jesus' counterquestion was a reasonable one: the answer to it would apply, *a fortiori*, to their original question; since they decline to answer they have forfeited the right to a reply. Besides, if they have missed the meaning of John's mission they will not accept a statement of Jesus about his own authority.

9-19. The Wicked Vinedressers
(Mk 12:1-12; Mt 21:33-46)

9 And he began to tell the people this parable: "A man planted a vineyard, and let it out to tenants, and went into another country for a long while. 10 When the time came, he sent a servant to the tenants, that they should give him some of the fruit of the vineyard; but the tenants beat him, and sent him away empty-handed. 11 And he sent another servant; him also they beat and treated shamefully, and sent him away empty-handed. 12 And he sent yet a third; this one they wounded and cast out. 13 Then the owner of the vineyard said, 'What shall I do? I will send my beloved son; it may be they will respect him.' 14 But when the tenants saw him, they said to themselves, 'This is the heir; let us kill him, that the inheritance may be ours.' 15 And they cast him out of the vineyard and killed him. What then will the owner of the vineyard do to them? 16 He will come and destroy those tenants, and give the vineyard to others." When they heard this, they said, "God forbid!" 17 But he looked at them and said, "What then is this that is written:

'The very stone which the builders rejected
has become the head of the corner'?

18 Every one who falls on that stone will be broken to pieces; but when it falls on any one it will crush him."

19 The scribes and the chief priests tried to lay hands on him at that very hour, but they feared the people; for they perceived that he had told this parable against them.

All three synoptists have given this parable and a comparison of the three versions is instructive. Matthew has two groups of servants who are maltreated or killed; in Mark three are sent, one after another, but then the third is followed by "many others"; Luke describes the sending of three successive servants—surely closest to the original form. In all three versions the sending of the son is distinct. This parable also occurs in the gospel of Thomas and presents a climactic series of three messengers, that is, two servants and the son; and, very likely, this is how the original parable ran. Again, in Mark (12:8), the son is murdered in the vineyard and his body is cast out of it; in Matthew (21:39) and Luke (20:15) he is killed outside the vineyard. Otherwise the three versions are much the same: allegorical traits are present in all, but these touches give greater relief to a factor which was present from the first.

9. The introduction (v. 9a) is typically Lucan. The hearers must have recalled, spontaneously, the familiar passage Is 5:1-7—"My beloved had a vineyard on a very fertile hill . . . the vineyard of the Lord of hosts is the house of Israel . . . and he looked for justice, but behold, bloodshed." From the start this vineyard (of the parable) is Israel and the vinedressers are the leaders of Israel (cf. v. 19).

10-12. The servants represent the long line of prophets sent by God to his people; it is natural that other versions of the parable should have heightened the symbolism by touches such as those we have noted in Mark and Matthew (cf. Lk 11:49-51; 13:34).

13f. The brutal and apparently meaningless treatment not only of the servants, but of the son too, does not necessarily mean that we are dealing with an allegory instead of a parable, because, indeed, the story might have been drawn from life. Palestine in the first century A.D. was plagued by absentee landlordism and the landlord's agents would not have been welcome visitors. The seemingly futile murder of the owner's son can be explained too, for the murderers conclude that the original owner has died and that his heir has come to claim the property. If they get rid of him the vineyard will have no claimant and they may hope to remain in possession.

15. This detail (cf. Mk 12:8) underlines the identification of the son with Jesus, who died outside the walls of Jerusalem (Jn 19:17; Heb 13:12); it follows, too, that the vineyard is taken to represent the city.

16. This (v. 16a) is the original ending of the parable; the horrified exclamation (v. 16b) shows that the hearers had indeed seen the point of it. Jesus had put before them a sketch of Israel's history and had warned them that unless they speedily repented, they would see God's vineyard pass from their hands forever. Even though Luke (v. 9) does say that the parable was addressed to "the people", Mark (11:27; 12:12; cf. Lk 20:19) explicitly presents it as Christ's final warning to the Sanhedrin.

17. The three synoptists conclude by quoting Ps 118(117):22, a verse which does not really fit the meaning of the parable. We begin to see the reason for the presence of the psalm-text at this point when we realize that in the early Christian preaching, it was a favorite proof-text for the Resurrection and exaltation of Christ (cf. Ac 4:11; 1 Pt 2:4-7). In the parable, however, Jesus was accusing the Sanhedrites of plotting his death; there was no reference to the Resurrection. Though the psalm-text was not part of the original parable the reason for its insertion is manifest: the early Church could never speak of the death of Jesus without proclaiming his Resurrection.

18. Luke, who alone includes this comment (Mt 21:44 is not authentic), has in mind two Old Testament sayings. In Is 8:14 Yahweh will become for Israel "a stone of offense and a rock of stumbling"; in Dn 2:34f, 44f the kingdom of God is a "stone cut out from a mountain by no human hand" which will break in pieces all world empires. The evangelist sees in Jesus the fulfillment of these Messianic texts: those who collide with him, like the unbelieving Jews, will be broken; and when he comes again, as the great judge, he will "crush them". From first to last, it is a grim warning.

19. The Jewish leaders did look behind the story to the owner and vineyard and servants of their own religious history. What was more disturbing, they recognized Jesus' claim to be the Son and they saw that they had been cast as the wicked vinedressers. They did not like what they had been asked to see.

20-26. Tribute to Caesar
(Mk 12:13-17; Mt 22:15-22)

20 So they watched him, and sent spies, who pretended to be sincere, that they might take hold of what he said, so as to deliver him up to the authority and jurisdiction of the governor. **21** They asked him, "Teacher, we know that you speak and teach rightly, and show no partiality, but truly teach the way of God. **22** Is it lawful for us to give tribute to Caesar, or not?" **23** But he perceived their craftiness, and said to them, 24 "Show me a coin. Whose likeness and inscription has it?" They said, "Caesar's." 25 He said to them, "Then render to Caesar the things that are Caesar's, and to God the things that are God's." 26 And they were not able in the presence of the people to catch him by what he said; but marvelling at his answer they were silent.

20. Luke has entirely rewritten Mk 12:13. The scribes and chief priests, having decided to rid themselves of Jesus (v. 19), plan to bring a political charge against him; Luke omits mention of Pharisees and Herodians (Mk 12:13) and speaks of specially chosen agents.

21f. Their fulsome flattery does not disguise the malicious intent behind the trick question. The issue raised concerned the annual tax which the Romans levied on every adult male, a tax resented by Jews both because it was a sign of subjection and because it had to be paid in silver coinage stamped with the emperor's head (a violation of the Jewish Law against images). Jesus is presented with a dilemma; if he maintained that it was unlawful to pay the tribute he would leave himself open to a charge of treason; if he said that the payment was lawful he would alienate popular support.

23f. Jesus turns the tables on his adversaries by getting them, in effect, to answer their own query. They are able to produce the coin in question, a silver denarius, thus admitting that they have accepted Roman coinage and with it the economic and political order of Rome.

25. Since they, in practice, acknowledge the authority and enjoy the benefits of Rome, they have a duty to pay that government its due in obedience and tribute. It does not follow, of course, that the demands are equal: man's debt of loyalty to Caesar is conditional; to God it is absolute. It is obvious that the narrative has built up to this climax; the saying is what matters, the details only serving to set it in relief.

26. The trap set by the chief priests and scribes (v. 20) has not sprung; they still fear popular reaction (cf. 19:48; 20:19). This passage is the classic Pronouncement Story, in which a narrative leads up to and concentrates on a saying or pronouncement of Jesus. The relations between Church and State, the clash of civil and religious rights, are nothing new. The early Christians had to face this problem and that is why the saying of Jesus (v. 25) was remembered and treasured; it was the basis of future discussion on the relationship of Church and State (cf. Rm 13:1-7; 1 Pt 2:13-17).

27-40. The Resurrection of the Dead
(Mk 12:18-27; Mt 22:23-33)

27 There came to him some Sadducees, those who say that there is no resurrection, **28** and they asked him a question, saying, "Teacher, Moses wrote for us that if a man's brother dies, having a wife but no children, the man must take the wife and raise up children for his brother. **29** Now there were seven brothers; the first took a wife, and died without children; **30** and the second **31** and the third took her, and likewise all seven left no children and died. **32** Afterward the woman also died. **33** In the resurrection, therefore, whose wife will the woman be? For the seven had her as wife."

34 And Jesus said to them, "The sons of this age marry and are given in marriage; **35** but those who are accounted worthy to attain to that age and to the resurrection from the dead neither marry nor are given in marriage, **36** for they cannot die any more, because they are equal to angels and are sons of God, being sons of the resurrection. **37** But that the dead are raised, even Moses showed, in the passage about the bush, where he calls the Lord the God of Abraham and the God of Isaac and the God of Jacob. **38** Now he is not God of the dead, but of the living; for all live to him." **39** And some of the scribes answered, "Teacher, you have spoken well." **40** For they no longer dared to ask him any question.

Unlike the preceding questions, the query of the Sadducees [56] is not concerned with the authority of Jesus or with his attitude to Rome; the issues it raises are religious and theological. At the same time the motives of the questioners are no better—they think to ridicule Jesus.

27. For the denial of the resurrection of the dead cf. Ac 23:8.

28. The question is based on the Law of levirate marriage (a Law which, most likely, was no longer practically in force). The provision of levirate (from the Latin *levir* = brother-in-law) was the following: if brothers dwelt together and one of them died childless, a surviving brother was expected to marry the widow, and the firstborn son of this marriage was legally regarded as the son and heir of the deceased (Dt 25:5-10).

[56] See pp. 289f.

29-33. Doubtless, this was a stock question.

34-36. Luke has omitted Mk 12:24 and has entirely rewritten Mk 12:25. He distinguishes two ages: marriage is an institution of this age, necessary for the continuation of the race; but in the world to come there will be no marriage. The reason is that those who have risen are, like the angels, immortal—there is no longer any place for marriage as a means of propagating the species or as a legal relationship. Furthermore, the risen ("children of the resurrection" is a Semitism) are children of God, sharing in God's life and glory and raised above earthly preoccupations.

37f. Cf. Mk 12:26f. Jesus argues from Ex 3:6: the text implies that Abraham and the patriarchs are still alive because God could not be named after a dead thing—a rabbinical argument which impresses the hearers (v. 39). For v. 38b—added by Luke—cf. Gal 2:19; Rm 6:10: all who await the resurrection have life from God, the source of life.

39f. These scribes were obviously Pharisees and were pleased with Jesus' refutation of the Sadducees (cf. Ac 23:7-9). Luke has omitted the question on the greatest commandment (Mk 12:28-34)—he has dealt with it in 10:25-27; but he reproduces Mark's conclusion (cf. Mk 12:34).

41-44. David's Son
(Mk 12:35-37a; Mt 22:41-46)

41 But he said to them, "How can they say that the Christ is David's son? **42** For David himself says in the Book of Psalms,

'The Lord said to my Lord,
  Sit at my right hand,
43 till I make thy enemies a stool for thy feet.'

44 David thus calls him Lord; so how is he his son?"

This passage, independently transmitted by Mark, has been attached by Luke to the foregoing discussion; he abridges and stylistically improves the text of Mark.

41. Now it is Jesus' turn to take the offensive. He is not denying the explicit datum of Old Testament Messianism (Is 9:2-7; 11:1-9; Jer 23:5f; 33:14-18; Ezek 34:23f; Ps 89[88]:19-37), but is intent on showing that this does not exhaust the true notion of Messiah.

42f. "In the Book of Psalms" (cf. 24:44; Ac 1:20; 13:33)—Luke only, in the New Testament, refers to the book by its title.

44. If David can speak of the Messiah as his "Lord" he must regard him as somebody more than his son—the phrase makes David's son greater than David himself. In other words, Jesus means that "son of David" is, by itself, an inadequate description of the Messiah. The passage implies that Ps 110(109):1—a common Christian proof-text (cf. Ac 2:34; 1 Cor 15:25; Heb 1:13; 1 Pt 3:22)—was already interpreted Messianically in 1st-century A.D. Judaism.

45-47. Warning against the Scribes
(Mk 12:37b-40; cf. Mt 23:1-36)

45 And in the hearing of all the people he said to his disciples, **46** "Beware of the scribes, who like to go about in long robes, and love salutations in the market places and the best seats in the synagogues and the places of honor at feasts, **47** who devour widows' houses and for a pretense make long prayers. They will receive the greater condemnation."

Luke has addressed this warning to the disciples; otherwise his text is almost verbally the same as Mark's.

45. An editorial link.

46f. Cf. 11:45-48—ostentation, vanity, greed and hypocrisy of the scribes condemned. Widows were likely to subscribe generously toward the upkeep of certain rabbis, especially if these had a reputation for piety; the husbands of married women would have been less susceptible!

21:1-4. The Widow's Mite
(Mk 12:41-44)

1 He looked up and saw the rich putting their gifts into the treasury; **2** and he saw a poor widow put in two copper coins. **3** And he said, "Truly I tell you, this poor widow has put in more than all of them; **4** for they all contributed out of their abundance, but she out of her poverty put in all the living that she had."

This episode closes the long series of discussions; it and the previous passage were probably linked in the tradition by the catchword "widow".

1f. By omitting reference to "the multitude" (Mk 12:41), Luke draws a clear contrast between the "rich" and the "poor widow"; he does not give the Roman equivalent (*quadrans,* Mk 12:42) for the two *lepta* (Greek)—the smallest coins in circulation.

3f. Generosity is not measured by the amount of the gift; the incident illustrates the theme of the gospel that the poor are nearer to God than the self-sufficient rich.

5-36. THE APOCALYPTIC DISCOURSE
(Mk 13:1-37; Mt 24:1-51)

In 17:22-37 Luke has treated of the Parousia, the glorious return of Jesus; here he takes up the same subject, but this time, like Mark and Matthew, in close association with the question of the destruction of Jerusalem. He follows Mark but with more changes than usual. This fact, and the clear distinction (much more obvious than in Mk/Mt) between the destruction of Jerusalem (21:5-24) and the End (21:25-36), are most satisfactorily explained on the assumption that Luke wrote after 70 A.D. (the date of the destruction of Jerusalem by the Romans). If this is granted, it is obvious why the apocalyptic terms of Mk 13:14-20 are translated into the plain language of Lk 21:20-24. Another factor is that Luke is more conscious of the delay of the Parousia. In short, Luke handles two distinct themes: one historical—the destruction of Jerusalem and the victory of the gospel; the other eschatological—the end of this age and the Parousia of the Son of man.

5-7. The Destruction of the Temple
(Mk 13:1-4; Mt 24:1-3)

5 And as some spoke of the temple, how it was adorned with noble stones and offerings, he said, **6** "As for these things which you see, the days will come when there shall not be left here one stone upon another that will not be thrown down." **7** And they asked him, "Teacher, when will this be, and what will be the sign when this is about to take place?"

5. "Some" in place of "one of his disciples" (Mk 13:1)—the discourse is no longer addressed only to the disciples. Luke omits Mark's reference to the Mount of Olives (Mk 13:3); the setting is still in the Temple. In Luke's scheme, during this last period in Jerusalem, Jesus is in the Temple by day and on the Mount of Olives by night.

6. "The days will come"—introducing an oracle of woe: this splendid Temple is doomed.

7. In Mark (13:3) four disciples question Jesus privately. The question of v. 7 concerns the destruction of the Temple; in his reply Jesus distinguishes this event from the end of the world: the fall of Jerusalem will not mark the End.

8-19. The Warning Signs
(Mk 13:5-13; Mt 24:4-14; 10:17-21)

8 And he said, "Take heed that you are not led astray; for many will come in my name, saying, 'I am he!' and, 'The time is at hand!' Do not go after them. **9** And when you hear of wars and tumults, do not be terrified; for this must first take place, but the end will not be at once.

10 Then he said to them, "Nation will rise against nation, and kingdom against kingdom; **11** there will be great earthquakes, and in various places famines and pestilences; and there will be terrors and great signs from heaven. **12** But before all this they will lay their hands on you and persecute you, delivering you up to the synagogues and prisons, and you will be brought before kings and governors for my name's sake. **13** This will be a time for you to bear testimony. **14** Settle it therefore in your minds, not to meditate beforehand how to answer; **15** for I will give you a mouth and wisdom, which none of your adversaries will be able to withstand or contradict. **16** You will be delivered up even by parents and brothers and kinsmen and friends, and some of you they will put to death; **17** you will be hated by all for my name's sake. **18** But not a hair of your head will perish. **19** By your endurance you will gain your lives."

8. By his addition of the phrase "the time is at hand" (cf. Dn 7:22), Luke strengthens the warning against false messiahs who preach that the end of the age is imminent.

9. "The end will not be at once" is a stronger expression than Mark's (13:7) and emphasizes the delay of the Parousia: these events precede the fall of Jerusalem but they do not herald the End.

10f. The editorial phrase "then he said to them" marks a transition from the warnings of v. 8f to the prophetic passage which follows; Luke adds "pestilences" (cf. Jer 14:12; 21:7,9; Ezek 5:12,17), "terrors and great signs from heaven" (cf. 2 Mc

5:3), and omits Mark's "this is but the beginning of the sufferings" (Mk 13:8) because he sees the beginning in the persecution of the disciples (vv. 12-19). The language consciously echoes
traditional Old Testament images of disaster (cf. Is 8:21; 13:13;
19:2; Jer 21:9; 34:17; Ezek 5:12; Am 4:6-11; 8:8; 2 Chr 15:6)
and could well be applied to the destruction of Jerusalem, seen
as a divine intervention and as a prefiguration of the end of the
world.

12. Of more immediate concern to the disciples is the persecution they must face (cf. Ac 4:3; 5:17f, 40f; 6:12). Luke omits
Mk 13:10 because the gospel has been preached to the end of
the earth (Ac 1:8; 28:30f).

13. Profession of faith in such circumstances will be the
supreme testimony to the gospel.

14f. Luke has rewritten Mk 13.11, to avoid a repetition of
12:11f. The wording of v. 15 recalls Ac 6:10—the martyr Stephen.
It is Christ himself (Mk 13:11; Lk 12:12—the Holy Spirit) who
will inspire the disciples (cf. Ac 4:14; 6:10; 26:28)—their victory
will be really his.

16f. A paraphrase of Mk 13: 12-13a: the world's hate, and
martyrdom for some, will be their fate (cf. Mi 7:6; Lk 12:52f),
yet they must remain confident.

18f. V. 18 is a proverbial expression (cf. 1 Sm 14:45; 2 Sm
14:11; 1 Kg 1:52; Lk 12:7; Ac 27:34). The two verses follow on
vv. 14f (vv. 16f may be regarded as a parenthesis): steadfast,
supported by Christ, the disciples will come through the persecution (cf. Ap 3:10)—v. 16b refers to a small minority. In this
context of persecution the optimistic atmosphere is that of Acts;
but Luke intimates that Christians must anticipate a long period
of tribulation.

20-24. Siege of Jerusalem
(Mk 13:14-20; Mt 24:15-22)

20 "But when you see Jerusalem surrounded by armies, then know
that its desolation has come near. **21** Then let those who are in Judea
flee to the mountains, and let those who are inside the city depart, and
let not those who are out in the country enter it; **22** for these are days
of vengeance, to fulfill all that is written. **23** Alas for those who are
with child and for those who give suck in those days! For great distress shall be upon the earth and wrath upon this people; **24** they will

fall by the edge of the sword, and be led captive among all nations; and Jerusalem will be trodden down by the Gentiles, until the times of the Gentiles are fulfilled."

The text of Mark has been drastically rewritten: in v. 20 the "desolating sacrilege" (Mk 13:14) in the Temple has become the siege of the holy city: v. 21 replaces Mk 13:15f (already used in Lk 17:31) and v. 22 is a new addition. A vivid description of the fate of the city (v. 23f) replaces the vague prophecy of Mk 13:19f; reference to the Christian remnant (Mk 13:20) is omitted. The most reasonable explanation of this procedure is that Luke has worked over the text of Mark in the light of the historical fate of Jerusalem. The suggestion that Luke has not written after this event, but has cleverly used biblical texts relevant to the siege of Jerusalem in 587 B.C., is undoubtedly a serious one and has much in its favor; but it is quite in the manner of Luke to be guided by biblical parallels and to imitate Old Testament language.

20. The opening phrase echoes Mk 14:1, the rest is Luke's composition; as clearly as in 19:43 the siege of Jerusalem is described.

21. In the initial stages of the siege there is yet the possibility of flight.

22. Proper to Luke, it gives the reason for the flight of the disciples: the fate of the city is sealed. This is the judgment of God foretold by the prophets (cf. Dn 9:26).

23. Mk 13:17 refers to the difficulties of flight. Luke (v. 23a) applies the *woe* to those in the doomed city; in v. 23b he adapts Mk 13:19 to fit the fate of Jesus. Mk 13:18 has been omitted, perhaps because of its obscurity, but, more likely, because the siege did not take place during winter but during April—September, 70 A.D.

24. The merciful shortening of the days of wrath (Mk 13:20) is left aside; doubtless because the prophetic doctrine of the remnant would be unfamiliar to Luke's Gentile readers. The fate of Jerusalem is summed up in three points: part of the inhabitants will be slain; the rest will be sold into slavery (cf. Jos BJ VI 9, 3, § 420); the city will be "trodden down" by the Gentiles (Titus stationed the tenth legion on the site of the ruined city— cf. Jos BJ VII 1, 2, § 5; 1, 3, § 17). Luke may well have been aware

of all this. "Until the times of the Gentiles are fulfilled": Luke
has set an undetermined period between the destruction of
Jerusalem and the End (vv. 25-28). This "time of the Gentiles"
is, perhaps, the period in which the vineyard, taken from the
Jews, has been given to the care of others (cf. 20:16); it is the
same as the period of the Church. The fall of Jerusalem makes
manifest to all that the "time of Israel", which really ended with
the ministry of Christ and the founding of the Church, had
indeed come to an end. Like Paul (Rm 11:25f) and Ap 11:1f,
Luke appears to entertain a hope of a final return of Israel—when
the "times of the Gentiles" are fulfilled.

25-28. The Coming of the Son of Man
(Mk 13:24-27; Mt 24:29-31)

25 "And there will be signs in sun and moon and stars, and upon
the earth distress of nations in perplexity at the roaring of the sea and
the waves, 26 men fainting with fear and with foreboding of what is
coming on the world; for the powers of the heavens will be shaken.
27 And then they will see the Son of man coming in a cloud with
power and great glory. 28 Now when these things begin to take place,
look up and raise your heads, because your redemption is drawing
near."

Now the discourse turns to the end of the "times of the
Gentiles" and to the judgment of mankind.

25f. Luke's apocalyptic description, based on Mk 13:24, has
been influenced by Is 13:10 and Ps 65 (64):8; more clearly, too,
the whole world is involved (v. 26).

27f. Cf. Mk 13:26—the fulfillment of Dn 7:13f. Luke leaves
aside Mk 13:27.

28. Looks back to the signs of v. 25f. The cosmic events which
will terrify the nations will indicate to the followers of Christ
that the time of persecution is ending: their "redemption" (a
Pauline word, cf. Rm 3:24; 8:23; Eph 1:7) is *drawing near.*
These signs before the End do not contradict 17:20f and 21:34f.
The End will be preceded by signs, yet the Son of man will
appear suddenly like lightning.

29-33. The Time of This Coming
(Mk 13:28-32; Mt 24:32-36)

29 And he told them a parable: "Look at the fig tree, and all the trees; 30 as soon as they come out in leaf, you see for yourselves and know that the summer is already near. 31 So also, when you see these things taking place, you know that the kingdom of God is near. 32 Truly, I say to you, this generation will not pass away till all has taken place. 33 Heaven and earth will pass away, but my words will not pass away."

The introductory formula (v. 29a) is proper to Luke; he has added "all the trees"—so departing from the Palestinian local color. He has changed the "he", that is, the Son of man of Mk 13:29, into "kingdom of God" (v. 31); otherwise the two versions are in close agreement. As originally spoken by Jesus, the parable must have referred to the disaster which was overhanging Jerusalem; and while Luke, going back beyond vv. 25-28, may regard the signs of vv. 20-24, it is surely more natural that the parable and its comment agree with the immediate context (vv. 25-28,34-36). In other words, for the evangelist, the parable refers to the signs of the End. It is true that, strictly speaking, v. 32 will not suffer this interpretation, but Luke may well have taken "this generation" in the broad sense of "mankind"—for his statement has no temporal value but, like v. 33, underlines the constancy of God's design. Thus, he has omitted Mk 13:32 with its reference to time.

34-36. Watchfulness

34 "But take heed to yourselves lest your hearts be weighed down with dissipation and drunkenness and cares of this life, and that day come upon you suddenly like a snare; 35 for it will come upon all who dwell upon the face of the whole earth. 36 But watch at all times, praying that you may have strength to escape all these things that will take place, and to stand before the Son of man."

Luke has replaced the passage Mk 13:33-37 (cf. Lk 12:35-40) with an admonition to watchfulness (cf. 1 Thes 5:1-11), one influenced by his realization of the delay of the Parousia.

34f. Christians must be constantly on their guard against dissipation and absorption in worldly affairs (cf. 8:14; 12:22; 17:26-

30): the End will come suddenly, "like a snare" (cf. Is 24:17). "That day", the day of judgment, is the other aspect of the "day of redemption" (v. 28). The universality of the final judgment is emphasized.

36. Vigilance (Mk 13:33; Lk 18:1) and prayer (18:1) will win for them strength to support the dangers and temptation of the last trials and will enable them to stand (among the redeemed) in the presence of the Son of man come in his glory.

37-38. Jesus' Last Days

37 And every day he was teaching in the temple, but at night he went out and lodged on the mount called Olivet. 38 And early in the morning all the people came to him in the temple to hear him.

This summary statement links up with 19:47. Jesus spent the nights, not in Bethany (cf. Mk 11:11), but at the Mount of Olives, in the open (cf. 22: 39,47). The wording suggests a fairly long period of activity (cf. 19:47). There is an undeniable literary contact with Jn 8:1f; significantly, a few manuscripts have inserted here the passage on the woman taken in adultery (Jn 7:53–8:11).

VI. THE PASSION 22–23

In his Passion narrative Luke still follows Mark, but not as closely as elsewhere. To a notable extent he has arranged the order of events so as to give a clearer and smoother account, and here, as elsewhere, his theological ideas give a personal coloring to the narrative. Ultimately, however, the more satisfactory arrangement is due to the fact that he is evidently following a special source (besides Mark), one related to the Johannine tradition.

22:1-2. The Plot of the Sanhedrin [57]
(Mk 14:1f; Mt 26:1-5)

1 Now the feast of Unleavened Bread drew near, which is called the Passover. 2 And the chief priests and the scribes were seeking how to put him to death; for they feared the people.

Very close to Mark. 1. Strictly speaking, Passover and feast of Unleavened Bread are not identical: the Passover meal was eaten on the night of 15th Nisan, the first of the seven days of Unleavened Bread; Mark (14:1) has clearly distinguished them.
2. "They feared the people" looks back to 20:19. Luke omits Mark's "not during the feast" because, in fact (according to the Synoptic tradition), Jesus was crucified on the feast. He omits the anointing at Bethany (Mk 14:3-9), doubtless because he has described a similar incident in 7:36-50; besides, the action of Judas follows neatly after the decision of the Sanhedrin.

3-6. The Betrayal
(Mk 14:10f; Mt 26:14-16)

3 Then Satan entered into Judas called Iscariot, who was of the number of the twelve; 4 he went away and conferred with the chief
[57] See p. 291.

244

priests and captains how he might betray him to them. **5** And they were glad, and engaged to give him money. **6** So he agreed, and sought an opportunity to betray him to them in the absence of the multitude.

Apart from the addition of v. 3, Luke has only slightly re-touched the text of Mark.

3. His explicit attribution of Judas' action to the influence of Satan is a new and powerful theological insight (cf. Jn 13:2,27). At the beginning of the Passion narrative it is made clear that the machinery now set in motion against Jesus is guided by the Adversary. Now is the "opportune time" (4:13), the moment of the last combat, when, just as at the temptation in the wilder-ness, Jesus and Satan stand face to face (cf. 22:53). "Chapter 22, v. 3 completes the circle of redemptive history, for Satan is now present again. Now the period of salvation, as it was described in 4:18-21, is over and the Passion, which is described by Luke and also by John as a work of Satan, is beginning."[58]

4. The "captains" are the officers of the Temple police (cf. v. 52; Ac 4:1; 5:24,26).

6. Luke notes Judas' acceptance of the terms and the need for stealth.

7-13. Preparation for the Passover
(Mk 14:12-16; Mt 26:17-19)

7 Then came the day of Unleavened Bread, on which the passover lamb had to be sacrificed. **8** So Jesus sent Peter and John, saying, "Go and prepare the passover for us, that we may eat it." **9** They said to him, "Where will you have us prepare it?" **10** He said to them, "Be-hold, when you have entered the city, a man carrying a jar of water will meet you; follow him into the house which he enters, **11** and tell the householder, 'The Teacher says to you, Where is the guest room, where I am to eat the passover with my disciples?' **12** And he will show you a large upper room furnished; there make ready." **13** And they went, and found it as he had told them; and they prepared the passover.

Luke differs from Mark in having Jesus take the initiative; he also specifies that the two disciples were Peter and John.

7. The first day of Unleavened Bread is meant (v. 1), that is,

[58] H. Conzelmann, *op. cit.*, p. 80.

15th Nisan. The Jewish day was reckoned from sunset to sunset. Very likely Mark, for the benefit of his Gentile readers, has used the Graeco-Roman system—midnight to midnight; and Luke has followed him in this. Thus, since 15th Nisan began at sunset (and 14th Nisan ended at the same time), the sacrifice of the Passover lamb towards the close of 14th Nisan and the eating of the Passover meal a few hours later, early on 15th Nisan, would both, by our reckoning, fall on the same day.[59]

8. The companionship of Peter and John is a theme common to Luke and to the fourth gospel (cf. Lk 8:51; 9:28; 22:8; Ac 1:13; 3:1f,11; 4:13,19; 8:14; Jn 13:23f; 18:15f; 20:3-9; 21:7,20f).

9-12. Water was normally carried by women; a man carrying a jar of water would be conspicuous. Probably, Jesus had already made arrangements with his host.

13. Preparation for the Passover meal would include the purchase, sacrificing, and roasting of the lamb; the purchase of unleavened bread, herbs, and wine; and the trimming of lamps. Luke has placed the announcement of the betrayal at the close of the meal (vv. 21-23) and not at the beginning as in Mk/Mt. Thus he achieves an uninterrupted sequence and more effectively presents the institution of the Eucharist as the climax of the Passover meal.

14-20. The Lord's Supper
(Mk 14:22-25; Mt 26:26-29; 1 Cor 11:23-25)

14 And when the hour came, he sat at table, and the apostles with him. **15** And he said to them, "I have earnestly desired to eat this passover with you before I suffer; **16** for I tell you, I shall not eat it until it is fulfilled in the kingdom of God." **17** And he took a cup, and when he had given thanks he said, "Take this, and divide it among yourselves; **18** for I tell you that from now on I shall not drink of the fruit of the vine until the kingdom of God comes." **19** And he took bread, and when he had given thanks he broke it and gave it to them, saying, "This is my body [which is given for you. Do this in remembrance of me." **20** And likewise the cup after supper, saying, "This cup which is poured out for you is the new covenant in my blood."]

The first problem that presents itself is a celebrated textual one: the choice of "longer" or "shorter" text—depending on the

[59] See pp. 292ff.

acceptance or rejection of vv. 19b-20. The longer text is represented by the majority of manuscripts and versions; vv. 19b-20 are missing from Codex Bezae and the Old Latin (v. 20 is omitted by some Syriac manuscripts). Westcott and Hort pronounced in favor of the shorter reading and many critics have followed them (cf. RSV). The matter cannot be decided on textual grounds alone and internal evidence strongly supports the authenticity of vv. 19b-20. In favor of the longer text we may note its symmetrical structure—two parallel panels, vv. 15-18 and 19f, each composed of corresponding elements: Passover meal of v. 15f and bread of v. 19; cup of v. 17f and cup of v. 20. Again, the fact that vv. 19b-20 differ only in detail from 1 Cor 11:23b-25a suggests that both Paul and Luke have echoed the liturgical text with which they were familiar, doubtless the one in vogue in Antioch and then in the Pauline churches. The presence of two cups (vv. 17,20), over which Jesus had pronounced a blessing, disconcerted certain copyists. To judge from the manuscript evidence, the first cup was regarded as being sufficiently eucharistic and the other was set aside. It is also likely that the words of v. 17 were closer to the liturgical formula which was familiar to the scribes in question.

14. A consciously solemn introduction to the Supper (cf. Mk 14:17); the "hour" may be an echo of the Johannine "hour". The title "Apostles" (in place of Mark's "Twelve") is in keeping with the solemnity of the setting.

15-18. It is often argued that Luke here follows a special source. In fact, it is far more likely that he has rewritten Mk 14:25. The eschatological saying (vv. 16,18), placed by Mark after the institution of the Eucharist (Mk 14:25), is better situated before that event, as here; but its new situation is due to Luke's deliberate arrangement. His literary construction is dominated by a theological idea: the Eucharist is the Christian Passover. Thus, before describing the institution of the Eucharist, he gives a schematized description of the Passover meal. The juxtaposition of the two rites brings out their difference: the old must be "fulfilled" (v. 16b) by something new in the kingdom which is to come (v. 18b). But now the outlook is no longer purely eschatological as in Mk 14:25; in its Lucan context the Passover meal and the wine (vv. 16,18) suggest the Eucharist, and the "kingdom of God" suggests the domain in which this paschal rite will find expression, that is, the Church. Significantly, Luke does not speak of "new" wine (Mark). In implying that Jesus will again eat and drink in the kingdom, he may have in mind the post-Resurrection meals which he (24:30,41-43; Ac 10:41) and John (Jn 21:9-14) alone mention.

19f. Literary dependence on 1 Cor 11:24f (more accurately, on the liturgical tradition which Paul has reproduced) is undeniable. The minor retouches of Luke are meant to achieve a better parallelism and are also suggested by the text of Mark. The following literal translation of the texts of Luke and Paul brings out the parallelism.

Lk 22:19f	*1 Cor 11:23b-25*
	The Lord Jesus, on the night that he was betrayed,
And, having taken some bread,	took some bread,
when he had given thanks	and when he had given thanks
he broke (it)	he broke (it)
and gave (it) to them,	
saying:	and said:
"This is my body	"This is my body
which is given for you.	which is for you.
Do this as a memorial of me."	Do this as a memorial of me."
And the cup likewise	And likewise the cup
after supper, saying:	after supper, saying:
"This cup (is)	"This cup is
the new covenant in my blood	the new covenant in my blood:
which is poured out for you."	
	Do this, as often as you drink it, as a memorial of me."

Though Lk 22:19f is parallel to vv. 15-18, it concerns something entirely new: the bread of v. 19 is no longer, like the Passover lamb of vv. 15f, ordinary food, but the body of Christ; the cup of v. 20 is not filled with the wine of the Passover meal, but with the blood of Christ. While RSV (margin) has "is given" and "is poured out" it seems that the participles *didomenon* and *ekchunnomenon* refer to the immediate future, hence "will be given", "will be poured out". Jesus announces his approaching death and presents it as a sacrifice, like that of the victims whose blood sealed the Sinai covenant (Ex 24:5-8)—but a redemptive sacrifice. For, in speaking of blood "poured out for you" (Mk: "for many") in view of a "new covenant", Jesus had in mind the Servant of Yahweh whose life had been "poured out" and who had borne the sins of "many" (Is 53:12); God had given him as "a covenant to the peoples, a light to the nations"(Is 42:6; cf. Lk 4:17-21). Jesus lets it be understood that his imminent death is going to replace the sacrifices of the Old Law and deliver men, not from temporal captivity but from the bondage of sin; he is about to inaugurate the new covenant which Jeremiah had foretold (Jer 31:31-34). "Do this in remembrance of me": the disciples must repeat what he had done and said, his actions and his words. It is not, however, a mere commemoration but the renewal of a rite by means of which the sacrifice of the living Christ is made present in bread and wine: their action will be as real and efficacious as that of Jesus (because *he* will act in and through them). The gestures, the words, will be repeated, but the reality will persist unchanged: the sacrificial offering of the body and blood of Christ made once for all. And thus the Lord, in an abiding and substantial presence, will be with his own to the end of time.

21-23. Announcement of the Betrayal
(Mk 14:17-21; Mt 26:20-25; cf. Jn 13:21-30)

21 "But behold the hand of him who betrays me is with me on the table. 22 For the Son of man goes as it has been determined; but woe to that man by whom he is betrayed!" 23 And they began to question one another, which of them it was that would do this.

By giving the announcement of the betrayal at this point, Luke has avoided the difficulty, present in Matthew and Mark, that Judas still remained for the meal after he had been unmasked.

21. Suggested by Ps 41(40):10, but adapted to fit this context.

22f. Luke emphasizes the divine preordination of events and omits the terrible saying of Mk 14:21c. He places the anxious questioning of the disciples (of one another, not of Jesus as in Mark—cf. Jn 13:22) at the end (v. 23; cf. Mk 14:19).

24-30. Greatness in the Kingdom
(Mt 20:20-28; Mk 10:35-45)

24 A dispute also arose among them, which of them was to be regarded as the greatest. **25** And he said to them, "The kings of the Gentiles exercise lordship over them; and those in authority over them are called benefactors. **26** But not so with you; rather let the greatest among you become as the youngest, and the leader as one who serves. **27** For which is the greater, one who sits at table, or one who serves? Is it not the one who sits at table? But I am among you as one who serves.

28 "You are those who have continued with me in my trials; **29** as my Father appointed a kingdom for me, so do I appoint for you **30** that you may eat and drink at my table in my kingdom, and sit on thrones judging the twelve tribes of Israel."

While Mark and Matthew have the journey to the Mount of Olives immediately after the institution of the Eucharist, Luke adds some farewell words of Jesus in the supper room (vv. 24-38)—thus anticipating the discourse of John (Jn 13:31–14:31). Mark and Matthew have the episode of vv. 24-27 after the demands of the sons of Zebedee; Luke has it here, in the context of the Passover meal, because of the reference to sitting at table (v. 27).

25. The title *Evergetes* (benefactor) was assumed by many of the Ptolemies and Seleucids.

26. In the kingdom of Jesus, those who hold authority must be the servants of those whom they govern: the principle of authority is admitted, but the manner of its exercise is bluntly characterized as service. Happily, in our day, we are taking a second look at these words of the Master. John L. McKenzie comments: "Too frequently the leaders of the Church have counted on the Spirit for what the Spirit does not give and counted on themselves for what the Spirit does give. One wonders whether the Spirit is present with all its force in the Church when the words 'obedience' and 'due submission' and 'duly constituted authority' are heard in the Church more frequently than the word 'love'. One could suspect an effort to substitute for the power of love the power of domination; and one is reminded of the kings and magnates of the Gentiles." [60]

27. This is not a veiled reference to the feet-washing of Jn 13:4-17; it is a simple example by way of answer to the question of v. 24—the repetition of *tis meizōn* ("who is the greatest") forms an *inclusion* which marks the passage as a unit. Throughout his ministry Jesus had served his disciples but had never ceased to be their Master.

28-30. The passage seems to be a combination of two sayings: vv. 28,30b (occurring, in another context, in Mt 19:28) and vv. 29,30a (proper to Luke); it has been added here by means of the catchword "table" (vv. 30,27,21—and the general context of the Passover meal).

28. In its present context the saying probably points to the betrayal of Judas: the others are those who have remained faithful.

29f. In virtue of the royal power which Jesus already possesses he can make provision for his faithful Apostles: they will have part with him in the Messianic feast (cf. 14:15-24) and, for the earthly phase of the kingdom of Christ, they will participate in his authority over all its subjects ("judging" used in the biblical sense of "ruling over"—cf. Jg 3:10; 10:2f; 12:7-13). Luke does not say *twelve* thrones (cf. Matthew), doubtless with Judas in mind. Another, and perhaps more satisfactory, interpretation is to regard the passage in the light of Lk 24:26: as Christ through suffering entered into his glory, so the disciples, the companions of his trials (v. 28), will share his glory: that is, their reward.

31-34. Peter's Denial Foretold
(Mk 14:27-31; Mt 26:31-35)

31 "Simon, Simon, behold, Satan demanded to have you, that he might sift you like wheat, 32 but I have prayed for you that your faith may not fail; and when you have turned again, strengthen your brethren." 33 And he said to him, "Lord, I am ready to go with you to prison and to death." 34 He said, "I tell you, Peter, the cock will not crow this day, until you three times deny that you know me."

Originally these were two distinct sayings (vv. 31f proper to

[60] J. L. McKenzie, *op. cit.*, p. 186.

Luke and vv. 33f Marcan); note the change of names (vv. 31, 34).

31f. Unlike Mark and Matthew the scene is still the supper room (cf. Jn 13:36-38). Repetition of the name strikes a note of solemnity; Simon—"because Jesus speaks to him as to a weak man who does not deserve the name of Peter".[61] Satan demanded to have Simon as he sought to ruin Job (Jb 1:6-12; 2:1-7); he makes his final onslaught not only against Jesus (22:3), but against his Apostles for whom the Passion will be a "sifting", a profound spiritual trial. Simon will stumble and deny his Master but the prayer of Jesus had not been inefficacious; deep down, his faith in the Messiahship of Jesus had not failed. When Peter will have "returned", will have come to his senses (cf. 22:62), he will become the strong support of his brethren. In Luke this prophecy of Peter's denial looks forward to his restoration to leadership of the Apostles (cf. Jn 21:15-19).

33f. Substantially the same as Mk 14:29-31 but rather freely rewritten.

35-38. The Testing Time

35 And he said to them, "When I sent you out with no purse or bag or sandals, did you lack anything?" They said, "Nothing." **36** He said to them, "But now, let him who has a purse take it, and likewise a bag. And let him who has no sword sell his mantle and buy one. **37** For I tell you that this scripture must be fulfilled in me, 'And he was reckoned with transgressors'; for what is written about me has its fulfillment." **38** And they said, "Look, Lord, here are two swords." And he said to them, "It is enough."

Peculiar to Luke. The sayings have been influenced by the experience of the Christian community.

35. This looks back to the time before the time of trial. The reference is to 10:4, the sending of the seventy-two, and supports the view that 9:1-6 and 10:1-16 are not distinct discourses.

36. But the exhilarating (cf. 10:17) period of the Galilean ministry is over: their Master is now going to his death and they, as his associates, will find all men's hands against them. The hostility they will have to face is depicted in symbolic terms: a purse in order to buy food (no longer given freely), a sword to win it by force. "The instruction to sell their coats and buy

---

[61] M.-J. Lagrange, *op. cit.*, p. 553.

swords is an example of Jesus' fondness for violent metaphor (cf. Mt 23:24; Mk 10:25), but the disciples take it literally, as pedants have continued to do ever since." [62]

37. The reason is that the disciples will share the fate of their Master. Jesus quotes Is 53:12 and thus explicitly identifies himself with the Suffering Servant of Yahweh. For him, the decisive moment has come.

38. The disciples, still "slow of heart" (24:25), take the words of Jesus literally. The phrase "It is enough" does not refer to the swords but closes the discussion; doubtless the words were tinged with sadness—*"on peut soupçonner un sourire indulgent, et non sans mélancolie"*.[63]

39-46. At the Mount of Olives
(Mk 14:26,32-42; Mt 26:30,36-46)

39 And he came out, and went, as was his custom, to the Mount of Olives; and the disciples followed him. **40** And when he came to the place he said to them, "Pray that you may not enter into temptation." **41** And he withdrew from them about a stone's throw, and knelt down and prayed, **42** "Father, if thou art willing, remove this cup from me; nevertheless not my will, but thine, be done." **43** And there appeared to him an angel from heaven, strengthening him. **44** And being in an agony he prayed more earnestly; and his sweat became like great drops of blood falling down upon the ground. **45** And when he rose from prayer, he came to the disciples and found them sleeping for sorrow, **46** and he said to them, "Why do you sleep? Rise and pray that you may not enter into temptation."

Luke abridges Mark more drastically than usual but, at the same time, makes his own contribution from another tradition.

39. Only now do Jesus and the disciples leave the supper room to go "as was his custom" (cf. 21:37; Jn 18:2) to the Mount of Olives. At this point Luke omits the prophecy of the disciples' desertion and the promise of a post-Resurrection appearance of Jesus in Galilee (Mk 14:27f); he has anticipated the foretelling of Peter's denial which Mark puts on the way to the Mount of Olives (Mk 14:29-31).

40-46. Luke omits the choice of the three disciples who were to keep vigil with Jesus, also the thrice repeated prayer, together

---

[62] G. B. Caird, *op. cit.*, p. 241.
[63] M.-J. Lagrange, *op. cit.*, p. 558.

with the three references to the weariness of the disciples. He does not give the Semitic place-name "Gethsemane" (cf. Mk 14:32-42).

40. Luke reiterates at the close of the scene (22:46) the admonition to pray which Mark puts later (Mk 14:38). "Temptation" is the eschatological trial, the great Messianic trial (cf. 11:4): the sufferings which must precede the era of salvation (cf. 24-26). At his hour of trial, Jesus chooses to drink the cup, he chooses the cross; the disciples must pray that they, too, in their turn, will make the right choice.

41f. Luke's more elegant style is obvious: Jesus "withdrew" about "a stone's throw"; he "knelt down" rather than "fell on the ground" (Mk 14:35). Luke omits Jesus' request that this hour might pass from him (Mk 14:35). In Luke's presentation Jesus does not look for human comfort; instead, by his repeated warning (vv. 40, 46) he seeks to fortify his disciples; prayer is the weapon against temptation. It is an angel who strengthens Jesus for the hour of death.

43f. These verses, proper to Luke, though missing from important manuscripts like Codex Alexandrinus and Codex Vaticanus, are, nonetheless, authentic. Their omission can be readily explained on theological grounds: the representation of the Lord strengthened by an angel, and the portrayal of the too human details of the agony. For the same reasons it is inconceivable that they should be a later insertion. Besides, the style is Lucan. The soul of Jesus is troubled in the first place, an anguish that reacts on his body (v. 44) and so the "strengthening" is primarily spiritual; the ministration of the angel symbolizes God's compassion for his Son and his anwer to that Son's prayer (cf. Heb 5:7). Throughout, Luke has drawn attention to the prayer of Jesus, and here is the culmination: in anguish—vividly foreseeing, and humanly shrinking from, the horrors of the Passion, burdened, above all, by his love for his own people and for all men—he prayed more earnestly. He himself, in his trial, this "temptation", puts into practice his own recommendation to the disciples (vv. 40,46). If Paul could understand so clearly that the power of God can support our weakness (cf. 2 Cor 12:10; Phil 4:13), Jesus himself has experienced, with a clarity we cannot imagine, that weakness and that strength. The extreme spiritual anguish of Jesus reacted on his body: his sweat became *like* great drops of blood. The expression may indicate the intensity of the sweat; it does not necessarily imply that it is a sweat mixed with blood—though this is, perhaps, the more natural interpretation. At any rate, it is a striking illustration of the reality of Christ's humanity. This whole passage on the agony of our Savior should not only remind us of the cost of our redemption but, above all, should be a powerful encouragement to us; for indeed, our High Priest is no stranger to suffering; he knows the demands it can make on our human nature and he can fully sympathize with our human lot (cf. Heb 4:15; 5:7-9).

45. A delightful example of Luke's delicacy of feeling: the disciples were "sleeping *for sorrow*" and not simply because "their eyes were very heavy" (Mk/Mt).

46. With v. 40 this forms an *inclusion*, rounding off the passage.

47-53. The Arrest
(Mk 14:43-52; Mt 26:47-56; Jn 18:2-11)

47 While he was still speaking, there came a crowd, and the man called Judas, one of the twelve, was leading them. He drew near to Jesus to kiss him; **48** but Jesus said to him, "Judas, would you betray the Son of man with a kiss?" **49** And when those who were about saw what would follow, they said, "Lord, shall we strike with the sword?" **50** And one of them struck the slave of the high priest and cut off his right ear. **51** But Jesus said, "No more of this!" And he touched his ear and healed him. **52** Then Jesus said to the chief priests and captains of the temple and elders, who had come out against him, "Have you come out as against a robber, with swords and clubs? **53** When I was with you day after day in the temple, you did not lay hands on me. But this is your hour, and the power of darkness."

A much abbreviated version of Mark. Luke cannot bring himself to state that the traitor actually kissed Jesus (cf. Mk 14:45), and he also omits reference to the desertion of the disciples (Mk 14:50). Jesus is not at once arrested (cf. Mk 14:46) and, as in John (18:4-11), is perfectly in command of the situation.

48. The hour of the Son of man has come: already the cup is overflowing—the betrayal is signaled by a friend's token of friendship.

49f. One of the disciples (Simon Peter—Jn 18:10) struck off the man's ear—the *right* ear as in John, thus inflicting greater dishonor (cf. Mt 5:39).

51. Jesus' remark echoes that of v. 38: the disciples still do not understand. The healing of the servant's ear, given by Luke only, is a gesture that this evangelist could not overlook.

52-53a. It is surprising, to say the least, that the chief priests and the elders should have been present in person at the arrest. On the other hand, the saying of v. 53a (cf. Mk 14:49; Mt 26:55) strikingly resembles Jesus' answer made before Annas (Jn 18:20), a saying that could have been addressed only to the Jewish authorities. It is likely that a reply of Jesus made at the appearance before Annas (not recorded by the synoptists) is anticipated at this point.

53b. Jesus points out that only now, and not earlier, could his enemies have laid hands on him; but God had willed that this should be their hour—or rather the hour of the prince of darkness whose instruments they were, like Judas (v. 3). Now is the "appointed time" (4:13) and Satan had launched his final assault on Jesus.

54-62. Peter's Denial
(Mk 14:66-72; Mt 26:69-75; Jn 18:15-18, 25-27)

54 Then they seized him and led him away, bringing him into the high priest's house. Peter followed at a distance; **55** and when they had kindled a fire in the middle of the courtyard and sat down together, Peter sat among them. **56** Then a maid, seeing him as he sat in the light and gazing at him, said, "This man also was with him." **57** But he denied it, saying, "Woman, I do not know him." **58** And a little later some one else saw him and said, "You also are one of them." But Peter said, "Man, I am not." **59** And after an interval of about an hour still another insisted, saying, "Certainly this man also was with him; for he is a Galilean." **60** But Peter said, "Man, I do not know what you are saying." And immediately, while he was still speaking, the cock crowed. **61** And the Lord turned and looked at Peter. And Peter remembered the word of the Lord, how he had said to him "Before the cock crows today, you will deny me three times." **62** And he went out and wept bitterly.

54a. Only now does Luke state that Jesus was arrested. The high priest is not named but, very likely, Annas is meant (cf. Jn 18:13). Luke names Annas before Caiaphas in 3:1 and Ac 4:6 and it is altogether credible that this influential man would have been popularly called high priest, and may have been still regarded as the legitimate high priest: his deposition by the Romans would have seemed invalid. The "house" therefore is the house of Annas, not the official residence of the high priest.

54b-60. Peter's questioners are different in each of the gospels: Mark (a maid, the same maid, the bystanders), Matthew (a maid, another maid, the bystanders), Luke (a maid, "someone else", "another"), John (the portress, "they", "one of the servants of the high priest"). In Mark the denials of Peter become more vehement each time; in Luke there is a decrescendo (vv. 57, 58, 60); especially in vv. 60f he has toned down the vehemence of Peter's denial (cf. Mk 14:71). It seems very likely that Mk 14:66-72 combines two narratives: the first (14:66-68) ends with Peter going out into the forecourt and the cock crowing (this last detail, though omitted in many manuscripts, should be retained); in the other (14:69-72) two denials precede the cockcrow. It is noteworthy that in John the first denial (Jn 18:15-18) is separated from the others (18:25-27) by the interrogation before Annas (18:19-24). Luke, by omitting reference to Peter's exit and to the first cockcrow (Mk 14:68), has removed the traces of a composite narrative.

61f. It would seem that, after a brief interrogation by Annas (cf. Jn 18:19-24), Jesus spent the rest of the night in the courtyard of Annas' house; he had only to turn and look at Peter who sat by a fire in the middle of the courtyard. A typically Lucan touch is the look of Jesus that moved Peter so deeply—here again is the merciful Savior. "Each of us can take to heart this observation of Luke, that deeply sensitive writer. When we find ourselves guilty of a denial of Christ, be it small or great, we should feel that this eloquent glance of the Lord is turned on us: 'You had promised to be faithful, and now see what you have done' and, like Peter, we should be stirred to sincere repentance." [64]

63-65. Jesus Mocked
(Mk 14:65; Mt 26:67f)

63 Now the men who were holding Jesus mocked him and beat him; **64** they also blindfolded him and asked him, "Prophesy! Who is

[64] P. Benoit, *Passion et Résurrection du Seigneur* (Paris: Cerf, 1966), p. 80.

it that struck you?" **65** And they spoke many other words against him, reviling him.

John (18:13-23) tells of an appearance of Jesus before Annas immediately after his arrest; then—likely in the early morning— he was taken to Caiaphas (18:24). And though Luke does not name Annas, his text is clarified by the information John has supplied. The "high priest's house" of Lk 22:54 is the house of Annas; his courtyard is where Peter denied his Master and where Jesus was mocked. On this assumption those who mock Jesus are the guards who, after an interrogation (cf. Jn 8:19-23), have charge of him until the morning session of the Sanhedrin. V. 64 shows the guards playing a brutal version of a guessing game with their prisoner; mindful of the religious charges brought against him, they declare that this "prophet" should find the game an easy one. Here Jesus is mocked by the Jews as prophet, just as he will be mocked by the Romans as king (Jn 19:2f).

66-71. Jesus before the Sanhedrin
(Mk 14:53-64; 15:1; Mt 26:57-66; 27:1f)

66 When day came, the assembly of the elders of the people gathered together, both chief priests and scribes; and they led him away to their council, and they said, **67** "If you are the Christ, tell us." But he said to them, "If I tell you, you will not believe; **68** and if I ask you, you will not answer. **69** But from now on the Son of man shall be seated at the right hand of the power of God." **70** And they all said, "Are you the Son of God, then?" And he said to them, "You say that I am." **71** And they said, "What further testimony do we need? We have heard it ourselves from his own lips."

Mark and Matthew speak of two sessions of the Sanhedrin, one at night which they describe in some detail (Mk 14:53,55-64; Mt 26:57,59-66), the other in the early morning, which they mention briefly (Mk 15:1; Mt 27:1). Luke speaks of one session only, and places it in the morning (Lk 22:66-71). During the night he has the denials of Peter and the mockery of Jesus by his guards. Mark/Matthew's presentation is frankly unlikely: a night assembly of the Sanhedrin is hard to accept and it is difficult to believe that the members of the Sanhedrin, so conscious of their dignity, would, immediately after the trial of Jesus, have

taken part in the crude mockery scene; in Luke this last is shown
as the guards' way of passing the night. In short, it can scarcely
be doubted that Luke owes his better arrangement to a personal
source distinct from Mark. Comparison with John not only confirms the order of Luke but helps to explain the presentation of
Mark/Matthew. Above (vv. 54-65) we have suggested that the
high priest in question is Annas. Luke omits the interrogation
before him (cf. Jn 18:19-23) but sets the mocking scene at the
courtyard of his house where Jesus was confined until morning.
Mark/Matthew, on the other hand, speak of two sessions, because there were two sessions; but they have substituted for the
private interrogation of Annas, held at night, the official process
of the Sanhedrin held next morning. The discrepancy between
Mark/Matthew and Luke/John is explained by this simple dis-
placement—one that easily happened in the oral tradition.

66. The morning session was that of the *presbyterion,* the
"assembly of elders", that is, the Sanhedrin, whose main compo-
nents were the chief priests and scribes. The place of the session
was, most probably, a special building near the Temple; the term
synedrion may refer to this place but, strictly speaking, it means
no more than "council".

The passage vv. 67-71 is based on Mk 14:61-64, with the customary Lucan modifications. Luke has omitted the saying about
the Temple (Mk 14:57f). The course of the trial has been schematized; the examination of witnesses has been set aside as superfluous.

67-69. In Mk 14:61 and Mt 26:63 Jesus is asked if he is "the
Christ, the Son of God", but Luke has separated the two titles:
"If you are the Christ, tell us" (v. 67) and "Are you the Son of
God, then?" (v. 70)—so reflecting the full Christian meaning of
"Son of God". The evangelist has a similar gradation in his Infancy narrative (1:31-33 and 1:35). In our passage the question
of v. 67a regards the Messianic dignity of Jesus. The first part of
his reply (v. 67b), proper to Luke, is Johannine in tone: cf. Jn
10:25 which comes after the same question (cf. Jn 3:12; 6:36,64;
8:45). The "power of God" (v. 69) explains the Jewish expression "Power" (= "God") (Mk 14:62). Luke avoids saying that the
Sanhedrites "will see" the Son of man or that he will "come with
the clouds of heaven" (Mk 14:62; cf. Dn 7:13), apparently to

avoid possible misunderstanding. In Dn 7:13 the Son of man is borne on "the clouds of heaven" into the divine presence; Mk 14:62 applies the image to the triumphal return of the risen Christ to his Father—this the Sanhedrites "will see". But later, in certain Christian milieux at least, this "coming on clouds" was applied to the Parousia (cf. 1 Thes 4:16f); Luke does not wish his readers to believe (mistakenly) that Jesus had announced his imminent Parousia. But he does declare that "from now on" (cf. 1:48; 5:10; 12:52; 22:18; Ac 18:6) the Son of man is exalted to the right hand of God (Ps 110[109]:1) because his imminent death is his entry into glory (cf. Lk 24:26; Ac 2:36). Jesus is the Messiah—but seated at the right hand of God—a Messiah of divine rank.

70f. The second question seeks to clarify this point: is Jesus claiming divine Sonship? Though Luke omits the term "blasphemy" (Mk 14:64), the reaction of the Sanhedrites shows that they regard him guilty of that crime: he, a man, had "made himself the Son of God" (Jn 19:7). More clearly than Mark/Matthew, Luke has brought out the reason why Jesus was condemned to death. If he does not mention the sentence, it is because it had to be ratified by the Roman authorities. It does not follow, of course, that the Sanhedrites were guilty of deicide (cf. 23:34; Ac 3:17); but they had rejected, and had compassed the death of, God's last messenger (19:44), their Messiah.

23:1-5. Jesus before Pilate
(Mk 15:1-5; Mt 27:11-14; Jn 18:28-38)

1 Then the whole company of them arose, and brought him before Pilate. 2 And they began to accuse him, saying, "We found this man perverting our nation, and forbidding us to give tribute to Caesar, and saying that he himself is Christ a king." 3 And Pilate asked him, "Are you the King of the Jews?" And he answered him, "You have said so." 4 And Pilate said to the chief priests and the multitudes, "I find no crime in this man." 5 But they were urgent, saying, "He stirs up the people, teaching throughout all Judea, from Galilee even to this place."

The Sanhedrin had decided that Jesus must die; it was necessary to have a sentence of death pronounced by the Roman procurator: the *ius gladii*, or power of execution, was reserved to Rome (cf. Jn 18:31).

1. The place of judgment was not the fortress Antonia which dominated the Temple but the former palace of Herod the Great, in the northeastern part of the city.

2. If Jesus were to be condemned by Pilate, the charge against him would have to be a political one, not a religious issue. In fact, the accusation is threefold: he has stirred up the people to revolt; more specifically, he has forbidden the payment of tribute to Caesar; and he has put himself forward as the Messiah-King and so as a rebel against Roman authority. The second charge is a blatant lie (cf. 20:20-25), and the others are deliberate misrepresentations of Jesus' work and claims.

3f. Pilate's reaction to the enigmatic reply of Jesus presupposes a longer interrogation similar to that of Jn 18:35-38. Luke emphasizes Pilate's testimony to the innocence of Jesus: the procurator three times declares his conviction that the prisoner is no criminal and offers no threat to Roman rule (Lk 23:4,14,21); similarly, in John, Pilate makes a triple declaration: "I find no crime in him" (Jn 18:38; 19:4,6). Throughout Acts, Luke is careful to show that the Roman authorities have always acquitted Paul of charges brought against him (Ac 16:35-39; 18:12-15; 19:31,35,41; 24:22f; 25:18,25f,31f; cf. 13:12); here he has shown the Roman procurator declaring that Jesus is no political criminal.

5. The charge is reiterated. Judea = Palestine (cf. Lk 4:44). For the range of the ministry cf. Ac 10:37.

6-12. Jesus before Herod

6 When Pilate heard this, he asked whether the man was a Galilean. **7** And when he learned that he belonged to Herod's jurisdiction, he sent him over to Herod, who was himself in Jerusalem at that time. **8** When Herod saw Jesus, he was very glad, for he had long desired to see him, because he had heard about him, and he was hoping to see some sign done by him. **9** So he questioned him at some length; but he made no answer. **10** The chief priests and the scribes stood by, vehemently accusing him. **11** And Herod with his soldiers treated him with contempt and mocked him; then, arraying him in gorgeous apparel, he sent him back to Pilate. **12** And Herod and Pilate became friends with each other that very day, for before this they had been at enmity with each other.

Peculiar to Luke. **6f.** Mention of Galilee (v. 5) suggested to Pilate a means of evading this troublesome affair. Herod Antipas (cf. 3:1) would have been in Jerusalem for the Passover; during his stay he would have resided at the former family residence of the Hasmonaeans in the western quarter of the city.

8-10. For Herod's curiosity cf. 9:9; his question seeks to satisfy it. This is not a trial, though the chief priests and scribes attempt to make it one.

11. Annoyed by the silence of Jesus, but also convinced that he was no dangerous rebel, Herod decided to make a mockery of the claims attributed to him. The "gorgeous apparel"—doubtless a cast-off princely robe—would mark him as "king"; it is a practical recognition of the baselessness of the charges. This scene of mockery is strangely like Mk 15:16-19 and Mt 27:27-30, where Jesus is mocked by the Roman soldiers, an episode omitted by Luke. It is likely that the Romans had played their part when the prisoner had returned from Antipas.

12. The enmity had been caused or aggravated by Pilate's massacre of Galileans (cf. 13:1); but now each was flattered by the recognition of the other. In Ac 4:25-27 we find Peter and John applying Ps 2:1f to the action of Herod and Pilate representing, respectively, the "kings" and "rulers" of the psalm.

13-25. Again before Pilate
(Mk 15:6-15; Mt 27:15-26; Jn 18:38b–19:16)

13 Pilate then called together the chief priests and the rulers and the people, **14** and said to them, "You brought me this man as one who was perverting the people; and after examining him before you, behold, I did not find this man guilty of any of your charges against him; **15** neither did Herod, for he sent him back to us. Behold, nothing deserving death has been done by him; **16** I will therefore chastise him and release him."

18 But they all cried out together, "Away with this man, and release to us Barabbas"—**19** a man who had been thrown into prison for an insurrection started in the city, and for murder. **20** Pilate addressed them once more, desiring to release Jesus; **21** but they shouted out, "Crucify, crucify him!" **22** A third time he said to them, "Why, what evil has he done? I have found in him no crime deserving death; I will therefore chastise him and release him." **23** But they were urgent, demanding with loud cries that he should be crucified. And their voices prevailed. **24** So Pilate gave sentence that their demand should be granted. **25** He released the man who had been thrown into prison for insurrection and murder, whom they asked for; but Jesus he delivered up to their will.

13-15. Pilate, forced to resume the trial, again professes his conviction that his prisoner is innocent; he can now add that Herod shares the same view.

16. The "chastisement" (scourging, cf. Jn 19:1) was a compromise suggestion. Here (or after v. 19) some manuscripts add v. 17 (cf. RSV margin) which appears to be an explanatory gloss (or note) based on Mk 15:6; Mt 27:15.

18-25. Luke omits Mk 15:6-11, so Barabbas appears abruptly. For the third time (v. 22) Pilate bears witness to the innocence of Jesus—in contrast to the attitude of the Jews who insistently demanded his death (vv. 21,23) while they sought the deliverance of a murderer (v. 25). Luke lays the blame squarely on the Jews (cf. Jn 18:38; 19:4,6) while he tends to minimize the culpability of Pilate (cf. Jn 19:11). This fact, and the omission of any reference to outrages by the Roman troops (cf. Mk 15:16-20), suggest that Luke has sought to present the role of Rome in the crucifixion in as favorable a light as possible. But, while acknowledging Jewish responsibility, we must not forget what Jesus himself will declare: they did not really know what they were doing (22:34).

26-32. The Road to Calvary
(Mk 15:20b-23; Mt 27:31b-34; Jn 19:17)

26 And as they led him away, they seized one Simon of Cyrene, who was coming in from the country, and laid on him the cross, to carry it behind Jesus. 27 And there followed him a great multitude of the people, and of women who bewailed and lamented him. 28 But Jesus turning to them said, "Daughters of Jerusalem, do not weep for me, but weep for yourselves and for your children. 29 For behold, the days are coming when they will say, 'Blessed are the barren, and the wombs that never bore, and the breasts that never gave suck!' 30 Then they will begin to say to the mountains, 'Fall on us,' and to the hills, 'Cover us.' 31 For if they do this when the wood is green, what will happen when it is dry?"

32 Two others also, who were criminals, were led away to be put to death with him.

26. Jesus was led away by Roman soldiers (cf. vv. 36,47). Simon was a Jew of the Diaspora, from Cyrene in North Africa, who now dwelt in Jerusalem; Luke omits the Marcan detail that he was "the father of Alexander and Rufus" (Mk 15:21). Luke's

phrasing "[they] laid on him the cross, to carry it behind Jesus",
is a conscious echo of the saying: "Whoever does not bear his
own cross and come after me, cannot be my disciple" (14:27).
He has presented Simon as the model of the Christian who walks
in the footsteps of his Master. The rest of this passage is proper
to Luke.

27. A morbidly curious crowd followed the three (cf. v. 32)
condemned men. The women are not those mentioned in 8:2f
(cf. 23:49); they are, perhaps, women who had known Jesus or
women who habitually attended to the last needs of condemned
criminals, and who prepared the spiced wine (cf. Mk 15:23).

28-30. Jesus is moved by thought of the sufferings that lie in
wait for these women and their children—in the war of 66-70
A.D. (cf. 21:20-24). Again the phrase, "the days are coming",
introduces an oracle of woe; v. 29b echoes 21:23, while the quotation of Hos 10:8 (v. 30) is found again in Ap 6:16.

31. If the innocent ("the green wood" = Jesus) suffers so, what
will happen to the guilty (the "dry wood" = the Jews)?

32. Luke mentions the presence of two criminals who were to
be executed with Jesus; in the other gospels these emerge more
abruptly.

33-38. The Crucifixion
(Mk 15:22-32; Mt 27:33-43; Jn 19:17-24)

33 And when they came to the place which is called The Skull,
there they crucified him, and the criminals, one on the right and one
on the left. 34 And Jesus said, "Father, forgive them; for they know
not what they do." And they cast lots to divide his garments. 35 And
the people stood by, watching; but the rulers scoffed at him, saying,
"He saved others; let him save himself, if he is the Christ of God, his
Chosen One!" 36 The soldiers also mocked him, coming up and offering him vinegar, 37 and saying, "If you are the King of the Jews, save
yourself!" 38 There was also an inscription over him, "This is the King
of the Jews."

Luke departs somewhat from the order of Mark. Omitting the
reference to spiced wine (Mk 15:23), he places the crucifixion
immediately after the arrival at Calvary. Then come the words
of forgiveness (absent from Mark) and the dividing of his clothing; the title over the Cross has been placed last, obviously as a
literary climax.

33. A combination of Mk 15:22,24a,27. Luke omits the Aramaic name Golgotha. He notes crucifixion with two criminals in accordance with Is 53:12; our attention had already been drawn to that Isaian text (Lk 22:37).

34a. Manuscript evidence for and against the verse seems evenly balanced; on internal evidence it is to be accepted. The fact that the saying seems to break the connection between vv. 33 and 34b is no argument against its authenticity since it is a Lucan insertion into the text of Mark. The prayer of Stephen (Ac 7:60) is surely meant to be an intentional parallel. Its omission by a goodly number of manuscripts can be explained on the grounds of an apparently excessive indulgence toward the Jews and a seeming contradiction of other sayings (cf. Lk 20:16; 21:24; 23:31). These words of forgiveness are not primarily for the soldiers, who are merely obeying orders, but for the Jewish leaders. These cannot be absolved from guilt in their calculated rejection of Jesus and in the manner in which they engineered his death. But they were motivated by fierce zeal for their religion (as Paul was to be), and they did, sincerely, believe Jesus guilty of blasphemy (22:70f). Above all, they were not, subjectively, guilty of deicide—as Paul explicitly acknowledges (1 Cor 2:8). This prayer of Jesus is not only perfectly in character; it is the climax of his condescension, so visible in the parables, towards these stubborn men.

34b. Like the other synoptists, Luke's reference to the division of the garments is brief; John (19:23f) has given a fuller account.

35-37. Luke divides the spectators into three categories: the people looked on (cf. v. 27); the rulers mocked Jesus; the soldiers joined in the raillery. In v. 35 Mark's title "the king of Israel" is given a turn more congenial to Luke's Greek readers and points to the Servant of Yahweh (cf. 9:35; Is 42:1). In vv. 36f the raillery is proper to Luke but the episode anticipates Mk 15:35f—with the omission of any mention of Elijah (cf. 9:36).

38. The title on the Cross is the climax of this mockery.

39-43. The "Good Thief"

39 One of the criminals who were hanged railed at him, saying, "Are you not the Christ? Save yourself and us!" 40 But the other rebuked him, saying, "Do you not fear God, since you are under the same sentence of condemnation? 41 And we indeed justly; for we are

receiving the due reward of our deeds; but this man has done nothing wrong." 42 And he said, "Jesus, remember me when you come in your kingly power." 43 And he said to him, "Truly, I say to you, today you will be with me in Paradise."

Proper to Luke. 39. In place of Mark's (15:32f) brief statement that the two crucified men also reviled Jesus, Luke declares that only one acted so.

40f. The other acknowledges the innocence of Jesus. It would seem that, in Luke's eyes, these two men symbolize Jews and Romans in their attitude to Jesus. The former, like the Jews, seeks in Jesus a Messiah who would arise in power and dramatically deliver Israel—and rejects him when these hopes are dashed (cf. 22:67-71); the other, like Pilate, admits that Jesus has done nothing wrong, and does not deny his Kingship (cf. 23:3f).

42. Further, he recognizes Jesus as the Messiah. He asks to be remembered when Jesus comes in his kingly power (or into his kingdom), that is, when he comes to inaugurate the Messianic age, an event which, in Jewish belief, would involve the resurrection of the dead.

43. Jesus, the Savior, assures the "good thief" that his prayer will be answered more promptly than he could have dreamed: this very day, after death, he will enter with Jesus into the life of God; he will be with Christ in the abode of happiness conjured up by the word Paradise—the heavenly dwelling-place (cf. Lk 16:22-26). "Paradise" is a Persian word, meaning park or garden; in the Septuagint it is used to render the "garden of Eden" (Gn 2:8) and eventually came to mean the future abode of the righteous. Here it is no more than an image; and Lagrange sagely observes that, instead of trying to situate "Paradise", it is more profitable to recall the words of Ambrose: *Vita est enim esse cum Christo; ideo ubi Christus, ibi vita, ibi regnum.*

44-49. The Death of Jesus
(Mk 15:33-41; Mt 27:45-56; Jn 19:25-30)

44 It was now about the sixth hour, and there was darkness over the whole land until the ninth hour, 45 while the sun's light failed; and the curtain of the temple was torn in two. 46 Then Jesus, crying with a loud voice, said, "Father, into thy hands I commit my spirit!"

And having said this he breathed his last. 47 Now when the centurion saw what had taken place, he praised God, and said, "Certainly this man was innocent!" 48 And all the multitudes who assembled to see the sight, when they saw what had taken place, returned home beating their breasts. 49 And all his acquaintances and the women who had followed him from Galilee stood at a distance and saw these things.

The three synoptists tell of cosmic phenomena and portentous happenings which accompanied the death of Jesus, such as darkness and the rending of the Temple veil; Matthew is the most elaborate and includes the resurrection of "many of the saints" (Mt 27:51-53). We should realize that here the tradition has clothed the event in the imagery of the Day of Yahweh (cf. Am 8:9f; Jl 2:10; 3:3f; Zeph 1:15): to the eyes of the first Christians the day of Jesus' death is the day of God's judgment and the beginning of the eschatological age, and we are dealing here with conventional, symbolic language.

44. The "darkness" covered the land (of Palestine) from noon until three in the afternoon. We might think of a severe *khamseen* or sirocco (with sand-laden winds obscuring the sun), but it is surely wiser to see an Old Testament image and grasp its theological implication: this is, in a real sense, the Day of Yahweh, the day of judgment. An eclipse of the sun would have been impossible at the full moon (the date of Passover was determined by the time of the full moon) and some manuscripts have "corrected" Luke's text to read: "the sun was darkened"; in fact, the better attested reading (*tou hēliou) ekliptontos* does not necessarily mean that the sun was eclipsed, but can simply mean that the sun's light failed—again conventional Old Testament language.

45. The rending of the Temple veil, placed after the death of Jesus by Mark/Matthew, is here given by Luke as a companion sign of the darkness—the transposition is made on literary grounds. The "curtain" may be the veil which divided the Holy of Holies from the Holy Place (cf. Ex 26:31f) or, perhaps more likely, the curtain which hung in front of the Holy Place and shut off the interior of the Temple from the view of those who stood in its outer courts. The rending of the veil is manifestly symbolic: the religion of Israel, the cult of the true God, until now shut off (by the veil) from the eyes of the Gentiles, is now open to all— the veil is gone, the new religion is universalist, open to all men.

For by his death Christ has opened the way, for all, to the heavenly sanctuary (Heb 10:19f).

46. Luke, who omits the citation of Ps 22(21):2 (cf. Mk 15:34), doubtless because it might be misunderstood, here gives as the cry of Jesus (Mk 15:37) another psalm-text (Ps 31[30]:6; cf. Ac 7:59f). The "loud cry" is a conventional phrase (cf. Lk 17:15; 19:37; Jn 11:43; Ac 14:10; 26:24).

47. Yet another witness to the innocence of Jesus. The term *dikaios*, "just", "innocent", especially after the praise of God, suggests that the centurion has seen in Jesus the perfect man whose martyr's death is a glory for God; the word has replaced Mark's "a son of God".

48. Luke adds this moving description of the repentant crowd. No evangelist tells of the reaction of the chief priests, scribes, and Pharisees.

49. The attitude of the friends of Jesus is described in terms of Ps 28(27):12; 88(87):9. The women are named in 8:2f.

50-56. The Burial of Jesus
(Mk 15:42-47; Mt 27:57-61; Jn 19:38-42)

50 Now there was a man named Joseph from the Jewish town of Arimathea. He was a member of the council, a good and righteous man, **51** who had not consented to their purpose and deed, and he was looking for the kingdom of God. **52** This man went to Pilate and asked for the body of Jesus. **53** Then he took it down and wrapped it in a linen shroud, and laid him in a rock-hewn tomb, where no one had ever yet been laid. **54** It was the day of Preparation, and the sabbath was beginning. **55** The women who had come with him from Galilee followed, and saw the tomb, and how his body was laid; **56** then they returned, and prepared spices and ointments.

On the sabbath they rested according to the commandment.

50f. Luke, typically (cf. 1:6; 2:25; Ac 11:24), adds that Joseph was a "good and righteous man", and explains that, though a member of the Sanhedrin, he had had no part in that body's action against Jesus. Arimathea is "a city of the Jews"—a geographical note added by Luke (cf. 4:31; 8:26). Like Simeon (2:25) Joseph "was looking for the kingdom of God", and so was favorably disposed towards Jesus; Matthew (27:57) and John (19:38) make him already a disciple.

52. The surprise of Pilate and his questioning of the centurion (Mk 15:44f) are omitted.

53. Luke specifies that the tomb had not been used (cf. Jn 19:41).

54. "The sabbath was beginning"—literally "the sabbath *was dawning*": a broad use of the expression to signify that the sabbath (which began at sunset) was imminent. John (19:31) has explained the reason for the urgency of these proceedings.

55f. The women of v. 49 saw the tomb and the body of Jesus laid in it; thus they are important witnesses of the Resurrection (cf. 24:3f). The preparation of spices and ointments before the sabbath began (Mk 16:1—"when the sabbath was past") is very likely a literary arrangement which enables Luke to move directly into the Resurrection narrative in 24:1.

VII. AFTER THE RESURRECTION 24

24:1-12. The Resurrection
(Mk 16:1-8; Mt 28:1-10; Jn 20:1-18)

1 But on the first day of the week, at early dawn, they went to the tomb, taking the spices which they had prepared. 2 And they found the stone rolled away from the tomb, 3 but when they went in they did not find the body [of the Lord Jesus]. 4 While they were perplexed about this, behold, two men stood by them in dazzling apparel; 5 and as they were frightened and bowed their faces to the ground, the men said to them, "Why do you seek the living among the dead?" 6 [He is not here, but has risen.] Remember how he told you, while he was still in Galilee, 7 that the Son of man must be delivered into the hands of sinful men, and be crucified, and on the third day rise." 8 And they remembered his words, 9 and returning from the tomb they told all this to the eleven and to all the rest. 10 Now it was Mary Magdalene and Joanna and Mary the mother of James and the other women with them who told this to the apostles; 11 but these words seemed to them an idle tale, and they did not believe them. [12 But Peter rose and ran to the tomb; stooping and looking in, he saw the linen cloths by themselves; and he went home wondering at what had happened.]

Luke differs from Mark most obviously in avoiding mention of apparitions of Jesus in Galilee. Textually, this chapter is remarkable for the number of "Western non-interpolations"—a technical term for verses or phrases not found in Codex Bezae and Old Latin (the Western Text) which thus present a shorter reading that may be original.[65] Though, in the text of Luke, these passages (in vv. 3,6,12,36,40,51,52) are enclosed in brackets (because the RSV has relegated them to the margin), our commentary makes it clear that we regard them as authentic.

1f. Luke abridges and alters (in the light of 23:56) Mk 16:1f,4 and omits 16:3.

3. He explicitly records failure to find the body (cf. Mk 16:5a).

[65] See pp. 29f.

"Of the Lord Jesus" is absent from Codex Bezae and Old Latin; in favor of authenticity, apart from the majority manuscript evidence, is the use of the title in Ac 1:21; 4:33; 8:16.

4-6a. Where Mark has "a young man" (16:5) and Matthew (28:2) "an angel of the Lord", Luke speaks of "two men" and John (20:12) of "two angels". The women are filled with religious awe (cf. 1:12; etc.); the rhetorical question implies the Resurrection of Jesus. The Western Text omits v. 6a which may possibly be an assimilation to Mk 16:6 or Mt 28:6; yet it is not an exact assimilation and the weight of manuscript evidence is in its favor.

6b-8. This is perhaps the most striking example of Luke's editorial freedom. Since, in his theological plan, the climax of his gospel must be in Jerusalem, he cannot, without bringing about an anti-climax, record the apparitions in Galilee. So he rewrites Mk 16:7 and changes the promise of an appearance in Galilee into a prophecy made by Jesus "while he was still in Galilee". Though this prophecy had been addressed to the Twelve (9:22, 44; 18:31) it was known to the women (v. 8).

9. Luke apparently contradicts Mk 16:8; the discrepancy is no doubt explained by the abrupt ending of Mark (cf. Mt 28:8).

10f. Three of the women are named; instead of Salome (Mk 16:1) Luke names Joanna (cf. 8:3). For the incredulity of the disciples, cf. Mk 16:14; Mt 28:17.

12. This verse is missing from the Western Text. It is argued that (in the rest of the manuscript evidence) it is an interpolation, based on Jn 20:3-10, intended to illustrate vv. 24 and 34 and to bring these verses into harmony with v. 11. But a later interpolation would surely agree more closely with the text of John where the point is the belief of the "other disciple", not the incredulity of Peter, and where there is no equivalent to "wondering at what had happened". This is one more of the many contacts wtih the Johannine tradition evident in Luke's Passion and Resurrection narrative. We may say that Lk 24:12 and Jn 20:2-10 represent a tradition earlier than that of Mark/Matthew, which relates, very simply, that Peter (the "other disciple" is a Johannine theme), informed by Mary Magdalen that the tomb was empty, hastened to the place, found the tomb empty as she had said, and, without seeing angels or Jesus, returned perplexed.

13-35. On the Road to Emmaus

13 That very day two of them were going to a village named Emmaus, about seven miles from Jerusalem, **14** and talking with each other about all these things that had happened. **15** While they were talking and discussing together, Jesus himself drew near and went with them. **16** But their eyes were kept from recognizing him. **17** And he said to them, "What is this conversation which you are holding with each other as you walk?" And they stood still, looking sad. **18** Then one of them, named Cleopas, answered him, "Are you the only visitor to Jerusalem who does not know the things that have happened there in these days?" **19** And he said to them, "What things?" And they said to him, "Concerning Jesus of Nazareth, who was a prophet mighty in deed and word before God and all the people, **20** and how our chief priests and rulers delivered him up to be condemned to death, and crucified him. **21** But we had hoped that he was the one to redeem Israel. Yes, and besides all this, it is now the third day since this happened. **22** Moreover, some women of our company amazed us. They were at the tomb early in the morning **23** and did not find his body; and they came back saying that they had even seen a vision of angels, who said that he was alive. **24** Some of those who were with us went to the tomb, and found it just as the women had said; but him they did not see." **25** And he said to them, "O foolish men, and slow of heart to believe all that the prophets have spoken! **26** Was it not necessary that the Christ should suffer these things and enter into his glory?" **27** And beginning with Moses and all the prophets, he interpreted to them in all the scriptures the things concerning himself.

28 So they drew near to the village to which they were going. He appeared to be going further, **29** but they constrained him, saying, "Stay with us, for it is toward evening and the day is now far spent." So he went in to stay with them. **30** When he was at table with them, he took the bread and blessed, and broke it, and gave it to them. **31** And their eyes were opened and they recognized him; and he vanished out of their sight. **32** They said to each other, "Did not our hearts burn within us while he talked to us on the road, while he opened to us the scriptures?" **33** And they rose that same hour and returned to Jerusalem; and they found the eleven gathered together and those who were with them, **34** who said, "The Lord has risen indeed, and has appeared to Simon!" **35** Then they told what had happened on the road, and how he was known to them in the breaking of the bread.

This delightful narrative is peculiar to Luke.

13. It is impossible to identify the site of Emmaus with certainty. The problem is complicated by a variant reading. Codex Sinaiticus and some dozen Greek manuscripts read "one hundred and sixty stadia", and the village may be identified with the Emmaus of 1 Mc 3:40; 4:3. It would appear, however, that the "one hundred and sixty" follows from this identification and that the reading goes back to Origen. "Sixty stadia" (about seven miles), attested by most manuscripts, is the better reading. The most likely site of Emmaus is Kulonieh (whose ancient name was Emmaus), even though this is only four miles from Jerusalem, to the west of the city. Emmaus was, apparently, the home of one or both of the disciples.

14-16. As they discussed the shattering experience of the preceding days Jesus appeared, evidently as though he had overtaken them. The disciples do not at first recognize the Lord (cf. v. 31); as in similar apparitions, a word or sign from him is necessary before he is recognized (cf. vv. 39-43; Jn 20:14-16,19f; 21:4-7).

17f. Jesus is going to prepare them for his self-revelation. At his question they stopped short, saddened by the import of it and amazed that one coming from Jerusalem could be in ignorance of what had taken place. Cleopas (possibly the Clopas of Jn 19:25) was probably Luke's source; or, more realistically, the name figured in the tradition known to Luke.

19f. Yet again responsibility for the crucifixion is placed squarely on the shoulders of the Jewish leaders. The disciples acknowledge that Jesus was a mighty prophet (cf. Ac 7:22); as a prophet his violent death was not exceptional (cf. 11:47-51; 13:34).

21. But they had seen in him something more—the Messiah, though their expectation was thoroughly Jewish. In v. 21b their disillusionment is forcefully expressed: before the death of Jesus they could still hope for a divine intervention—which might have taken place immediately after death, but certainly not as late as the third day!

22-24. The situation had been aggravated by the report of some women (cf. vv. 9,11); momentary hopes were dashed when some of the disciples, investigating the matter, had found only an empty tomb. The implication is that if Jesus were alive he would certainly have manifested himself to his disciples. "For them, Jesus is dead, and with him their faith in him." [66]

[66] J. Schmid, *op. cit.*, p. 357.

25f. The disciples, like the Jews in general, had not accepted *all* that the prophets had spoken: they had closed their eyes to the suffering of the Messiah (cf. 18:31; Ac 26:23); that is why the death of Jesus had been a fatal stumbling block. But, in God's design, the way to glory was the path of suffering (cf. 9:22; 22:69). Christ had suffered and so *had* already entered into his glory (*ouchi edei*, "was it not necessary" governs *eiselthein*, "enter")—cf. Jn 20:17, 19-23.

27. Starting with the Pentateuch, Jesus explained the Messianic prophecies. The statement is general—he need not have touched on *all* the Messianic texts—but it is a precious testimony to a Christian interpretation of the Old Testament. It is noteworthy that vv. 19f and 25-27 echo the theme, and the very words, of the *kerygma*, the mission preaching of the primitive Church, as we find it in the discourses of the early part of Acts (cf. Ac 2:22f, 29-36; 3:14f, 22-24): apostolic testimony and the Scriptures bear witness to Jesus of Nazareth who died and rose again.

28f. "He appeared to be going further"—not a feigned action; rather, everything depended on their invitation. In fact, they "constrained" him—Oriental etiquette (cf. Gn 19:3; Ac 16:15). Evidently, they had reached the home of one or of both.

30f. The breaking of bread is the occasion of their recognition of him. The expression "breaking of bread" is a technical term for the Eucharist (cf. Ac 2:42, 46; 20:7, 11; 27:35; 1 Cor 10:16). While it does not necessarily follow that here (and in v. 35) the Eucharist is meant, it is clear that Luke has deliberately used eucharistic language: Jesus *took bread, blessed, broke it, gave to them* (cf. Lk 22:19). And his lesson is that as the two disciples recognized Jesus in the setting of a meal shared with him, so Christians, in the eucharistic meal, make the same real encounter with their Lord. Their eyes had been opened—but Jesus had vanished from their sight; for now they believed that he was truly risen.

32. Now, too, they realized why it was that the "stranger's" exposition of the Scriptures had set their hearts aflame.

33f. Understandably, they hurried back to Jerusalem with the astounding news to find that Simon, too, had seen the risen Lord (cf. 1 Cor 15:5).

35. Again Luke draws attention to the "breaking of bread"—he is determined that his readers will not miss its significance. This whole passage, centered around the "liturgy of the word" (vv. 19-27) and the "eucharistic" meal (vv. 30f), has a marked liturgical coloring. It is an early catechesis, in a liturgical setting, highlighting the encounter with the Lord in the Eucharist.

36-43. Appearance of the Risen Christ in Jerusalem
(Jn 20:19-23)

36 As they were saying this, Jesus himself stood among them [and said to them, "Peace be to you"]. 37 But they were startled and frightened, and supposed that they saw a spirit. 38 And he said to them, "Why are you troubled, and why do questionings rise in your hearts? 39 See my hands and my feet, that it is I myself; handle me, and see; for a spirit has not flesh and bones as you see that I have." [40 And when he had said this, he showed them his hands and his feet.] 41 And while they still disbelieved for joy, and wondered, he said to them, "Have you anything here to eat?" 42 They gave him a piece of broiled fish, 43 and he took it and ate before them.

Jesus had appeared to Simon (v. 34) and to the two disciples (vv. 13-35); this time he appears to a greater number and goes out of his way to emphasize the reality of his resurrection.

36. Doubtless the same apparition as that of Jn 20:19-23. The phrase, "and said to them, 'Peace be to you,'" omitted by the Western Text, may be an interpolation after Jn 20:19. But it is at least equally likely that Luke and John have followed a common tradition.

37. The disciples were startled by his sudden appearance—"the doors being shut" (Jn 20:19). Their reaction is not inconsistent with v. 34; Lagrange observes: *"On leur avait dit que le Seigneur était ressuscité, mais qu'est-ce qu'un ressuscité?"* [67] Just as in the Emmaus narrative, a gesture or word is needed before the disciples recognize the risen Lord.

38-40. Jesus gently rebukes them for their fear and hesitation; then, in order to convince them, he shows, and invites them to touch, the hands and feet that bear the marks of the nails (Jn 20:20,25,27). V. 40 is missing from the Western Text and from certain Syriac manuscripts and again the suggestion that, in the

[67] *Op. cit.*, p. 612.

other witnesses, it has been taken from Jn 20:20 merit attention. Yet, it seems better to believe that Luke has followed a Johannine source and to accept the reading as authentic. Doubtless, it is Luke who changed the original "hands and side" (cf. Jn 20:20) to "hands and feet", since he had not mentioned the pierced side of Jesus (cf. Jn 19:34).

41-43. "They disbelieved *for joy*": In a final gesture of condescension Jesus ate some fish in their presence. Luke also has in mind the eucharistic significance of this "meal" (cf. Ac 1:4; Lk 24:30); this communion with Christ, in the setting of a meal, represents the encounter of faith in the Eucharist. A glorified body does not require food—but this is not to say that it cannot assimilate food. We might paraphrase Lagrange's question: "What is a glorified body?" This narrative, like the corresponding passage of John, is meant to prove that the Resurrection of Jesus is a physical fact, that the risen Christ is not a ghost but a real Person. Very likely it is a reply to objections that the Apostles had been misled by false impressions or by their imaginings; we are shown that the disciples, far from being susceptible, were, despite their doubts, persuaded that Jesus had risen.

44-49. Last Instruction
(Ac 1:3-8)

44 Then he said to them, "These are my words which I spoke to you, while I was still with you, that everything written about me in the law of Moses and the prophets and the psalms must be fulfilled." **45** Then he opened their minds to understand the scriptures, **46** and said to them, "Thus it is written, that the Christ should suffer and on the third day rise from the dead, **47** and that repentance and forgiveness of sins should be preached in his name to all nations, beginning from Jerusalem. **48** You are witnesses of these things. **49** And behold, I send the promise of my Father upon you; but stay in the city, until you are clothed with power from on high."

At the close of his gospel Luke summarizes the last commission of Jesus to his disciples; this he repeats at the beginning of Acts. More pointedly, the outline and words of this passage echo the apostolic kerygma of Acts (just as we have noted in respect to vv. 19f,25-27 above).

44. Jesus recalls the occasions on which he had warned them that he, in fulfillment of the will of God enshrined in the Scriptures, would have to suffer, die, and rise again (cf. 9:22,44; 17:25; 18:31-33; 22:37). The phrase "Moses and the prophets and the psalms" stands for Law, prophets, and writings, the Jewish threefold division of the Old Testament. "While I was still with you": Jesus has entered into his glory (cf. v. 26) by his exaltation to the Father (Jn 20:17); his relations with the disciples are not what they were before his glorification.

45-48. He gives them a new understanding of the Old Testament, an insight that will enable them to see how and where it "bears witness to him" (cf. Jn 5:39). This reinterpretation of the Old Testament is a basic element of the primitive kerygma: the dawning of the age of fulfillment (v. 44; cf. Ac 2:16; 3:18; 3:24); the suffering of the Messiah and his Resurrection on the third day (Ac 2:23f; 3:13-15; 4:10). The kerygma always includes the proclamation of repentance and forgiveness of sins, a proclamation to all men—the universalist note is very much at home in Luke (Ac 2:38f; 3:19f; 4:12). These are the points which Paul developed in his discourse at Antioch of Pisidia (Ac 13:26-41). The message of salvation will go forth from Jerusalem, preached by the Apostles who are witnesses of the fulfillment of the prophecies (cf. Ac 1:8), men who had seen the risen Christ and who can attest that this Lord is the same Jesus with whom they had lived (Ac 1:21; 2:32; 3:15; 5:32; 10:39-42; 13:31). The disciples are convincing witnesses and efficacious missionaries because they have seen the Lord and have believed in him; all who would, effectively, bear witness to Christ must have encountered him in personal and living faith. Today, when the call of the apostolate is urgent and the role of witness is seen as the obligation of every Christian, we are more keenly aware that religion is not the acceptance of a body of doctrine or the adherence to a code of laws, but attachment to a Person. Knowledge of Christ, in the biblical sense of acceptance and commitment, is the essence of Christian life; it is obviously the first requirement of an apostle. The Good News is the straightforward proclamation of events that manifestly followed a pattern traced by God, the fulfillment of a divine plan. It was inevitable that this proclamation, couched in terms of the Old Testament, should itself become a new chapter in the written word of God. In this passage

Luke has shown us, on the authority of the Lord, that our preaching of Christ must be, first and last, scriptural.

49. Jesus assured the disciples that he would send upon them "the promise of the Father" (cf. Ac 1:14), that is, the promised Holy Spirit (cf. Jl 2:28; Ac 2:16-21). Hence, they are bidden to stay in the city until they will be "baptized with the Holy Spirit" (Ac 1:4f). This is perfectly in accord with Luke's plan: in order to end his gospel at Jerusalem he studiously avoids mention of the apparitions in Galilee (cf. 24:6). In this final charge Jesus looks to the future. His work is done; now begins the work of his disciples, the mission to the world.

50-53. The Ascension
(Ac 1:9-14; cf. Mk 16:19)

50 Then he led them out as far as Bethany, and lifting up his hands he blessed them. **51** While he blessed them, he parted from them [and was carried up into heaven]. **52** And they [worshipped him, and] returned to Jerusalem with great joy, **53** and were continually in the temple blessing God.

Luke has undoubtedly given the impression that all the events of chapter 24 had taken place on Easter Sunday (cf. vv. 1,13,33, 36,44,50). This arrangement is editorial and the passage vv. 44-53 is a telescoped version of Ac 1:3-14. Though it is true that Jesus did ascend to his Father on Easter day (cf. Jn 20:17), it is clear that the Ascension in question here is the same as that of Acts—the final, visible departure of Christ forty days (Ac 1:3) after the Resurrection.

50f. "As far as Bethany": in Acts the place of ascension was "the mount called Olivet" (Ac 1:12)—Bethany lies on the eastern slope of the Mount of Olives. With his hands raised in blessing (cf. Lv 9:22; Sir 50:22) Jesus parted from them (Ac 1:9). Though missing from the Western Text, v. 51b is authentic; its omission can be explained on the grounds of apparent discrepancy with Acts (ascension after forty days).

52f. The phrase "worshipped him, and" (cf. Mt 28:17) is missing from the Western Text; it may have been omitted because it read somewhat incongruously after the departure of v. 51. The joy of the disciples, at the moment of parting, though at first sight surprising, is explained by their realization that "the Lord has risen indeed" (v. 34). And they have his assurance that, very soon, they will be "clothed with power from on high" (v. 49). Their minds have been opened to understand the Scriptures: now they have grasped the plan of God and they realize that Christ, their Lord, has triumphed. Thankfully, they hasten to glorify God in his Temple. Luke has closed his gospel as he began it, in the Temple; yet all is changed, changed utterly! He has shown the "time of Israel" yielding to the "time of Christ". And now, about to begin his account of the word of salvation going forth from Jerusalem to "the end of the earth" (Ac 1:8), he leaves us at the beginning of a new age, the "time of the Church".

ADDITIONAL NOTES

1. The Kingdom of God

The basic idea of the "kingdom of God" is that of the "rule" or "reign" of God. This corresponds to the meaning of the Aramaic *malkutha* (the term used by Jesus): "kingship", "kingly rule", "sovereignty". But, while the reign of God is the primary idea, that of domain or kingdom is also necessarily implied; there can be no reign, in any real sense, without a kingdom.

Jesus, in speaking of the kingdom of God, obviously took it for granted that his hearers would know what he meant. He spoke of something already familiar to them, and he did not have to begin by explaining the term. In the Old Testament, however, the expression occurs only rarely and then in the later books (e.g. Tb 13:1; Ps 146[145]:11f; Dn 2:37; Wis 10:10). In non-biblical Jewish literature, however, there was frequent reference to the kingdom of God. This was largely due to a tendency to avoid mention of the name of God or to speak of him in abstract terms. For instance, in Is 24:23, instead of "Yahweh shall reign", the Aramaic version reads: ". . . the kingdom of God will be manifest." Yet, although the name is not prevalent, the reality of the kingdom of God is very much in evidence in the Old Testament, and the synoptists' use of the term has Old Testament roots (cf. Nm 23:21; 1 Sm 12:13; Is 52:7; 1 Chr 29:11).

In the teaching of Jesus the kingdom is, first and foremost, an intervention of God in history. This is also true of the Old Testament concept; but in the New Testament view, the divine intervention is made manifest in the coming of the Son of God. God intervenes in history; in other words it is he who establishes the kingdom, it is his work. He is like the owner of the vineyard, like the king who gave a feast. And he, too, grants vitality to the kingdom so that it grows, from within, like a seed, so that it spreads out, irresistibly, as leaven permeates the mass of dough. Although it is the work of God, nevertheless, in the concrete, the kingdom is identified with the work and with the very Person of Jesus Christ.

This insistence on the supernatural origin of the kingdom and on its intrinsic power does not mean that the idea of a domain can be ignored. God, in establishing his reign among men, sets up a kingdom in which he will be acknowledged as King and over which he will reign. This is why there is question of entering into the kingdom (Lk 13:29; 18:24f). This is the reason it is like a feast in which those who belong to the kingdom have a place (13:28). In the interpretation of the parable of the Cockle, we read that the Son of man will send his angels who will "gather out of his kingdom all causes of sin and all evildoers" (Mt 13:41). In these and similar passages, it is clear that a kingdom is meant and not a reign only.

The question may be asked whether, in the teaching of Jesus, the kingdom is already present, or whether he sees it as something lying wholly in the future. The truth of the matter is that he considered it under both aspects, for it has this twofold aspect. In many passages of the gospels, it appears as a future reality (cf. Lk 10:9,11; 21:31), and many of the parables refer to a kingdom that awaits its completion and perfection: the Sower, the Mustard Seed (Lk 8:5-8; 13:18f). But these same parables just as obviously presuppose that the kingdom is already present, and what they teach is that, despite every obstacle, it will come to fulfillment—the mustard seed grows and the sown grain ripens to harvest. This double aspect follows from the heavenly origin of the kingdom.

In Jesus, bound up with his own Person and activity, the reign of God is present, but as an initial salvation which awaits fulfillment. The intervening period is the era of the Church, and its activity in the service of the perfect reign that is to come. Because in Jesus and his works God's reign with its saving power is actually in operation, its final phase is certain; there is an indissoluble link between the dawn of God's reign and its coming full manifestation in glory. The kingdom of God designates a dynamic reality which comes from heaven, which is revealed to the disciples of Jesus and which takes body, little by little, under the form of the true Israel. But the fulfillment remains an object of hope and the present era of salvation looks to its consummation.

2. Messianism

Israel had broken with the prevalent cyclic conception of time: in the biblical view history was meaningful; it had a beginning and, tending toward a God-given goal, it will have an end. It was a view that was particularly applicable to the history of Israel, dominated by the idea of covenant and presented in the Bible as *Heilsgeschichte*. This original conception of history is the basis of Messianic hope. Messianism, in the widest sense of the word, is Israel's expectation of a glorious destiny. More precisely, it is the expectation of an ultimate era of salvation that involves the manifest inauguration of the kingdom of God. This reign will first be established over Israel and then, through Israel, it will extend to all mankind. It is to be observed that Messianism consists essentially in confident expectation of the establishment of God's reign; there was, at first, no mention of a Messiah. And even when, with the passage of time, the figure of a Messiah did emerge, he was always regarded as God's instrument in the bringing in of his kingdom—an event which called for a special intervention of God in person. The Messiah was never the object of Israel's Messianic expectation; he was the one through whom that expectation was to be fulfilled. Instinctively, we think first of the Messiah who has come and we measure all the past by him. But Israel looked to a future that was vague even to the prophets who were granted a glimpse into it, and to eyes not fully enlightened the Messiah of the future did not stand out as a sharply defined figure.

Messianic expectation ran through the whole of Israel's history and the essential feature of that hope was there from the beginning, but the centuries and events brought clarification and refinement. That constant hope was accompanied by a steady growth in the appreciation of the election of Israel and of her true destiny. The figure of the Messiah emerged and began to assume an increasingly important role in the nation's hope.

The noun "Messiah" (*mashiah*) comes from a verb meaning "to anoint", "to rub with oil", a verb that in the Old Testament is reserved almost exclusively for sacred anointing, consecration by oil. The derived substantive designates the subject of anointing and is applied only to persons. In ancient Israel there is frequent mention of royal anointing; it is certain that, before the exile, the king was the Anointed One *par excellence.* From the moment that the oracle of Nathan (2 Sm 7:12-16) had fixed the hope of Israel on the dynasty of David, each king of that line became in turn the actual "Messiah" through whom God would accomplish his purpose in regard to his people. And the accession of each new king brought renewed hope, with the expectation of peace and justice and prosperity—the blessings of the Messianic age—and eventual rule over the whole world.

When the ultimate failure of the monarchy was evident, and when it did in fact come to an end, Israel's prophets and theologians looked again at the facts. The one constant element was the unconditional promise to the Davidic dynasty—that could not fail. But since the monarchy was no more, the only possibility now was that God would, in the future, raise up a son to David and through him bring about his reign over Israel and over mankind. Messianic expectation was no longer centered in a dynasty but on a person. True, this was still a son of David, but he was not just one of a line: he was an extraordinary person of the future. This Messiah was seen as a King, but he was presented too as a prophet—the Suffering Servant of Yahweh (Is 53), and as the glorious Son of man of the end-time (Dn 7:13f). And while Jesus was greeted by the people as Son of David, he preferred to present himself as one who, through suffering, would enter into his glory.

Nathan's oracle to David (2 Sm 7:8-16) is the foundation of dynastic Messianism and the first link in an unbroken chain that reaches to the New Testament (cf. Mt 1:1). "The prophecy is built round a contrast: David is not to build a house (a temple) for God (2 Sam 7:5); God is to build a house (a dynasty) for him, v. 11. The substance of the prophecy is the perpetuity of the Davidic dynasty in Israel, vv. 12-16. David himself thus understood it (vv. 19,25,27,29; cf. 23:5); so also Ps 89(88):29-37; 132(131):11f. The oracle, therefore, stretches beyond Solomon, David's immediate successor, to whom it is applied by v.

13 (an addition) and by 1 Chr 17:11-14; 22:10; 28:6 and 1 Kg 5:19; 8:16-19. There is an interplay of light and shade in the prophecy, however, and it allows us a glimpse of one privileged descendant who is to enjoy God's special favor." [68]

Jewish eschatology gave an important place to the expectation of a Messiah: a royal Messiah everywhere, a priestly Messiah in certain milieux. The agent of salvation appeared also as the Servant of Yahweh and as the Son of man, while the promises always looked to the inauguration of the kingdom of God. It is not easy to coordinate the data; the coming of Jesus alone shed full light on the prophecies and reconciled apparent contradictions. Yet, it is well to recall that what Jesus proclaimed was not primarily the coming of the Messiah, but the presence of the kingdom of God.

3. Son of God

In the gospels, Jesus is frequently called "Son of God". This designation is not quite as obvious as it appears; hence, it must be examined more closely. The biblical title "Son of God" does not necessarily imply divine Sonship. It can, and very often does, indicate adoptive sonship, which follows on the divine choice and establishes a particularly intimate relationship between God and his creatures.

In the Old Testament, the term is applied to angels (Jb 1:6; 36:7; Ps 29[28]:1), to the Chosen People (Ex 4:22; Wis 18:13), to the Israelites (Dt 14:1; Hos 2:1), to their leaders (Ps 83[82]:6), to the king (2 Sm 7:14; Ps 89[88]:27). In later Judaism, with the advent of individualistic religion (that is, of a more personal relationship between the individual and God), the pious man became a "son of God" (Sir 4:10; 23:1; Wis 2:16). Thus it seems that, at the time of Jesus, "Son of God" had no necessary Messianic connotation, while it could, of course, be applied to the Messiah.

In the Synoptic gospels the title "Son of God" is often colored by the evangelists' faith in the true Sonship of Christ. Frequently we must realize that whereas the title, *of itself,* does not go beyond the Messianic significance, it is often clear that an

[68] *The Jerusalem Bible,* p. 391.

evangelist, *when he wrote his gospel*—in the light of his post-Resurrection faith—had in mind the divine Sonship in the strict sense. Thus, we must not suppose that the title had originally the full meaning in the mouth of Satan (Lk 4:4), or of the demoniacs (4:41). The declaration of the centurion at the foot of the Cross is a striking case in point. According to Mark, he says: "Truly this man was the Son of God!" (Mk 15:39), whereas Luke has: "Certainly this man was innocent!" (Lk 23:47). This title even at the Baptism (Lk 3:22) and at the Transfiguration (9:35) did not, for its hearers, imply more than the special divine favor bestowed on the Messiah.

The title "Son of God" is, of course, open to the meaning of true divine Sonship. In fact, Jesus did suggest this. He speaks of "my Father's house" (Lk 2:49) and calls God "my Father" (22:29; 24:49). So, too, he never speaks of "our Father", but always of "my Father" or "your Father". The most explicit text of all, which is quite in the style of John, but undoubtedly belongs to the Synoptic tradition, clearly asserts his divine Sonship: "All things have been delivered to me by my Father; and no one knows who the Son is except the Father, or who the Father is except the Son and any one to whom the Son chooses to reveal him" (10:22). These statements, confirmed by the Resurrection, give to the title "Son of God" the properly divine meaning which it has, for example, in the Pauline epistles.

4. Son of Man

The title "Son of man" is a literal translation of the Aramaic expression *bar enash*, which simply means "man". But, in its emphatic form (*nasha*), the second noun is capable of conveying the notion "*the* man", and hence of being used in a special Messianic sense. As found in the gospels, the origin of the title goes back to Daniel. In a judgment scene, Daniel saw "one like a son of man", that is, a human figure, in contrast to four beasts (representing world empires); and, again in contrast to the beasts' origin from the depths of the sea, he saw him appear "on the clouds of heaven". This son of man was presented to the Ancient of Days (God) and received universal and everlasting dominion. As presented in Dn 7:13f, the figure certainly appears as an individual. Yet, in the interpretation of the vision (Dn 7:26f), "son of man" stands for the "saints of the Most High"— the Messianic people, the purified remnant of Israel. It appears that the "saints of the Most High" and the "son of man" must stand for the same reality, at once collective and individual: the Messianic people and the Messiah who represents and contains them.

It must be admitted that this mysterious figure, coming on the clouds of heaven and receiving universal dominion and an everlasting kingdom, evokes a conception "which is very different from that of the traditional Messiah—an earthly king, descended from David, who conquers his enemies in war. This leader has become a transcendent personage, of heavenly origin, who receives his dominion by a sovereign and direct intervention of God".[69] Although it is probable that in certain restricted circles a Messiah was awaited who was "Son of man", it is understandable that, among the Jews, the title never became a current Messianic one. Despite this, or rather, as we shall see, precisely because of this, "Son of man" does designate the Messiah who had come.

Before turning to the use of "Son of man" in Luke, we have to consider another Old Testament concept that is closely linked to this title in the gospels. In Second Isaiah (Is 40-55) four poems or canticles may be regarded as distinct, in some way, from the rest of the book: Is 42:1-9; 49:1-6; 50:4-9; 52:13–53:12. These have to do with a mysterious figure called the "Servant of Yahweh". While the identification of the Servant is a widely discussed problem, almost all scholars would agree that he is a Messianic figure. But, like the Son of man, it is hard to deny that the Servant has both corporate and personal characteristics; he is at one and the same time the Messianic people and the Messiah. What is undoubted is that Jesus made his own, and accomplished, the mission of the Servant. The Suffering Servant, no less than the heavenly figure of Daniel, stands behind the title, "Son of man".

5. The Messianic Secret

Son of man, then, expresses the complexity and the fullness of

[69] P. Benoit, *Exégèse et Théologie* I (Paris: Cerf, 1961), p. 136.

the Messianic idea, but it remains a mysterious title. Why should Jesus have used a mysterious title? In order to answer this question, another feature must be taken into account, one that is found in other gospels too, but which is most obvious in Mark. Throughout that gospel, Jesus is at pains to hide his Messiahship. The devils know him and cry out: "You are the Son of God"—and he commands them to be silent (Mk 1:25,34; 3:11f; cf. Lk 4:35, 41). Silence is enjoined after notable miracles. For instance, after he had raised the daughter of Jairus, he turned to those who were present "and he strictly charged them that no one should know this" (Mk 5:43; cf. 1:44; 7:36; 8:26; Lk 8:56; 5:14). Again, when at Caesarea Philippi Peter had recognized his Messiahship, and later when he was transfigured before Peter and James and John, he admonished them to tell nobody until he had risen from the dead (Mk 8:30; 9:9; cf. Lk 9:21; 9:36). From time to time he withdrew from the crowd on secret journeys (Mk 7:27; 9:30). He gave his disciples private instructions (e.g. 4:10f, 33f).

We might say that the Messianic secret lies behind almost every narrative in Mark. Nevertheless, it must be admitted that the warnings to preserve silence, as found in the gospel, are artificial and stereotyped to some extent. Sometimes silence is imposed when its observance is impossible, for example, at the raising of the daughter of Jairus (Mk 5:21-43; cf. Lk 8:49-56), and at the healing of the deaf mute (Mk 7:36f) and of the blind man (8:26). Yet, the theme is not Mark's invention; it occurs notably in Mt 9:27-31 which has no parallel in Mark.

A partial explanation of the reticence of Jesus may be found in the conflict between his own Messianic consciousness and the prevalent false notions about the Messiah. Jesus was indeed the Messiah, but he did not present himself as Son of David; instead, he called himself Son of man because, although not a current Messianic title, it could—as in fact it did—designate the Messiah. He imposed silence because the idea of Messiahship, as he conceived it—the spiritual Messiahship of a suffering Messiah— would be unacceptable to most of his contemporaries.

This explanation does not go deep enough, however; we must seek a more profound reason for his conduct. In the first place, he could not really explain who he was until his death and Resurrection had shed their light on his Person. Then, too, the strangeness of the title he had chosen and the veiling of his Messianic dignity expressed a condition of revelation itself—the appeal to human liberty. Jesus continually asked the question: "Who do you say that I am?"

6. The Pharisees

The Hasidim movement of the Maccabean period (cf. 2 Mc 14:6) survived, in later times, in two branches: Pharisees and Essenes. The Pharisees (whose name means the "separated ones") emerged during the reign of John Hyrcanus (135-104 B.C.). During his reign and that of his successor, Alexander Jannaeus (104-76 B.C.), they cut themselves adrift from, and stood in opposition to, the Hasmonean dynasty. Later they refused to take an oath of allegiance to Herod the Great; they practiced passive resistance but avoided embroilment in political affairs; and they maintained a similar attitude toward the Roman authorities. However, they also "separated" themselves from the "people of the land"—the mass of the people "who knew not the Law" (Jn 7:49). Like the Hasidim before them, they were champions of the Torah and, since they had withdrawn from political activity, their religious character became more and more marked.

On the whole, the Pharisees came from the middle classes. According to Josephus, the members of the party numbered 6,000 in the time of Herod, and those in sympathy with their views must have been more numerous. What set them apart was an exact and detailed knowledge of the Mosaic Law and of the "traditions of the Elders", the oral interpretation of the Torah. Insistence on the oral tradition was at once the strength and the weakness of Pharisaism. On the one hand it offered a means of adapting the prescriptions of the Torah to changing circumstances. It also meant that the Pharisees were more open to the acceptance of new ideas; thus, they readily gave assent to doctrines such as personal immortality, judgment after death, the resurrection of the body, and the existence of angels. While stressing the action of divine Providence, they also insisted on human freedom. They looked forward eagerly to the establishment of the kingdom of God on earth and they had a lively

Messianic expectation. As moral theologians they were much more open and progressive than the Sadducees.

On the other hand, preoccupation with the oral prescriptions —which they set on a par with the written Law—could and did lead to legalism and even to puerile casuistry. The severe indictment of the Pharisees in Mt 23 lists some of the extremes of their legalistic interpretation. They had turned the observance of the Torah into an insupportable burden and since, in their view, faithfulness to God was expressed through faithfulness to the whole Torah (written and oral) they had effectively "shut the kingdom of heaven against men" (Mt 23:13). Besides, pride in their knowledge and observance of the Law led to self-righteousness, an attitude strikingly illustrated in the parable of the Pharisee and the Publican (Lk 18:9-14).

Even though the Pharisees despised "the common breed without the law", their influence over the people was immense. They were zealous for the Law, their religious ideals were high, and their moral conduct was often exemplary. Paul himself bears witness to the sincerity of his former life: ". . . as to the Law a Pharisee . . . as to righteousness under the Law blameless" (Phil 3:5f). Besides, their independent attitude toward the Roman authorities appealed to the people. Not that the Pharisees were extremists; indeed, they cautioned against open revolt. Although their faults were glaring and although their opposition to and rejection of the Messiah was a national tragedy, we cannot but admire the faith and courage that survived the shattering experience of two Jewish wars (66-70; 132-135 A.D.) and we cannot but marvel at the spirit, bequeathed by them, that has enabled Judaism to survive (against all reasonable expectation) to the present day.

7. The Sadducees

The Sadducees (their name probably means "Zadokites", descendants or partisans of Zadok, Solomon's priest—1 Kg 2:35) first appear as an organized party in the time of John Hyrcanus (134-104 B.C.). It is due partly to the conflict of Sadducees and Pharisees that the Jews eventually lost their political independence: the appeal of both parties to Rome led to Pompey's intervention in 63 B.C. The conflict was not surprising; the two parties differed widely in social structure as well as in outlook and practice. "In general the Pharisees belonged to the middle classes, the Sadducees to the wealthy priestly aristocracy. The Pharisees claimed the authority of piety and learning, the Sadducees that of blood and position; the Pharisees were progressive, the Sadducees conservative; the Pharisees strove to raise the religious standards of the masses, the Sadducees were chiefly concerned with Temple administration and ritual, and kept themselves aloof from the masses." [70]

The Sadducees stressed the importance of the Law of Moses, especially the regulations governing the priesthood and sacrifice. However, they are not simply to be identified with the priesthood; they also included members of the lay aristocracy. In fact, they took their stand on the Torah alone (in the strict sense of the written Law) and rejected the oral tradition. Hence, they denied the resurrection of the dead, personal immortality, and recompense beyond the grave, as well as the existence of angels and devils (cf. Ac 23:8). Since they interpreted the Law very literally, in moral matters they held extremely rigid views. Politically, they easily accepted Roman rule because the preservation of the status quo was to their advantage. It is readily understood that they did not have the sympathy of the people and had little influence in the religious and moral sphere. When the Temple and its cult came to an end, they had no further *raison d'être* and they, too, disappeared from history.

8. The Scribes

Scribes first appeared in the reign of Solomon as educated civil servants; they were the originators and authors of the wisdom literature in Israel. In postexilic times, the scribe was one versed in the Law, like Ezra (Ez 7:6, 11f; Neh 8:1). In the first century A.D., the scribes, who were lawyers, moralists and theologians, were the guides and teachers of the Jewish community: "The scribes sit on Moses' seat; so practice and observe whatever they tell you" (Mt 23:2). They were named "lawyer",

[70] R. H. Pfeiffer, *History of New Testament Times* (London: Black, 1963²), p. 56.

"teacher", "doctor of the Law", and were given the title of *rabbi* ("my master"). Some of them were celebrated founders of schools like Hillel and Shammai in the early part of the 1st century A.D.; others had great authority, like Gamaliel, St. Paul's master (cf. Ac 5:34-39; 22:3).

Although in the gospels the scribes are most often associated with the Pharisees, the terms "scribe" and "Pharisee" are not identical. For one thing, the scribes, even in the narrower sense of doctors of the Law, were in existence long before the Pharisee party emerged. Then, too, there were scribes with Sadducee leanings who held and taught the tenets of that party. However, it remains true that the great majority of scribes inclined to Pharisaism and their position as teachers of the people greatly increased the influence of the Pharisees.

9. The Sanhedrin

The beginnings and original composition of the Sanhedrin are not clear, but, under the Roman procurators, it had assumed a precise form and character. It was a senate of priests and laymen with seventy members—not counting the high priest who was *ex officio* president of the assembly. The Sanhedrites were divided into three groups: the heads of the priestly families, the elders (representing the lay aristocracy), and the scribes. The third group was Pharisaic in spirit, the others were Sadducees. Paul skillfully played on this division when he was brought before the Sanhedrin (Ac 23:1-9).

Under the procurators, the Sanhedrin had considerable power. It could handle all cases involving infringement of the Torah: this included the civil as well as the religious sphere, since Judaism knew one Law only. The council had its own police force and could arrest malefactors and punish them when convicted. It might pass sentence of death; but the sentence had to be ratified by the Roman procurator (cf. Jn 18:31).

10. The Samaritans

The Samaritans of New Testament times were descendants of the heterogeneous people planted in Samaria after 721 B.C. The seeds of the enmity between them and the Jews were sown in the early days of the return from the Exile; the final break came in the time of Alexander the Great when (according to Josephus) the schismatic temple was built on Mt. Gerizim. When their temple was destroyed by John Hyrcanus in 128 B.C., they continued to maintain their cultic autonomy and to celebrate their Passover on the sacred mountain—a rite that they have faithfully followed to the present day (though now only a pitiful handful of them survives). Their sacred Scripture was (and is) the Pentateuch alone.

In the time of Jesus they formed a small group localized in Samaria. With regard to doctrine they were monotheists, and they venerated Moses as the prophet *par excellence* who had given them the Torah. They believed that, from the days of the high priest Heli, God had been angry with his sinful people. However, they looked for the coming of a Messianic figure— the *Taheb*—another Moses (cf. Dt 18:15). Jn 4:25 makes allusion to this Messianic expectation. Several gospel texts reflect the bitter feeling between Jews and Samaritans (e.g. Jn 4:9; 8:48; Lk 9:52-54). With supreme courtesy Jesus held up a Samaritan as the model of Christian charity; and Ac 8 relates how Samaria welcomed the Good News.

11. The Date of the Crucifixion

All four gospels agree that Jesus died on the *parasceve* of the sabbath, that is, on a Friday (Mk 15:42; Mt 27:62; Lk 23:54; Jn 19:31) but the date (the day of the month) of his death is disagreed upon by the Synoptics and John.

Synoptics: Jesus ate the Passover meal on 15th Nisan (according to our reckoning the evening of the 14th—the Jewish day began immediately after sunset) and died on the afternoon of 15th Nisan.

John: Jesus died on 14th Nisan (at the hour that the Passover lambs were immolated in the Temple).

Passover always fell on the 15th Nisan, whatever day of the month it should happen to be. The Paschal lambs were slaughtered in the Temple on the afternoon of 14th Nisan, i.e. after 2:00 p.m., and were eaten the same day after sunset—which was 15th Nisan by Jewish reckoning. From the 2nd century B.C. this was always the rule when Passover and sabbath coincided.

In detail, we observe that, according to the synoptists, the last supper eaten by Jesus with his disciples was a Passover meal. He had the preparations made for the Passover on the "first day of Unleavened Bread", that is, on 14th Nisan (Mk 14:12 and parallels; cf. 14:14 and parallels). On taking his place at table he remarked: "I have earnestly desired to eat this Passover with you before I suffer" (Lk 22:15). But, John begins his account of the Passion in this way: "Before the feast of the Passover" (Jn 13:1); and at the trial scene before Pilate he remarks that the Jews refused to enter the praetorium "so that they might not be defiled, but might eat the Passover" (18:28). Jesus was condemned to death on the "day of the Preparation for the Passover" (19:14) and was crucified on the same day (19:42). John's dating is confirmed by 1 Cor 5:7: Jesus *died* on the day the Paschal lamb was immolated, that is, 14th Nisan.

A strong case can be made for the Synoptic dating, and it may be argued that John had changed the date of the death of Jesus for theological reasons. Yet, it is perhaps more likely that the Paschal character of the Last Supper, stressed in the Synoptic tradition, has upset the chronological perspective, and that the perspective has been restored in the fourth gospel. We recognize with John that Jesus died on 14th Nisan and with the synoptists that the Last Supper was a Paschal meal—although it anticipated by twenty-four hours the Passover of the Jews. Various explanations of this last factor have been proposed, but it seems best to acknowledge that Jesus freely anticipated the Paschal meal. "Unable to celebrate the Passover on the Friday (though, indeed, he celebrated it in his own Person on the cross, Jn 19:36; 1 Cor 5:7), Jesus instituted his new rite in the course of a supper which, in consequence, became endowed with the characteristics of the old Passover." [71]

The crucifixion must have taken place between 26 and 36 A.D. —the term of Pilate's procuratorship. Since we have accepted the view which dates the death of Jesus to Friday, 14th Nisan, we can limit our scope to the years in which these factors were verified: 27, 30 and 33 A.D. When we consider that the public ministry opened in 28 A.D. (cf. Lk 3:1f) and lasted more than two years, but less than three years (John), we see that the years 27 and 33 are eliminated. Hence, we may assert, with some

[71] *The Jerusalem Bible*, p. 59.

confidence, that Jesus died on Friday, 14th Nisan, 30 A.D., that is to say, on April 7, 30 A.D.

12. Midrash

In modern biblical studies, the word *midrash* may mean a rabbinic method of exegesis, or a special literary form. Rabbinic midrash, as a literary form, is a literature concerned with the Bible; it is "a literature about a literature". Though extremely varied in detail, it may be reduced to two main types:

1. The form of midrash which is most limited in scope is the halakah. It is based on the legal texts of the Torah and its purpose is to find in them rules of conduct and of action that fit later times and circumstances. While halakic midrash could find a place in synagogal sermons, it is understandable that its privileged *Sitz im Leben* was the discussions of the rabbinical schools.

2. The most widely occurring and elastic form of midrash is the haggadah. This is an interpretation of the non-legal texts of the Torah and of the rest of Scripture. The viewpoint was varied (moral exhortation or doctrinal commentary) and the methods diverse (varying from a simple explanation of a text to a free narrative built on a text). Haggadic midrash is notably homiletic and the origin of much of it may be found in the liturgical assemblies. It is the commentary on, and an interpretation of, the text read in synagogue worship. However, the *pesharim* of Qumran, commentaries on prophetical texts which applied these texts to the history of the sect, also fit into this category.

From the viewpoint of literary structure, midrash may be exegetical (verse by verse exposition of the text), homiletical (traditional interpretation of texts presented in the form of homilies), or narrative (a completely rewritten biblical narrative embellished with legends and non-biblical traditions). But always the starting point of midrash is a text of Scripture. Its aim is to actualize a biblical text in face of a new situation, to learn what the text has to say to us here and now, to draw out from it all the lessons it contains. An excellent biblical example of haggadic midrash is found in the homily of Wis 11–19.

This brief outline of the characteristics and purpose of midrash should justify our contention that it is not correct to label Luke's Infancy narrative, or any part of it, midrash.

SELECT BIBLIOGRAPHY

The bibliography lists books and articles which have been especially helpful in the preparation of this commentary.

(1) *Commentaries*

Caird, G. B., *The Gospel of St. Luke.* Harmondsworth, Middlesex: Penguin Books, 1963.

Creed, J. M., *The Gospel According to St. Luke.* New York: St. Martin's Press, 1965.

Ginns, R., "St. Luke" in *A Catholic Commentary on Holy Scripture.* London: Nelson, 1953, pp. 744-775.

Lagrange, M.-J., *Évangile selon Saint Luc.* Paris: Gabalda, 1941⁵.

Lampe, G. W. H., "Luke" in *Peake's Commentary on the Bible.* London: Nelson, 1962².

Marchal, L., *Évangile selon Saint Luc.* Paris: Letouzey, 1950².

Osty, E., *L'Évangile selon Saint Luc* (BJ), Paris: Cerf, 1961³.

Plummer, A., *The Gospel According to St. Luke.* Edinburgh: Clark, 1922⁵.

Schmid, J., *Das Evangelium nach Lukas.* Regensburg: Pustet, 1960⁴.

Stuhlmueller, C., *The Gospel of St. Luke.* Collegeville, Minn.: The Liturgical Press, 1960.

Tinsley, E. J., *The Gospel According to Luke.* New York: C.U.P., 1965.

(2) *Other Literature*

Ahern, B. M., *New Horizons: Studies in Biblical Theology.* Notre Dame, Ind.: Fides, 1963.

Audet, J. P., "L'Annonce à Marie" in *Revue Biblique* 63 (1956), pp. 346-374.

Barrett, C. K., *Luke the Historian in Recent Study.*

Bauer, J. B., editor, *Bibeltheologisches Wörterbuch.* Graz: Styria, 1962², I and II.

Benoit, P., *Exégèse et Théologie.* Paris: Cerf, 1961, I.

—— *Passion et Résurrection du Seigneur.* Paris: Cerf, 1966.

—— "L'Enfance de Jean-Baptiste selon Luc 1" in *New Testament Studies* 3 (1956-57), pp. 169-194.

—— " 'Et toi-même, un glaive te transpercera l'âme' (Lc 2:35)" in *The Catholic Biblical Quarterly* 25 (1963), pp. 251-261.

———— and Boismard, M.-E., *Synopse des Quatre Évangiles en Français*. Paris: Cerf, 1965.

Bloch, R., "Midrash" in *Dictionnaire de la Bible (Supplement)* 6 (1960), pp. 1263-1281.

Brown, R. E., *New Testament Essays*. Milwaukee: Bruce, 1965.

Cerfaux, L. and Cambier, J., "Luc" in *Dictionnaire de la Bible (Supplement)* 4 (1957) pp. 545-594.

Conzelmann, H., *The Theology of St. Luke*. New York: Harper & Row, 1960.

Cullmann, O., *Christ and Time*. Philadelphia: Westminster Press, 1964.

Derrett, J. D. M., "Fresh Light on St. Luke XVI" in *New Testament Studies* 7 (1960-61), pp. 198-219; 364-380.

Dodd, C. H., *About the Gospels*. New York: C.U.P., 1952.

———— *According to the Scriptures*. London: Nisbet, 1952.

———— *The Parables of the Kingdom*. New York: Scribner's, 1961.

Dupont, J., *Les Béatitudes*. Bruges: Abbaye de Saint-André, 1958².

———— *The Sources of Acts*. New York: Herder & Herder, 1964.

George, A., "Parabole" in *Dictionnaire de la Bible (Supplement)* 6 (1960), pp. 1149-1177.

Harrington, W. J., *Explaining the Gospels*. Glen Rock, N.J.: Paulist Press, 1963.

———— *A Key to the Parables*. Glen Rock, N.J.: Paulist Press, 1964.

———— *Record of the Fulfillment: The New Testament*. Chicago: The Priory Press, 1966.

———— "The Annunciation" in *Doctrine and Life* 13 (1963), pp. 306-315.

Hermans, L., *The Bible on the Childhood of Jesus*. London: Sheed & Ward, 1965.

Hunter, A. M., *Interpreting the Parables*. London: SCM Press, 1960.

Jeremias, J., *Paroles de Jésus*. Paris: Cerf, 1963.

———— *The Parables of Jesus*. New York: Scribner's, 1964².

———— *The Central Message of the New Testament*. New York: Scribner's, 1965.

Jones, A., *God's Living Word*. Glen Rock, N.J.: Paulist Press, 1965.

Kee, H. C., Young, F. W. and Froehlich, K., *Understanding the New Testament*. Englewood Cliffs, N.J.: Prentice-Hall, 1965².

Lagrange, M.-J., *The Gospel of Jesus Christ*. London: Burns & Oates, 1938.

Laurentin, R., *Structure et Théologie de Luc 1—2*. Paris: Gabalda, 1957.

———— *Jésus au Temple. Mystère de Paques et Foi de Marie en Luc 2:48-50*. Paris: Gabalda, 1966.

Léon-Dufour, X., editor, *Vocabulaire de Théologie Biblique*. Paris: Cerf, 1961.

———— *Les Évangiles de l'histoire de Jésus*. Paris: Éditions du Seuil, 1963.

—— "The Synoptic Gospels" in Robert, A. and Feuillet, A. (editors), *Introduction to the New Testament*. New York: Desclée, 1966.

Lyonnet, S., "Le récit de l'Annonciation et la Maternite Divine de la Sainte Vierge" in *L'Ami du Clergé* 66 (1956), pp. 39-41.

Marchel, W., *Dieu Père dans le Nouveau Testament*. Paris: Cerf, 1966.

McKenzie, J. L., *Dictionary of the Bible*. Milwaukee: Bruce, 1965.

—— *The Power and the Wisdom: An Interpretation of the New Testament*. Milwaukee: Bruce, 1965.

Schnackenburg, R., *The Moral Teaching of the New Testament*. New York: Herder & Herder, 1965.

Taylor, V., *The Person of Christ in New Testament Teaching*. New York: St. Martin's Press, 1958.

—— *The Jerusalem Bible*. Garden City, N.Y.: Doubleday, 1966.

Vaganay, L., *Le Problème Synoptique*. Paris: Desclée, 1954.

Wikenhauser, A., *New Testament Introduction*. New York: Herder & Herder, 1958.

Wright, A. G., "The Literary Genre Midrash" in *The Catholic Biblical Quarterly* 28 (1966), pp. 105-138; 417-457.